# THE LOGIC OF
# POLITICAL VIOLENCE

# THE LOGIC OF POLITICAL VIOLENCE

*Lessons in Reform and Revolution*

Craig Rosebraugh

ARISSA MEDIA GROUP
Portland, Oregon

THE LOGIC OF POLITICAL VIOLENCE
Copyright © 2004 by Craig Rosebraugh

Arissa Media Group
P.O. Box 6058
Portland, Oregon 97228
Tel: (503) 972-1143
info@arissamediagroup.com
http://www.arissamediagroup.com

Printed and bound in the United States of America.

First Edition, 2004.

Library of Congress Control Number: 2003096953

International Standard Book Number: 0-9742884-1-1

Cover design and illustrations by Matthew Haggett.

Arissa Media Group, LLC was formed in 2003 to assist in building a revolutionary consciousness in the United States of America. For more information, bulk requests, catalogue listings, submission guidelines, or media inquiries please contact Arissa Media Group, LLC, P.O. Box 6058, Portland, Oregon 97228. Tel: (503) 972-1143
info@arissamediagroup.com • http://www.arissamediagroup.com

*By our own inactions,*
*by our own refusal to*
*confront the political structure*
*that is causing relentless atrocities,*
*we are guilty of allowing*
*a heightened degree of*
*violence and injustice to exist.*

# CONTENTS

# ACKNOWLEDGMENTS

I would like to thank Bobby Buchanan, Chris Hables Gray, Tomás Kalmar, Margo MacLeod and Goddard College for their support of this project. I would also like to thank A.H. for providing exceptional last-minute editing assistance.

# *Introduction*

I was first introduced to the idea of nonviolence while attending a community college in Portland, Oregon in the early 1990s. Contained within a class on peace and conflict studies was a segment on nonviolence, particularly as practiced by Gandhi during the Indian civil rights issues in South Africa and the independence movement in India. The class instructor was extremely energetic and obviously motivated by his own personal beliefs to promote Gandhi in the best light possible. I instantly became intrigued and developed a new found respect for the legendary man in the loincloth.

My studies during this period were limited largely to one biography of Gandhi, written by Louis Fischer, assigned by the class instructor. In this book, I learned the basics of Gandhi's personal and political life, and his thoughts and practices of nonviolence. Although I was admittedly excited and inspired by this brief glimpse into Gandhi's life, my thoughts and studies of nonviolence ended there, at least for a few years.

As a scholar and political activist living and trying to make positive changes in the United States I was immediately struck by state-sponsored guidance telling me how to act. From day one of my involvement many years ago through to this day I have heard that if one desires to pursue social and/or political change in this country there are "correct" and "proper" methodologies in place to make these pursuits a reality. After all, this is a democracy, one that boasts itself as the freest land in all the world. If the people truly aim to change societal laws and norms, by God that is their right and there are proper channels to go through to ensure success. *All social and political change in the United States has come about this way*, I have been constantly told.

As a young activist I quickly learned what these rules were that were time tested and thus would ensure success. The rules of the game are as follows:

## RULES FOR THE GAME OF
## SOCIAL AND POLITICAL CHANGE
## IN THE UNITED STATES OF AMERICA

1. You have the right to pursue social and political change as long as you follow the rules below.

2. All social and political change in the United States has come about ONLY through nonviolent methodologies and these are the ONLY methods which are permitted to be used.

3. With few exceptions, all activity must stay within the realm of behavior which is sanctioned or approved by the government. This directly relates to engaging in activities which are lawful and thus permitted by the government.

4. One rare exception to rule #3 has been the occasional use of nonviolent civil disobedience when unjust laws were broken for the greater good of society. While it is doubtful any unjust laws exist within the United States in current times, if an individual did decide to commit an unlawful act of nonviolent civil disobedience, he

or she must be prepared to submit to all penalties under the law resulting from this behavior.

*Note to #4: On the extremely rare occasion when one may decide that a law is unjust and therefore should be broken, it is best to coordinate this activity with the local, state, or federal policing forces to ensure safety for the participants and the general public.

5.      You have the right to pursue social and political change as long as you follow the rules above.

As I personally became active in anti-war protests and animal rights issues in the early 1990's, nonviolence was a recurring theme, and I began to expose myself to the subject a bit further. At that time I began to learn the philosophy of incorporating a universal application of compassion towards all and the idea of the circle of life, that all beings on this planet are connected and interrelated. For these reasons, I then adopted a strict vegetarian diet attempting to follow the idea that one should make every effort to walk as lightly on the earth as possible for a minimum destructive presence.

A couple of years later, while attending Marylhurst University in the Portland area, I enrolled in a specialized study course focused entirely on Gandhi and his nonviolence perspective. This is where my interest in the practical capabilities of nonviolence blossomed. Like my community college instructor, my professor at Marylhurst was equally, if not more, adhered to a sound support and promotion of Gandhi and his nonviolence principles. The professor considered the Gandhian philosophy to be an unstoppable force that could change the world. I began to be sold on the idea.

After reading many other books by Gandhi, King, Thoreau, and others, on the philosophy of nonviolence, I began to see the need to include this practice into my personal attempts to pursue social justice. As Gandhi had done countless times with the burning of passbooks in South Africa to the Salt March and fasting in India—to name just a few examples—I began to engage in active nonviolence, in the form of civil disobedience, to further progress the struggles for justice I was pursuing.

It felt good. Here I was, a white young man from a middle class background, risking my freedom for the good of society. As my arrest record grew, I increasingly became noticed and respected within the self-described "militant" activist circles, particularly those which also promoted and engaged in civil disobedience. I became so convinced of the potentiality of nonviolence as a means for achieving revolutionary change that I felt compelled to further study the subject. Soon I began to teach the philosophy in activist workshops, conferences, and even in some high schools, colleges, and universities where I was invited to guest lecture.

Over the course of a few years I watched the nonviolence process appeal to an increasing number of people both who participated in and supported the practice. It didn't register with me at the time that the overwhelming majority of people who came to my workshops and supported or engaged in nonviolence as a political tool were white and from a middle-to upper-class background. Oblivious to this fact, I was proud to be teaching what I believed to be the *only* methodology by which to pursue social and political change.

In the mid 1990's I was forced to rethink my own nonviolence absolutism after being confronted psychologically with the notion of property destruction for a political cause. Still involved in animal advocacy issues at the time, I became increasingly intrigued with a group known as the Animal Liberation Front, or A.L.F., that engaged in burglary, theft, vandalism, and even arson to further the animal rights movement. The group, founded in England in the 1970s and active in the U.S. since the early 1980s, made sense to me on a purely strategic level. As I determined the main motive behind industrialized animal exploitation was financial gain, there was a definite intelligence to the notion that property destruction could be beneficial. After all, it was clear that the various businesses that use animals on a daily basis are motivated purely by profit. So naturally if some animals were taken or property was damaged businesses would stand to lose finances. In theory, if enough losses were placed on a given business or even industry it would force that entity out of commission.

All of this theory behind the A.L.F. fit into my own nonviolence principles without much conflict at first. After all, the A.L.F. even had in its own code of conduct a specific clause that stated no life is permitted to be taken during any of their actions - human or nonhuman animal. So on a certain level the group was nonviolent - as it pertained to protecting human and animal life. Throughout its existence (the group is still active today) the A.L.F. has prided and promoted itself as being a nonviolent organization.

Yet, while a first and foremost goal of the group appeared to be to rescue animals from places of neglect, exploitation and murder, I also realized it was an aim of the group to financially force companies out of business. As a devoted nonviolence believer and practitioner, I repeatedly stumbled on the concept of force. I could use any word I wanted to describe the intended outcome of the A.L.F. activity but the notion remained the same. The group on a particular level is attempting to force —against their will—companies entirely out of business. This idea of force or coercion was fiercely opposed by Gandhi in his Satyagraha principles. He felt that under no circumstances was force or coercion to be used in a nonviolent pursuit of social change. I was very conscious of this fact, a complexity that presented me with a decent amount of inner turmoil.

Finally, after much thought on the matter, I decided that I would mold my own definition of nonviolence to include the use of property destruction as long as no lives were harmed in the process. I knew there was a great amount of logic to the idea that if industrialized animal abuse were motivated primarily by profits then one of the only methods of stopping it would be to remove that financial draw. I allowed my inner conflict over the use of coercion to be stuffed away in the back of my mind, where it would remain for some time.

In mid 1997, I began acting as a national spokesperson for the A.L.F. and was always certain to highlight the notion publicly (and even in my own mind) that this was a nonviolent group working to stop large-scale violence from occurring. Later that year, if for no other reason than I was a visible activist who publicly supported property destruction, I became the spokesperson for the North American Earth Liberation Front, or E.L.F. While the E.L.F. is concerned with stopping environmental destruction, its tactics are quite similar to those of the A.L.F. For me especially, the primary commonality in the conduct of the two organizations was the devotion to protecting human and animal life.

While the two groups had their similarities, the E.L.F. grew to be in a far different league than its animal counterpart. The A.L.F. had, throughout its history in the United States, primarily engaged in small scale theft, burglary and vandalism with arson being an extreme rarity. With the birth of the E.L.F. in the United States in the mid 1990s, large scale arson came to be used on an increasing basis. (Perhaps the largest and still most recognizable action the group has taken credit for is the $12 million fire that destroyed five structures at Vail Ski Resorts, Inc. in October 1998.) Throughout my entire time as a spokesperson for the E.L.F.

- November 29, 1997 through September 5, 2001 - I justified in my own mind the tactics of the group being nonviolent as they had never harmed a human or nonhuman animal. Through hundreds and hundreds of interviews with the news media I explained the organization's ideology and defended its own idea of nonviolence. While becoming a media poster-boy for radical environmentalism I simultaneously managed to continually dodge the needed in-depth analysis of the use of force or coercion and its relationship to nonviolence theology.

Acting as a spokesperson for these two controversial organizations (the E.L.F., has been considered the "number one priority" of the domestic terrorism unit of the FBI), I was taken through many new experiences which continually provoked me to re-evaluate my adherence to nonviolence. In early February 2000 I was awoken early in the morning to loud banging at the front door of my house accompanied by fierce screams from the FBI. Before I could even get to the door federal agents burst in and held me and two of my other roommates at gun-point before beginning a six-hour raid on the house. At the end of the day, FBI, BATF (Bureau of Alcohol, Tobacco, and Firearms), and U.S. Forest Service agents had seized hundreds of items of personal property from me, resulting in thousands of dollars in losses. While the attention from the federal government was not new (agents had repeatedly attempted to question me over the years, and I had received four federal grand jury subpoenas in 1997 and 1998), this new aggressive action by my government left a lasting impression.

This impression would only grow as the federal grand jury subpoenas continued to come. Over a year later, on April 5, 2001, federal agents again appeared for an early morning raid, this time on both my house and my business—a Portland, Oregon based baking company. Just as before, after six to seven hours, the agents left with boxes filled with thousands of dollars in personal property. Other than a few very minor items, I still to this day have not received my belongings back.

This chain of events peaked - at least thus far - with a subpoena I received to testify before the U.S. Congress on February 12, 2002 in a special session devoted to the "Emerging Threat of Eco-Terrorism." I was told that I was called to give information on the E.L.F., the most notorious "eco-terrorism" organization currently in operation in the United States. While facing at least a year in prison for not cooperating with the subpoena, I appeared along with my attorney, Stu Sugarman, in Washington, D.C., where I took the Fifth Amendment to all but two of the over fifty questions. (I confirmed that I had submitted a twelve-page written testimony to Congress and that I was a U.S. citizen.) During this proceeding, facing off with members of Congress attempting to make their constituents happy (thus furthering their own political careers), I was struck with the ridiculous nature of those *Five Rules for the Game of Social and Political Change in the United States of America.* Could an adherence to those rules really enable social and political change within the United States to become a reality?

# THE CASE OF THE UNITED STATES

It is an undeniable fact that the United States was founded on various forms of political violence. Whether it was the physical violence in fighting the European powers or the Native Americans, or the property destruction that came with incidents such as the famous tea dumping, the strategy of violence was implemented for one specific reason: Those involved believed there was no other recourse than to fight, by any means necessary, for their own ideas of liberty and justice. Certainly, this reality brought with it grave consequences, the most obvious being the genocide of Native Americans. But all judgments aside, the U.S. was founded on a campaign of political violence.

*What does this tell us?* In the nonviolence schools of thought, this example can easily demonstrate that wars and violence are immoral and flat-out wrong. Historians may casily argue that the very history of the U.S. constitutes a perfect model of the circle of violence theory. In this example, the very violence that enabled the country to be formed could be viewed as the predominant cause of the ongoing violence and unrest that American society has experienced over the years.

A nonviolence proponent might then conclude from this judgment that the only way to break this spiral of violence is through active nonviolence, through meeting aggressors with love, compassion, respect—and a bit of Gandhi's mythological *Soul Force.* Additionally, it is a commonly-asserted notion among supporters of nonviolence that the pursuit of transforming a violent society into one of peace and justice must begin at the personal level. Each individual, it is argued, must attempt to live out his or her own utopian visions, and when enough people do so nonviolently, the violent system will ultimately collapse. Through following this strict adherence to a *means must come before ends* policy, nonviolence practitioners proclaim that their utopian society will be lasting.

I disagree entirely with these presumptions. Various factors should have told us many years ago that the political system in the United States can only be changed through a campaign using many strategies, including political violence. One of these factors came with the very formation of the country. The War of Independence demonstrated that the original founders of the United States felt so strongly about their new land and eventual government that they would do anything to preserve and protect it. Whether it was through the use of conventional military tactics, guerrilla warfare, or even terrorism, the "Founding Fathers" of this land ensured their country would not be taken.

Throughout the various stages in U.S. history, during the various internal battles and external wars, governmental representatives did their best to walk in the same shoes as their predecessors. As a result, as the country continued to grow, the level of violence utilized by the U.S. government domestically and internationally also increased. There have been no indications from this historical timeline that those in power in the United States will hesitate, even for a split second, before engaging in violent defense and offense maneuvers when the governmental structure is actually threatened.

Another factor suggesting the necessity of violence in U.S. political and social movements is the very history of justice struggles within the country. Rule #2 in the *Game of Social and Political Change in the United States* says that "All social and political change in the United States has come about only through nonviolent methodologies and these are the only methods which are permitted to be used." This statement, while ingenious in its mythological and utopian qualities, is completely fictitious.

The formation of the country, which to many people was considered to be a justice pursuit, was already briefly touched upon. The abolitionist movement, for certain, utilized a variety of tactics and strategies to eventually force the U.S. government to outlaw slavery. Including a mixture of nonviolent tactics (such as educational campaigns, lobbying, and even the Underground Railroad) with violent slave revolts, the success of the movement was chiefly based on its diversity. Additionally, there is ample evidence to suggest that the various violent slave uprisings played at least an equivalent role to the less confrontational approaches.

Within the labor movement in the United States, advances were also accomplished through a blending of strategies. The nonviolent picket lines, boycotts, and strikes were just as crucial as the riots in producing tangible results. Those results, of course, were better working conditions and the eight-hour work day.

As I discuss in the section of this book on the civil rights struggle, the latter part of the movement included an exceptional increase in violence and the willingness to resort to Malcolm's *By Any Means Necessary* approach. While the nonviolent campaigns, of which King became the major focal point, were the lifeline of this particular endeavor, the violent riots and growth of the Black Power contingency in the 1960s forced the government to view King as the less threatening of two opponents. The U.S. government realized that, if it did not deal with King and agree to grant at least some reforms, it would have to answer to a growing, angry and determined, violent alternative.

In these four examples, deliberate political violence was used to aid in the progress of the justice struggles. But what about other historical justice pursuits, such as the suffragette movement, the anti-Vietnam War effort, the modern women's struggle, or even environmental advocacy? Was or has violence been a purposeful strategy that has produced a beneficial outcome for these issues? These questions touch upon one of the main points of the entire book.

# THE FAILURE OF REFORM

There is an important difference between the notion of reform and that of revolution. The reformist seeks to pursue social or political change under the existing power structure, while the revolutionary wants to tear apart *the* very power structure. Each and every example of justice movements listed above in the United States has been a reformist pursuit. As I will explain, the reformist nature of these struggles has been a key to their progress - where any progress did indeed occur.

In the abolitionist movement, the goal was to end slavery. There was not any recognizable threat to the entire political system of the country, nor any popular desire to create one. The only pressure that did come, the minute threat that was presented, was one of a purely political nature concerning the increasing public opinion in support of abolition. As difficult as the U.S. government made itself appear to give in to the abolition pressure, it could willingly grant this reform without losing its power and overall control.

In the suffragette movement, a similar story is repeated. While the

U.S. suffragettes engaged almost entirely in nonviolent behavior (unlike their British counterparts), many laws were broken during civil disobedience campaigns. Still, the popular movement leaders such as Susan B. Anthony, and the women in the trenches such as Alice Paul, were not attempting nor expecting to change the entire political system. They were targeting one piece of the oppression pie—the piece that still held women in a state of disenfranchisement. Owing to this reality, after a long fought battle, they acquired that one piece of pie, while the remaining pieces of oppression continued to multiply.

The same can be said for the labor movement, the civil rights struggle, and the anti-Vietnam War effort. In none of these three cases were there deliberate attempts or goals of overthrowing the political system. *Old Glory* was presumed to be fine; it just had a few wrinkles that needed to be ironed out. Just as in the previous examples, progress came only as a result of the justice struggles being reformist measures and was not meant to actually challenge the entire power structure of the country.

Nearly all political and social movements today within the United States follow a similar path down the doomed road of reformism. In the popular environmental movement, which began in the 1960s, advocates have been asking for, at minimum, a reduction in pollution, logging, and development. Even the most radical element of the struggle, including economic sabotage groups such as the Earth Liberation Front, have been seeking single issue changes under the existing power structure.

Union battles, anti-sweatshop labor pursuits, peace struggles, animal advocacy, and even police accountability campaigns have mirrored this same reformist mentality. My point is not to suggest that any of these single-issue injustices, past or present, are not worthy of attention and opposition. Rather, it is to make the well-founded argument that a, and perhaps *the*, key reason justice struggles have not come further in the United States is due to reformist rather than revolutionary practices.

As I have explained previously, in the history of the United States nearly all political and social movements have been reformist measures. They have not identified the political system within the United States as the common denominator of oppression and injustice and therefore targeted that structure for abolition. These single-issue pursuits have rarely threatened that political structure, and ample evidence suggests it was rarely even a desire. The goal, on almost every occasion, was to attempt to treat symptoms of a problem without ever identifying and targeting the primary disease. As a result, that disease has continued to grow and inflict increasing violence and oppression on a global scale.

The U.S. government, for obvious reasons, approves of, and to a degree supports, reformist measures. These campaigns, often times, are model examples of that very freedom U.S. citizens are privileged enough to hold. For many domestically, the ability to engage in reformist pursuits constitutes enough convincing proof that there are real checks and balances in place in the United States. *If there is any injustice occurring within this land, as U.S. citizens we have the right and ability to stop it!* Within the international political arena, U.S. domestic reform is also thought to act as concrete proof of the opportunity, freedom, and democracy that is supposed to make the United States such a great country.

Reformism is to blame for the lack of overall success in nearly all U.S. historical political and social movements. Even those struggles we identify as being successful—labor, civil rights, suffrage, modern women's, and abolition movements—arguably still have not achieved true success in the current time. Proof of this can be easily seen by glancing at the profiles of the Federal Government and top corporate CEOs. Has any woman or African American ever even come close to being elected into the oval office? While African Americans and women in general have made exceptional strides forward, the white, upper-class male is still in a position of political and societal domination.

Likewise, although better working conditions were obtained from the labor movement, the disparity between rich and poor continues to increase within the United States. The percentage difference between what CEOs and entry level employees take home also continually grows. As minimum wage requirements and other improvements increased, benefiting U.S. citizens to some degree, employers have increasingly looked overseas for cheaper labor. While child labor and sweat shop conditions may be illegal in the United States, U.S. corporations have taken advantage of horrific working conditions in countries overseas.

Historically, the various social and political movements within the United States have failed overall *because* they have not identified the political system itself as *the* primary problem. Thus, by their own limitations set under the guidelines of reformism—addressing single-issue injustices while supporting the overall political system—these pursuits were defeated from the start. They would never ultimately threaten the entire political system that, since the War for Independence, has been purposely structured to serve the wealthy, white man's interests and nothing else. The most these movements could achieve would be pressuring the government to give in to reformist measures, particularly as long as they posed no serious threat to the overall power and operations of the country.

# A REVOLUTION IS NEEDED
# IN THE UNITED STATES OF AMERICA

A political and social revolution is needed in the United States to destroy a system of governing that has proven itself unable to provide for the needs of its people. Furthermore, it is beyond necessary to rid the world of a political system that has demonstrated itself to be one of the greatest—if not *the* greatest—terrorist organizations in planetary history. Third, many examples over the course of U.S. history have proven that the U.S. political structure is unable to allow for further justice due to its very design - by and for the white, upper class, male. Reformist pursuits have repeatedly come up against a brick wall, being able to bite off, at most, an occasional piece of the oppression pie.

*Does a revolutionary atmosphere currently exist within the United States?* Definitely not. There are some necessary components, many of which can be seen by observing the frustration and anger amongst people engaging in various single-issue justice pursuits. Yet, the psychological determination to engage in a revolutionary movement is extremely rare, repressed by a potent propaganda campaign summarized in the *Five Rules for the Game of Social and Political Change in the United States.*

What might actually occur if U.S. government officials openly told their citizens that *if you see injustice that cannot be corrected by any other measure, you have the right—no, the obligation—to rebel and even to create a revolution to abolish this political system for one that can provide for justice?* What if this notion were purposely taught in schooling systems, through the news and entertainment media and by politicians, instead of the actual line that suggests an adherence to the Five Rules will actually solve political and societal grievances? Well it is not taught, specifically because revolution is never deemed appropriate to discuss in the context of current social and political justice movements within the United States. It is only politically and socially acceptable in historical terms, such as the moment before parents light their children's sparklers on the 4th of July.

As a result of this strong propaganda effort, only on rare occasions have single-issue social and political movements actually ever even placed a marginal degree of pressure on the government. When this pressure was applied, it came from the previously listed examples—all of which predominantly practiced a strict adherence to the Five Rules. Thus, since the Five Rules were followed—conduct which falls well within the safety zone of the U.S. political system—overall social and political change has never occurred.

It is feasible to assert that one main reason revolution is not discussed as a viable option to further justice movements in the United States is that a certain taboo is associated with the subject. That taboo, of course, is the topic of political violence. Revolution is seldom discussed in this country in any realistic terms due to the extreme hesitancy, particularly of the Left, to even contemplate using political violence to achieve justice. The old 'means-versus-ends' debate simply gets in the way.

*Could a successful political and social revolution within the United States be waged strictly on nonviolent terms?* The vast majority of liberal progressives seem to think so. Yet, from the examples I have already discussed, the likelihood of such a success is practically nil. The manner in which the United States was created, its historic and ongoing domestic and foreign policy behaviors, and the lack of effectiveness of past justice movements surely should provide some indication.

Contained within the chapter on nonviolence is an explanation of the requirements of nonviolent campaigns. One primary and unsurpassable factor that must be present for any nonviolent campaign to be successful is the ability of the opponent to have a working conscience, to be able to see the evil in his or her own actions and to voluntarily change. Nonviolence proponents rule out the use of any force, so the opponent must be able to give in to nonviolent pressure coming directly from the justice movement or even indirectly from the global political arena—which in turn may be pressuring the primary opponent specifically in reaction to the nonviolent justice campaign.

Throughout the history of the United States, each regime change has proven itself in opposition to this very basic theoretical nonviolence requirement. The most basic questions that illustrate this behavior are: *Would someone engage in a horrendous act of injustice or allow one to continue if he or she had a healthy working conscience? Would people directly or indirectly approve of and support this injustice if they had the ability to see the evils of their own actions and voluntarily change? How could individuasl in this state, of knowingly participating in a terrible atrocity, be compelled by a nonviolent campaign to relinquish all of their power, prestige, and position?*

Within this introduction I have argued three main points. The first is that the pursuit of reform in the United States has proven to be a fruitless venture. Secondly, I have shown why a political and societal revolution is necessary in the United States. Third, I have demonstrated that a revolution in the United States must be comprised of a variety of strategies—but it cannot be successful without the implementation of political violence.

\*

I will say in all honesty from the outset that my primary concern both with this work and in my life is attempting to create major social and political change within the United States. This is the reason I have undertaken this project. It is not meant to be another lengthy set of words on pages of paper, but rather a tool for contemplation and action. Since 1990, the birth of my political life, I have struggled to find the answers to the social change equation. *How can we actually create social and political change within the United States?* The arguments over strategies, over nonviolence versus violence, appear ageless. This book is meant as a necessary addition to the debate.

Before launching into the first section it will be useful to clarify a few definitions. First and foremost, I feel it is necessary to define social change and political change. What is actually meant by these terms? In the simplest terminology, social or political change refers to making society or the political system different. Rarely is there a visible identifiable factor associated with social or political change to differentiate between the positive and negative. While in theory it is possible to discuss and even work toward negative social change, rarely is this ever an admitted actuality. (Even Hitler in his own warped way would have proclaimed he was pursuing *positive* social change). By and large, when the terms social and political change are discussed, the usual underlying notion is that it is positive.

Positive social change broadly refers to the creation of differences within a society. While this may include political change—a difference created within the political system of the country—it is not absolutely a necessary component of the social change process. An individual living in a city who, out of a desire to bring the community closer together and less reliant on outside commodities, organizes and plants a community garden is not necessarily creating any change within the political arena. However, the act could definitely fall within the social change category.

Political change, on the other hand, does involve social change. It would be difficult to imagine any change within the political system having no effect whatsoever on the society merely due to the system's role in representing society. The change might be minute, but nevertheless, in most cases you cannot have one without the other.

Social and political change fall into two major categories: that of reform and that of revolution. These are important terms that will be frequently referred to throughout the book. In this work I specifically define a reformist as one who seeks social and/or political change, but under the existing power structure. The reformist definitely identifies one or more problems in need of correcting but otherwise genuinely believes the existing political system is beneficial. There are far too many examples to list of reformist measures currently in the United States, but a few would include the mainstream peace, environmental, and animal rights movements. Of course, it needs to be stated that there are some exceptions in each of these examples, but overall these movements have demonstrated a desire to promote positive social and political change while maintaining the current political system.

On the other hand, I refer to a revolutionary as one who seeks to fundamentally change the entire political system. A revolution may involve both political and social change, as we shall observe in the case of Castro's Cuba. Yet, under these definitions I am convinced it is not possible to have a successful social revolution without changing the entire political system. Therefore, I do not refer to social change on its own as revolutionary but as a reformist pursuit.

As far as the methodologies for social and political change, I divide them into two major categories: violent and nonviolent, with a hell of a lot of gray area in between. In relation to social and political change, the terms nonviolence and violence are widely discussed and debated. *Just what is meant by nonviolence?* Nonviolence, like many words, is difficult to define because people tend to describe it consciously or subconsciously in association with various nonviolence theorists. Person #1, who takes an absolutist stand behind Gandhian principles, would never admit or advocate that coercion plays any role in the nonviolence process. Yet person #2, who may have studied Martin Luther King, Jr., for example, may openly admit that there are certainly elements of coercion and "mental force" involved in nonviolent campaigns. Even on a personal level, my own definition of nonviolence has fluctuated back and forth considerably over the years.

Through all of my experiences and after much contemplation, I have come to a personal definition that I am using for this book. For me nonviolence begins with the absence from any physical injury to a life form, whether it be human, animal, or any of the various plant species we and the planet depend on for survival. Most definitions of nonviolence will share this most rudimentary point. Additionally though, I go further to define nonviolence as including the absence of nearly all mental force and coercion. Let me unpack this. In a nonviolent campaign, those seeking to create positive change normally will use a variety of strategies— short of violence—*to allow the opponent to see the evils in his or her own actions and voluntarily change.* More realistically, whenever a nonviolent campaign has been successful, it has been historically due to the opponent being coerced into changing. It was not a wholly internal decision on the part of the opponent, but rather a decision greatly affected by outside influences pressuring and molding the opinion.

Two simple examples to illustrate my point were the enfranchisement and desegregation campaigns in the U.S. civil rights movement. The white man did not willingly, on his own accord, just decide one day to grant African Americans the ability to vote and exist in desegregated zones. Instead, after lengthy and devoted campaigns were waged by African Americans—primarily nonviolent except for the massive, violent repression from whites—the white man became coerced or "mentally forced" into granting these most basic human rights within the legal system.

Now, in the above definition of nonviolence, I stated that it consists of action that is *absent of nearly all mental force and coercion.* Largely in line with Gandhian principles, this definition would include civil disobedience as long as there was absolutely no resisting and a certain degree of respect maintained toward the opponent. Also in line with Gandhi, I exclude the use of property destruction as being completely nonviolent.

I also find it necessary to differentiate pacifism from nonviolence —to a certain extent. Pacifism, in one of its popular definitions, refers to the "belief that war and violence are morally unjustified" (Oxford Dictionary, 2001, Berkeley Books, NY). With this definition there simply is no connotation implying any action or need thereof. Sitting on the couch doing nothing but thinking of how violence and war are unjustified may not constitute nonviolence in its most active sense, but it clearly fits into the pacifist category. While pacifism can be a form of nonviolence, I am primarily interested in the active application of nonviolent strategies to pursue social and/or political change. Some examples may include nonviolent civil disobedience campaigns, working directly within the political process, public education, protests, and more. Nonviolence, as one of the two primary subject matters of this work, will be discussed at length throughout this book.

With this most basic definition of nonviolence, it is simple to suggest that violence then incorporates all other strategies of action—physical harm, mental harm, unlimited force, coercion, etc. While this is seemingly true, I am strictly concerned with political violence, or violent acts committed in pursuit of positive social and/or political change rather than random acts with no realistic intended goal. Throughout the book I will refer to politically-motivated violence as simply political violence. Examples of political violence may include bombings, assassination, insurrection, guerrilla war, property destruction, terrorism, and more.

I decided to devote the first part of this book to a series of seven historical cases. Each of these cases provides crucial lessons as to why a political and social revolution is needed in the United States. This first section thus raises theoretical issues concerning nonviolence and political violence, which I discuss in Part Two. Finally, in my conclusion, I apply my findings to the current social and political change movements existing in the United States.

If, after reading this book, you remain in your easy chair and are not compelled to act or continue your action, I have failed in my efforts. As I stated earlier my one aim with this work is to assist in creating the much-needed political and social change within the United States. My one desire is that people act, that everything possible is done to ensure that this and future generations have a better world to live in. If we refuse to act, if we refuse to engage in every possible action to create change, aren't we ourselves allowing an incredible amount of violence to continue by our own inactivity?

# PART ONE

# HISTORICAL CONTEXT
## *Cases and Lessons from History*

Contained within this first section are seven historical case studies examining both nonviolence and political violence in terms of social and political change. While all historians make deliberate decisions on what cases to study and what information both to include and to exclude to strengthen their given arguments, I have carefully selected cases that assist in bringing the following issues to the table of debate regarding the social and political change process: *How can we best pursue social and political change in the United States? Is political violence ever a necessary and legitimate strategy in working toward justice? Is revolution a necessity in the United States?*

In this section I begin by taking a look at perhaps one of the most controversial topics in nonviolence theology, the case of *Jewish Resistance to Genocide in World War II Europe*. I specifically chose this case to demonstrate the ineffectiveness of nonviolent pursuits when faced with a morally-incompetent opponent. Hitler demonstrated very early on that he and his forces did not, under any circumstances, have a healthy, working conscience. Even before the bulk of murders took place in the various death camps, his SS forces were slaughtering Jews in the streets at random.

In this case, the *business-as-usual* policy of attempting to go about everyday activities as though nothing were wrong was highly implemented among the majority of Jews inside ghettos and camps. The business-as-usual practitioners spoke out against those who supported, promoted, and engaged in literally any resistance to the Nazis' *Final Solution* program. It is not that much unlike the members of mainstream justice movements today who condemn one another's actions, oftentimes assisting the opposition in catching and prosecuting those who have broken the given norms or laws in place. Just as the Judenrats often turned in rebels to the Nazis, today one can easily witness a peace and nonviolence proponent attempting to stop property destruction by force (as was the case in the streets of Seattle during the 1999 World Trade Organization meetings) or popular environmental organizations working with the FBI and U.S. government to stop radical eco-saboteurs.

The very business-as-usual policy practiced by enormous numbers of Jews during the Nazi era is mirrored today in the United States heavily among the Left as sheep following the enlightenment path of the Five Rules, careful to continually avoid the politically-violent wolves. Just as the Judenrats commonly preached to Jewish masses to live their lives as though nothing were wrong, in the business-as-usual mentality, single-issue nonviolence reformists act in total adherence to the Five Rules, blind to any realistic analysis of their failure. *This is the way I go about social and political change. If I have a grievance, this is the way to address it. It has always been this way and will always be.*

This very mentality suggests that nonviolent action and an adherence to the Five Rules—when both have been proven fruitless in a given situation—stem more out of a desire to appease a personal, individual conscience than an actual expectation to ever see tangible results. Most often this is shadowed by the almighty religious phenomenon of means-versus-ends: *As long as the means are correct* (meaning nonviolent and within the boundaries specified by the Five Rules) *the ends are a certainty.* Rarely is the reality ever addressed that an adherence to this logic enables a greater degree of violence and injustice to exist.

As I identify in the case of the Nazi holocaust, the "good Jews" who were among the vast majority in offering little or no real resistance to Hitler's agenda *permitted* the severe extent of the outcome. By 'no real resistance' I am referring both to actual pacification as well as more active forms of nonviolent resistance. Neither showed any sign whatsoever of working, except on behalf of Hitler's plans to annihilate the entire Jewish population.

Today in the United States, those who adhere to the Five Rules of conduct are, by their own inactions, allowing a heightened degree of violence and injustice to exist. Just as Hitler's regime demonstrated its willingness to use unceasing violence to accomplish its warped plan, the U.S. government has also, historically and even to this date, presented itself as a relentless aggressor bound to defend itself from any and all attacks by any means necessary. Knowing this, to engage in a justice struggle in the United States by only following the Five Rules of conduct is to tacitly enable the government to continue its murderous policies without any significant opposition. Thus, by its own inactivity, by its own refusal to actually confront and threaten the power of the United States government, the absolutist nonviolent Left is allowing a greater degree of violence to plague the global arena.

To demonstrate reformist limitations, I chose to include, as one of the primary examples of successful nonviolent application often discussed by nonviolence proponents, a study of the civil rights movement. African Americans suffered inconceivable atrocities throughout U.S. history, especially as they began to rise up in defiance of the white man's set norms. Rape, torture, and murder were common forms of white repression that came in response to merely seeking enfranchisement, desegregation, and other equal rights. After all the predominantly nonviolent efforts waged in the 1940s, 1950s, and 1960s by African Americans, the most that was accomplished were minor reforms. These minor reforms consisted of some enfranchisement, desegregation, and a heavy dose of lip service by the white power structure that the African American was then equal.

Yet, even to this day, African Americans still are far from experiencing any overall equality with whites in power. Similar to poor whites, women, and other "minorities," African Americans continue to take a back seat to well-off whites. This is precisely due to the fact that the structure of the political system in the United States was not seriously questioned or challenged during the civil rights struggle. The primary focus of the movement was aimed at cleaning the rotten food out of the same old refrigerator. My point here is that the very refrigerator was not built correctly, to preserve all the varieties of food, and so the very unit, the structure, the refrigerator itself is *causing* the food to go rotten. The refrigerator needs to be destroyed.

Similar to the civil rights struggle, I brought in the *Movement in the United States Against the War in Vietnam* to discuss the downfalls of single issue reformism, in one of the largest justice efforts in U.S. history. Nearly all of the U.S. peace and anti-war movements have had a similar trait in common: Each has been specifically focused on a particular action either taken or threatened by the U.S. government. Whether it be war in the Middle East, Asia, or even the building of nuclear weaponry at home, each subject in modern times has sparked a single issue opposition. Just as the 1960s were filled with anti-Vietnam War activity, today in the United States, peace and anti-war activists voice their outrage over U.S. military action taken in Afghanistan and Iraq.

The primary problem with this single-issue approach is that 1) no anti-war movement in the United States has ever stopped the government from engaging in military activity, and 2) even if one anti-war or peace movement did see progress during a given time, there is every reason to believe the U.S. government would not be deterred from continuing on with its militaristic policies elsewhere. In the case of the anti-Vietnam War movement, the popular misconception is that the peace activism actually forced the U.S. government to pull out of Vietnam. While there is evidence that Nixon was, at least partially, psychologically disturbed by the growing movement, his answer was not to stop the war but to initiate his policy of *Vietnamization*. This rather ingenious policy, directly aimed at reducing public support for the anti-war cause, allowed him to continue on with the military action for another five years.

It is difficult to fathom how a massive movement, consisting of hundreds of thousands of people, could not create enough pressure on its own to achieve change and justice. But indeed, the Paris peace agreement signed in 1973 was more a result of the success of the Viet Cong than any overwhelming pressure from the U.S. anti-war effort. The movement surely carried with it a level of pressure against the U.S. governmental policies in Vietnam, but it was not enough to force an end to the conflict.

Even if a historical or current peace movement did actually succeed in preventing or stopping a U.S.-sponsored war, there is ample evidence to suggest that the U.S. government would not stop its current military action elsewhere or in the future. This evidence, as I have explained previously, comes directly from the historical record of U.S. foreign and domestic policies. The political structure in the United States, maintained and controlled by and for the white, upper-class man, has demonstrated that it will stop at nothing to defend itself. Unless a successful movement abolishes that very political structure, it will certainly continue to act aggressively in a militaristic, violent nature. The single-issue mentality, of *stop this war*, only serves to *allow* more wars to be waged for this pseudo-democratic government and its economy.

The case of the Algerian Revolution, in which nationalists successfully ousted the French, provides further crucial lessons to those concerned with justice struggles in the United States. While political differences between the Algerian case and that of the current U.S. society are abundant, there are also some striking similarities. Perhaps most important, the rebel organizations operating inside Algeria—such as the FLN —did *not* enter into an already existing revolutionary atmosphere. These groups demonstrated, by horrifically successful uses of terrorism and other political violence, that revolutionary conditions can actually be *created*.

In terms of justice movements operating inside the United States, this example is crucial. Like the Algerian situation, nearly every "progressive" individual in the United States would agree that revolutionary conditions do not exist in this country. Therefore, the mere suggestion of revolution—even as an abstract topic—is commonly dismissed and allegedly would only be considered once those unstated conditions suddenly appeared.

The level of discontent in the United States, similar to that in colonized Algeria, is remarkably high. From an organizing perspective, the Algeria case suggests that it may indeed be possible to transform that frustration, anger, resentment, and feeling of alienation into positive revolutionary behavior. Likewise, it does seem quite feasible that strategies could certainly be implemented to produce the conditions necessary for revolution in this country, just as they were in Algeria.

Some, such as myself, would argue that those conditions already exist and have existed for many years. A terrorist government, plaguing the world with capitalist-driven violence, geared towards benefiting the white, upper-class male, should be proof in itself. But when its track record of exploitation, murder and destruction has been, at best, consistent and, at worst, continually increasing, the obligation for a political and societal revolution is immediate and pressing.

Others within the so-called "progressive" or Left-leaning movements often contend that revolutionary conditions may only be present when all other options of achieving justice have been exhausted. Additionally, it is commonly thought that the time for revolution might only arise when the government has proven itself to be so horrific and unstoppable, there simply exists no other plausible alternative. Yet, these two very notions constitute a severe gray area, undefined, and therefore never fully reachable.

*Every* other effort and strategy short of a full scale, fundamental political and societal revolution in the United States has been exhausted. As I have previously shown, the numerous single-issue, reformist pursuits have failed, by their own limitations, to produce the needed changes to allow for any true resemblance of justice. Even the massive movements, such as the civil rights and anti-Vietnam War struggles, were not enough to address the primary cause of many injustices. Rather, they, like other political and social justice movements in the United States, only served to reinforce the U.S. farcical democracy while allowing the political system to grow unchallenged. This growth, of course, has only meant an increase in both domestic and foreign state-sponsored violence, terrorism, and destruction.

The U.S. government has also proved itself to be a horrific and unstoppable disease, the necessary prerequisite for many within the Left to even theoretically contemplate revolution. How many more innocent men, women, and children will have to be murdered by the U.S. government before self-described "progressive" and "compassionate" people will agree the time has come to rise up in revolt? How much more of the natural environment—which we *all* rely on for our mere existence—must be destroyed before people finally realize that it is time to actually confront the very political system enabling the destruction? Hopefully, these realizations will come before it is too late.

The FLN organization in Algeria also provided an excellent example of the possibility of a revolutionary group holding its own and politically defeating a larger, more powerful opponent. Realizing it could never achieve victory over the French militarily, especially by using the conventional military terms of the French, the FLN intelligently refrained from even attempting this uneven bout. Instead, the FLN sought to create and sustain an unsettled, unstable atmosphere inside French ruled Algeria. This demonstrated to the French that no matter how much effort was placed into controlling and repressing Algerians, they still could not produce a stable atmosphere or demonstrate full control.

Through a campaign consisting largely of terrorist strategies, the European immigrants who settled in the area under French rule were literally frightened back to their home continent. As a result, the power and ability of the French to rule Algeria slowly diminished, and it became clear the colonialist regime was not welcome in the predominantly Moslem-based land. Thus, in 1962, after a bloody and incredibly violent battle with organizations such as the FLN, the French were forced to grant Algeria independence.

Inside the United States, another dismissal coming from the progressive sector of society is that any revolutionary effort would be annihilated by the U.S. government. Indeed, there is every indication this would certainly be the case if any insurgency were foolish enough to attempt to combat the United States using conventional military means. The case of the FLN in Algeria, however, demonstrates that the ability to win a battle against a more powerful opponent does certainly exist, especially when a variety of strategies are implemented.

This concept is further explored in the chapter examining the strategies of the Viet Cong used against the United States in the Vietnam War. The North Vietnamese should have been no match militarily for the almighty, U.S. forces—or so the U.S. government believed. With more advanced weaponry, better mobilization, and firepower, the U.S. government believed a quick and decisive victory was a certainty. Yet, through the political and armed strategies implemented by the North Vietnamese, the United States suffered its most embarrassing moment in U.S. military history.

Similar to the FLN, the success of the Viet Cong came as a direct result of its deliberate decision not to attempt to meet the U.S. military using conventional warfare. This would have only enabled the quick victory for the United States. Rather, armed strategies of guerrilla warfare and political strategies of successfully gaining widespread support among the local population and from the international political arena were utilized. As a result, President Nixon was forced to sign the 1973 Paris Agreement, effectively serving as evidence of the first, major U.S. military loss.

The case of Castro's Cuban Revolution also echoes the notion that popular forces can win a war against a stronger army. Castro's insurrectionary forces, at times numbering only a small handful, were able to successfully overthrow the Batista regime. This was only accomplished through highly unconventional means, primarily of guerrilla style warfare, where battles were not fought unless victory was a certainty.

Secondly, like the case in Algeria, the Cuban Revolution demonstrates that the insurrection itself can *create* the necessary revolutionary conditions. Additionally, it suggests a certain legitimacy to the belief that a revolution can begin well before the revolutionaries know precisely what it is they desire. In the case of the Cuban Revolution, Castro knew deep within his soul that his country needed something far more than just the overthrow of the Batista regime. He realized that unless the Cuban society was also transformed, a new corrupt regime would just replace Batista. Castro, especially at the beginning, had no thorough idea of the society he sought to create; he felt it was enough just to realize a different one was needed.

If the primary prerequisite for any revolution occurring in the United States were a mutually agreed-upon utopian dream by all members of "progressive" society, that revolution would never commence. This is precisely part of the reasoning behind the lack of progress in political and social justice movements within the United States. Among the liberal Left, justice seekers are continually caught up arguing amongst themselves over the perfect world they seek to create and the means to get them there. Unfortunately, this argumentative reality of the Left prevents any useful acknowledgment of commonalities, such as simply realizing that fundamental change is needed.

The Cuban Revolution also provides an excellent demonstration of the abilities of a few to change an entire nation. Unbelievably, Castro survived many failed insurrectionary attempts, as well as numerous assassination plots, to successfully gain control of the country. This example, on its own, suggests that in the United States an effective revolutionary movement may not be impossible.

Finally, I included the case of the 1916 Easter Uprising in Ireland to show an example of an obviously failed insurrection still having significance and a certain legitimacy. Just as in Algeria and Cuba, rebels engaged in insurrectionary behavior, not so much out of knowing precisely what sort of society they desired, as much as feeling a right and obligation to act against a perceived injustice. It is this very right and obligation that legitimizes the decision to revolt.

In the United States, this right and obligation to engage in revolutionary behavior should also be deemed legitimate. Even if insurgents have no idea what they seek to put in place of the current political system, it is still the right of all people living within the United States to start and participate in a revolution if all other means of addressing political and societal grievances have been exhausted. In the case of the United States, all other options were exhausted years ago.

Perhaps the most common example—in terms of nonviolent strategy—I have excluded from this section is that of Gandhi in his work in South Africa and then India. The Gandhian legacy, without any doubt, represents by far the most commonly-cited example of successful nonviolence application. This is especially true of western nonviolence scholars and activists. As I feel the Gandhian example is a necessary and crucial inclusion into the discussion of social and political change strategies, the particular case is used as a backdrop for the entire book, with particular emphasis in chapters 8 and 9.

I found these historic explorations into social and political change to be extremely helpful in formulating my own ideas about justice pursuits in the United States today and in the future. I can only hope that these lessons will also influence you. For unless we thoroughly digest lessons from history, we are doomed to repeat mistakes and failures of the past.

# CHAPTER ONE

# *Jewish Resistance to Genocide in World War II Europe*

One of the most striking dilemmas I have encountered while studying nonviolence theory and application was a question once posed to Mahatma Gandhi. During his use of Satyagraha in the Indian independence movement, Gandhi was asked whether or not his nonviolence theory could be successful if applied against a man such as Adolf Hitler and the Nazi forces. He replied that it could, but not without great sacrifices and casualties. Indeed, many followers of Gandhi, including theorists such as Joan Bondurant, Gene Sharp, Louis Fischer, and applicators such as Martin Luther King, Jr., would all agree with Gandhi that nonviolence can be used successfully against the most difficult opponents including Hitler.

Owing to the outcome of the Nazi's *Final Solution* program, in which at least five million Jews were systematically murdered throughout Europe, naturally there has been much skepticism in believing the power of nonviolence could have defeated Hitler's forces. Critics of Gandhi's assumption argue that nonviolence and passive resistance were utilized, often on a grand scale, with little or no success. Many identify the passivity of the Jews during World War II in Europe as directly contributing to the near success of the *Final Solution.*

It would be an absolute myth to proclaim that Jews in German-occupied Europe offered no resistance to the Nazis. Yet, I feel that is a common assumption held by a large percentage of the public that perhaps have not looked closely at the subject. I myself was never taught about Jewish resistance when I learned of the genocidal situation. After further examining the subject, I have become fascinated by the wealth of Jewish responses that did actually exist. Whether or not these responses were effective, whether there was enough of a response, whether the response was too late, or even if the correct response was made are all important questions to be considered.

My aim with this section is to not only describe the various types of resistance undertaken by Jews, but also to further analyze the resistance itself. This work therefore not only contains the various means of nonviolent resistance, but also includes the armed struggles undertaken by Jews against the Nazis. As most of the Jewish camps and resistance were in Eastern Europe, I will be devoting a majority of the discussion to this location. Western Europe will not be forgotten though and will be discussed at length. My hopes are that by digesting this work, you will not only have a more thorough knowledge of Jewish resistance in World War II Europe, but will also have a greater understanding of the role both armed resistance and nonviolence had in the final outcome.

# EASTERN EUROPE

Perhaps one of the most famous cases of resistance during the Nazi holocaust occurred in the Warsaw ghetto. Therefore, Warsaw seems like a fitting place to begin.

Warsaw has been the capital of Poland since 1596. Prior to the beginning of World War II, the Jewish population in Warsaw was 375,000, about thirty percent of the total population. Warsaw surrendered to German forces on September 28, 1939 and Germans entered the city the following day. Israel Gutman, a professor emeritus at the Hebrew University of Jerusalem, describes the plight of the Jews during the initial stages of the German invasion in an essay contained within *The Holocaust Encyclopedia.* He writes:

From the very first days of occupation, Jews were subjected to attacks, driven away from food lines, and seized
for forced labor. Religious Jews in traditional garb were
assaulted, and Jewish shops and homes were plundered.
The indiscriminate seizure of Jews for forced labor, regardless of age, sex, or health, paralyzed the community
as Jews kept off the streets (1990, p.685).

The climate for Jews in Warsaw continued to decline as Germans
established an official ghetto there in November 1940. Into the Warsaw
ghetto went Jews not only from Warsaw itself but also from many of
the outlying cities. At this time Jews were banned from reopening their
schools, banned from train travel, and restrictions were placed on owning
or leasing enterprises. In addition, Jews were ordered to give up their
radios and were required to wear the Star of David at all times. Germans
further terrorized Jews by murdering them in the streets at random, carrying out deportations to concentration camps, and seizing people for forced
labor.

Shortly thereafter, a Judenrat was set up in Warsaw. Judenrats
were a form of self government imposed on the Jews by the Nazis, largely
in Eastern Europe. A main purpose of the Judenrat was to instill a business-as-usual policy among Jews, most often in cooperation with Nazi
forces (Trunk, 1972, p. XXV). Additionally, the Judenrat was imposed
to allow the Germans a pseudo-acting government to address when they
wanted orders carried out.

Early on, some of these councils attempted to address the Nazis
on many of the atrocities committed against the Jews. In Warsaw, from
August 30 to September 19, 1940, the Judenrat addressed the Germans
regarding eighteen different problems. Some of these included trying to
stop the Germans from taking the furnishings from schools, and allowing tradesmen to continue their work. The Judenrat also petitioned the
Germans, arguing that it was unable to move some 130,000 Jews from the
"Aryan" sections of Warsaw into 50,000 small, one-bedroom apartments
existing in the ghetto.

During the first month the ghetto was sealed, 445 people died.
The number of deaths per month continued to rise from that time on. In
August 1941, the number of deaths reached 5,560 and from then on re-
mained between 4,000 and 5,000 per month (Gutman, 1990, p. 1609).

The first armed resistance group to be established in the Warsaw ghetto came largely as a response to conditions existing within the ghetto and news of mass executions of Jews in other eastern European areas by the Germans. Created between late March and early April 1942, the *Antifascist Bloc* was formed on the initiative of the communists inside Warsaw. The group also attracted individuals from the Zionist left who believed that the communists were supported by the Soviet Union. The Zionists presumed that the Soviets would be able to supply military backing and arms for the *Antifascist Bloc* in the ghetto. In reality though, these communists in particular had no direct contact with the Soviets and had little in the way of resources of their own.

The communists within the *Bloc* didn't support resistance within the ghetto itself, but rather wanted to use the ghetto as a resource for fighters in the partisan units operating outside the ghettos in Eastern Europe. Zionists, on the other hand, felt it was extremely crucial to struggle inside the ghetto. On May 30, 1942, the *Bloc* quickly demised after leading communists were arrested due to unrelated communist activity.

On July 28, 1942, the *Zydowska Organizacja Bojowa* (Jewish Fighting Organization; ZOB) was formed inside Warsaw. This armed group, created during the deportations occurring at Warsaw in 1942, at first primarily consisted of youth movements. *HaShomer ha-Tsa'ir, Dror,* and *Akiva* youth groups were the first to join the ZOB. The formation of the ZOB did not meet everyone's approval in the ghetto, especially some key figures who felt that a defense organization was not needed since Warsaw Jews were in no danger of being deported. Opponents also argued that any resistance within the ghetto could lead to its immediate liquidation. These concerns were also the primary factor in the delay of a resistance group operating in Warsaw before the deportations.

From July 22 to September 12, 1942, Germany conducted large-scale deportations in Warsaw. Approximately 300,000 Warsaw residents were transported out of the ghetto, and 265,000 of them were shipped to the Treblinka death camp. At this time the ZOB called on Jews inside Warsaw to "stand up for themselves and resist deportation" (Gutman, 1990, p. 1744). Most of the ghetto inhabitants, acting largely on fear, refused to act on the ZOB call and cooperated with the transport.

Owing to the fear instilled in ghetto residents and the reality of having few weapons, the ZOB was unable to launch any sort of massive resistance. Yet, the group did act on numerous occasions. On August 20, 1942, Joseph Szerynski, the head of the Jewish police in the ghetto at that time, was shot and severely wounded by a ZOB member. Szerynski had taken an active role in aiding the deportations. In addition, the ZOB set fire to German factories in the ghetto and interfered with the hunt for Jews. After two ZOB leaders, Josef Kaplan and Shmuel Braslav, were caught killed and all of ZOB's weapons were confiscated by the Germans on the same day, the ZOB decided to wait until after the deportation to resume planning for a revolt.

Only a mere 55,000 Jews remained in the Warsaw ghetto after this deportation. Of these, 35,000 were recognized as workers in German factories, and the other 20,000 went into hiding after escaping deportation. The Jews who were left finally understood what was actually occurring at Treblinka. This realization, in addition to the news from other ghettos about multiple deportations, led them to understand that they would soon be killed. "Many now said out loud that they regretted not having offered resistance to the deportations, and insisted that they would fight if an *Aktion* were again launched" (Gutman, 1990, p. 1744). (*Aktion* was the name given to the deportations and liquidations of ghettos and camps by the Nazis.)

Disagreements within the ZOB led the Revisionist Zionists to create their own group, *Zydowski Zwiazek Wojskowy* (Jewish Military Union; ZZW). For a short while, extreme tension existed between these two groups over strategies and whether or not they would even work together. Finally, after talks between representatives of both groups, the ZZW agreed to coordinate its actions with the ZOB. They both also agreed on a strategic plan to acquire weapons, and the division of the groups in the ghetto to prepare for the next deportation.

The ZOB decided to form a civilian branch called the *Zydowski Komitet Narodowy* (Jewish National Committee). This group was specifically created to collect funds for purchasing arms. Additionally, Polish underground leaders recognized this committee as an official organization authorized to represent Jews. This recognition was important, as Jews in the ghetto had been attempting to solicit assistance from the Polish underground, who previously were not easily addressed.

In late 1942, the ZOB found a supporter by the name of Arie Wilner who was on the "Aryan" side of Warsaw. Wilner had established connections with the *Armia Krajowa* (Home Army, AK), the military wing in Poland of the Polish government-in-exile in London, and the *Armia Ludowa* (People's Army)—the fighting force in Poland made up of the communists. The Home Army, AK, provided a small number of weapons to the ZOB and also trained them to make grenades out of explosives.

However, most of the weapons gained by the ZOB were bought from middlemen who had bought or stolen them from the Germans or their supporters. Using this new found assistance, the ZOB prepared for its first major revolt.

One of the next actions the ZOB took was removing those people from within the ghetto that had assisted the Germans in the first deportation. Among others, the ZOB killed Jacob Lejkin—acting chief of police during the deportation, and Dr. Alfred Nossig, who turned out to be a informer to the Nazis. These ZOB actions created fear in others who may have been collaborators and worked to neutralize them.

ZOB members also began publishing and distributing leaflets informing the ghetto residents of the fate of deportees and what was actually occurring at the Treblinka death camp. Most of the ghetto inhabitants didn't initially take too well to the leaflets, once again believing his type of action would only serve to create a quicker liquidation of the ghetto.

The second massive deportation at Warsaw began on January 18, 1943. Jews were ordered out of their apartments and told to show their identification papers for examination. Nearly all the Jews who remained in the ghetto refused to comply with these orders and went into hiding. After a few hours the first group of approximately 1,000 Jews was gathered by the Nazis. A group of resistance fighters, armed with pistols, deliberately infiltrated this group led by Mordecai Anielewicz. After a predetermined signal was given, the resistance fighters emerged from the group and fought the German soldiers. The group of 1,000 Jews quickly dispersed, and news from this uprising instantly made its way around the ghetto. On the same day, *Dror* youth group members engaged in armed resistance against the Germans from an apartment building within the ghetto.

The deportations ended only four days later on January 22, after Jews continuously refused to report when ordered, largely in response to news of the first day of uprisings. An estimated 5,000 to 6,000 Jews had been captured by the end of the deportations. Both Poles and Jews considered the resistance a great success, as only approximately ten percent of the entire ghetto population was actually captured. Yet, it was later realized that Germans were originally planning on only removing 8,000 people during this deportation *Aktion* and not liquidating the entire ghetto at that moment. Still, 2,000 to 3,000 people were saved due to the resistance actions at that time.

Over the next year, Jews within the ghetto constantly prepared for the next, and what would be the final, liquidation of Warsaw. Many underground bunkers were built and strategic plans were made for what they knew was inevitably coming. The ZOB steadily grew, and just before the final deportations began the group had some twenty-two fighting squads, each with fifteen fighters.

On April 19, 1943, at 3:00 a.m., Germans surrounded the ghetto with 850 soldiers and eighteen officers. As the Germans entered the ghetto in two sections they were met with fierce armed resistance that forced them to retreat. The center of the ghetto had been almost completely evacuated as Jews were either hiding in bunkers or in fighter positions in the apartments. Germans then strategically began going from structure to structure burning each, one at a time, to try and force everyone to come out. As a result of the intense heat and horrible air quality, the underground bunkers became unbearable. Yet, the Jews refused to surrender to the Germans, instead continuously attempting to move from bunker to bunker.

During the second week of the uprising, the bunkers continued to be the main area of resistance. Germans were made to go to each individual bunker and either throw in grenades or use gas to try and force everyone to emerge. On many occasions when Jews were forced out of the bunkers, many came out fighting, shooting at the first Germans whom they encountered. Although the Germans declared the Warsaw ghetto liquidated of Jews on May 16, 1943, many Jews still continued to hide in the bunkers and engage in armed resistance.

In addition to the armed resistance at Warsaw, approximately 20,000 Jews escaped from the ghetto during the last few months of its existence. They went into other areas of the city hoping to find refuge among the Polish people. A small but significant number of Poles did succeed in hiding Jews during this time period.

*

Perhaps one of the best-known camps created by the Germans was Auschwitz. Of the two thousand forced-labor and death camps that existed, Auschwitz was the largest operation. Built in mid-1940 by Jewish slave labor, the camp, located near the East German/West Poland border, initially held primarily Polish political prisoners. The camp soon grew as Birkenau (Auschwitz II) and Buna-Monowitz (Auschwitz III) were built in 1941 and 1942. Birkenau housed the main gas chambers and crematoria for the entire camp. Owing to the sheer size of the operation, transport trains arrived frequently. Jozef Buszko of Jagiellonian University in Krakow has described the process vividly:

> As the trains stopped at the *rampa* (railway platform) in Birkenau, the people inside were brutally forced to leave the cars in a great hurry. They had to leave behind all their personal belongings and were made to form two lines, men and women separately. These lines had to move quickly to the place where SS officers were conducting the Selektion, directing the people either to one side (the majority), for the gas chambers, or to the other, which meant designation for forced labor. Those who were sent to the gas chambers were killed that same day and their corpses were burned in crematoria, or, if there were too many for the crematoria to process, in an open space (1990, p. 109).

There was also a small third category of arrivals who were spared for an unknown time in order for medical experiments to be carried out on them. This consisted of mainly young Greek Jewish men and women.

The first small gas chamber was built in Auschwitz I. Using Zyklon B gas, the first experimental gassing took place on September 3, 1941. This consisted of killing 600 Soviet prisoners and 250 other ill prisoners chosen at random. As a result of this experiment, the four large permanent gas chambers were built at Birkenau. Each chamber, built to appear like shower rooms, was capable of gassing 6,000 people daily. Victims destined for the gas chambers were told they were being sent to work and that first they had to shower. The first Jews who fell victim to mass executions in the gas chambers in Birkenau were from Silesia.

One of the first documented cases of resistance at Auschwitz came on October 23, 1943. An unknown woman, who had just arrived on a transport train and was on her way with other women to the gas chambers, took a pistol from an SS guard and shot two other SS men. The other women in the grouping also resisted, and all of them were immediately executed when Nazi reinforcements arrived.

One of the most common forms of resistance, especially early on at Auschwitz, was escape. An estimated 667 prisoners did escape from this camp, but 270 of them were later captured nearby and killed.

In 1943, a multinational resistance group was formed in Auschwitz, largely on the initiative of Austrians. Referred to as the *Kampf-gruppe Auschwitz* (Auschwitz Fighting Group), this organization operated both in the main camp and in Birkenau. The main aim of this group was to assist other prisoners with food and medicine. In addition, they organized escapes, prepared for an uprising in the camp, conducted sabotage and documented the Nazi crimes against prisoners.

Perhaps one of the most famous and effective uprisings in all of the Nazi holocaust resistance occurred on October 7, 1944 in Auschwitz. One gas chamber was totally destroyed and another damaged when some of the *Sonderkommando* prisoners revolted.

Sonderkommando units consisted largely of Jewish prisoners who were assigned to the gas chambers and crematoria. Dragging the gassed bodies to the crematoria and cremating them was the primary function of the Sonderkommandos. The units would be frequently executed and new prisoners would be called to take their place. An unknown witness of the Sonderkommando operations wrote, "The Sonderkommandos, prisoners who serviced the whole operation and were periodically also liquidated, lived up in the attic. Some saw their own families entering the gas chambers" (Laska, 1983, p. 174).

Bruno Bettelheim, a former concentration camp prisoner, described the rebellion:

> In the single revolt of the twelfth Sonderkommando, seventy SS were killed, including one commissioned officer and seventeen non-commissioned officers; one of the crematoria was totally destroyed and another severely damaged. True, all eight hundred and fifty-three of the kommando died. But... the one Sonderkommando which revolted and took such a heavy toll of the enemy did not die much differently than all the other Sonderkommandos (Miklos, 1960, p. xiv).

Led by Roza Robota, the October 7 uprising in Auschwitz consisted of a group of young Jewish women. Robota had previously smuggled out gunpowder that she supplied to her Sonderkommando unit for the uprising. On January 6, 1945 Robota and four other women who took part in this revolt were executed.

The prisoners assigned to the Sonderkommando in Auschwitz also kept diaries hidden in the ground that were found after the war. These diaries documented the atrocities that occurred inside Auschwitz that the Nazis wanted so much to cover up and hide. The act of documentation has been considered by many to be a great part of the resistance effort.

It is difficult to imagine being forced to drag your own people, perhaps your own family members and friends, from the gas chamber to the crematoria to be incinerated. Even more difficult is the reality of knowing that the bodies are a result of a massive genocidal situation that doesn't seem to be sparing anyone. It is no wonder that many Jewish prisoners refused the duty of the Sonderkommando and were rather killed.

After the Sonderkommando uprising, the murders in the gas chambers stopped and Nazi officials gave the orders for the chambers to be demolished. This was one of the attempts by the Nazis to cover up their deliberate atrocities. On October 28, 1944 the last gassing occurred at Auschwitz. Various War Crime Investigation Commissions have reported that approximately four million men, women, and children, including Jews and non-Jews, died in Auschwitz (Laska, 1983, p. 174).

\*

In the various ghettos located inside Belorussia, Jews also struggled to stay alive by hiding, escaping, and/or joining the armed underground. Located in the western USSR, Belorussia had a Jewish population of 670,000 before the German invasion began on June 22, 1941. Thousands of Jews hid in bunkers and various other locations to escape the Germans. An estimated 12,600 people in Belorussia went into hiding upon the German occupation.

Underground organizations were extremely common in the ghettos of Belorussia. In 94 out of 111 ghettos or other locations with Jews, there were underground acts of resistance. Sixty-four of these had an organized underground (Cholawski, 1990, p. 171). The organizations assisted an estimated 25,000 Jews from Vilna, Novogrudok, and Polesye in escaping to the surrounding forests.

The two Vilna ghettos inside Belorussia were established September 3-5, 1941, after Germans had taken the city of Vilna from the Soviets, who had just recently acquired it from Poland. At this time the Jewish population in Vilna was at 57,000 (Arad, 1990, p. 1572). During a number of immediate *Aktions* carried out by the Nazis, Ghetto #2 in Vilna was liquidated between October 3 and October 21, 1941 just soon after its creation. By the end of the year, as a result of many *Aktions* performed by the Germans, only 23,500 Jews out of the original 57,000 were still alive. This included approximately 12,000 openly living in the ghetto, 8,000 who had gone into hiding and another 3,500 who had escaped to other towns in Belorussia or were hiding somewhere nearby, outside the ghetto.

The first major resistance in Vilna came with the establishment of the *Fareynegte Partizaner Organizatsye* (United Partisan Organization; FPO). On December 31, 1941, 150 members of the *Haluts* youth group in the ghetto attended a meeting. There the members were exposed to the declaration written by Abba Kovner, *Like Lambs to the Slaughter*. Kovner, a member of the *Ha-Shomer ha-Tsa-ir* Zionist youth movement, had fled Vilna earlier before the massive executions. When he came back to the ghetto he was informed of the massive murders.

Resistance, Kovner felt, was the only response that could be used. He then dedicated himself to the development of a Jewish fighting force. At the meeting of the *Haluts* group, Kovner's manifesto was read aloud. It stated in part:

> Hitler plans to kill all the Jews of Europe... the Jews of Lithuania are the first in line. Let us not go in like sheep to the slaughter. We may be weak and defenseless, but the only possible answer to the enemy is resistance (Levin, p. 823).

The FPO was then created on January 21, 1942 as a Jewish underground fighting organization operating inside the Vilna ghetto. For the first few months the main focus of the FPO was attempting to save Jews from execution. Shortly thereafter, the FPO adopted a new aim: to prepare for armed resistance if and when the ghetto would be liquidated.

Becoming increasingly organized, the FPO divided itself into underground cells. Simple weapons began to be manufactured inside the ghetto by the group, including hand grenades and molotov cocktails. Other, more sought-after weapons, such as guns, were more difficult to obtain. They either had to be purchased from the local population outside the ghetto or smuggled out of the German-captured weapons facility. Remarkably, the FPO was able to obtain pistols, some rifles, hand grenades, and even some submachine guns. At its height, the FPO had close to three hundred members with some sort of weapon available for each.

Attempting to make contact with other areas, the FPO also sent representatives to the Grodno, Bialystok, and Warsaw ghettos. There the members attempted to create some organization, push the idea of resistance, and inform others of the mass executions of Jews in Vilna and throughout Lithuania.

During this time period, the Nazis grew increasingly aware of the FPO's existence and activities. The FPO had also been involved with mining railways used by trains destined for the front lines, and with sabotaging equipment and arms in German factories. These acts did not go unnoticed, and German authorities sought to capture the leader of the FPO.

When the SS wanted an order carried out in the ghetto the Judenrat was commonly used, and this was no exception. On July 15, 1943, Jacob Gens, the chairman of the Vilna Judenrat, invited the FPO command to his house. Upon arriving, Gens immediately arrested FPO leader Yitzhak Wittenburg. As the security police were transporting Wittenburg to the ghetto gate, the FPO attacked, and Wittenburg was set free. Immediately, the FPO took up positions inside some of the ghetto houses preparing for a battle. The next day during a battle between the FPO and the ghetto police, many of the ghetto residents sided with the police rather than the FPO. These residents demanded that Wittenburg turn himself in to *save* the ghetto from the Germans (Arad, 1990, p. 471). Rather than face a battle sure to include massive casualties, Wittenburg turned himself in to the Germans. He committed suicide that same night.

After this incident, the FPO decided it needed to establish a partisan base in the forest, so FPO members would have a refuge if needed. So on July 24, 1943, a group of FPO men escaped from the Vilna ghetto and headed for the Naroch forest.

Throughout the German occupation of European countries during World War II, the partisan fighters played an important role in adding pressure against the Nazis. Gutman describes partisans as "irregular forces operating in enemy occupied territory, for the most part using guerilla tactics" (Gutman, 1990, p. 1108). Especially in Eastern Europe, partisan activities thrived in the forests where superior knowledge of terrain and support of the public was instrumental.

Jews, though, had perhaps the most difficult time joining the partisan units. Gutman writes:

> Moreover, the individual Jew or group of Jews who sought
> to join up with an existing partisan formation had special
> obstacles to overcome. They had to escape from a ghetto

and locate a partisan base in the forest, and even when
they finally joined a partisan unit they were not put on an
equal footing with the other fighters (1990, p. 1111).

On September 1, 1943, the Germans launched a deportation *Aktion*
to Estonia, which was one step toward the final liquidation of the entire
ghetto in Vilna. As the deportation began, FPO members mobilized and
took up positions in one section of the ghetto. They simultaneously called
on Jews to resist the call to report and to join the revolt. Unfortunately,
the majority of the ghetto residents believed they were merely being sent
to another work detail, so they ignored the FPO call and were deported.
Armed FPO members fought with the Germans that night for hours.

As a result of this day, the FPO realized that the total liquidation
of Vilna was coming soon, so they began moving their members into the
forest. The ghetto was liquidated on September 23, 1943, and that day the
last of the FPO members escaped to the forest via the city's sewer system.
A total of 600 to 700 people, including FPO members, left the Vilna ghetto
for the forests and joined up with the partisan units.

Also inside Belorussia, the Bialystok ghetto was created by the
Nazis shortly after the Germans seized the city of Bialystok from the Soviet Union on June 22, 1941. This same day, an estimated 2,000 Jews were
burned alive, tortured, or shot to death (Bender, 1990, p.210). During the
first two weeks, another 4,000 Jews were murdered from the Bialystok
ghetto.

It wasn't until August 1942 that an underground headquarters
was established in Bialystok. Referred to as *Block No. 1* or *Front A*, the
headquarters was a representation of the *Ha-Shomer ha-Tsa'ir, Bund*, and
Communist groups. Not until July 1943 did these three begin to work together in a united underground, just one month before the final liquidation
of the ghetto.

The main action of the Bialystok underground took place on August 16, 1943, when Germans surrounded the ghetto to begin the deportations. At 10:00 a.m., as thousands of Jews headed out for the deportations,
the underground revolted. Various cells of the underground went to predetermined positions to receive arms and launch the attack. For five days,
August 16-20, the underground fought with the Nazis. When it was nearly
over, rather than be captured by the Germans, the leaders of the revolt are
said to have committed suicide.

By the end of the uprising some 150 resistance members from the

Bialystok ghetto had escaped to join partisan units operating in nearby forests. These escapes from Bialystok began in December 1942, and partisan forces grew as a result. Many of the partisan units, particularly the Forois ("go out") unit, continually engaged the Germans in battle.

One last ghetto inside Belorussia that is worthy of attention concerning resistance is Minsk. The capital city in Belorussia, Minsk was taken by German forces on June 28, 1941. Prior to the German invasion, Minsk had a Jewish population of 30,000, which was about one-third of its total population.

The Minsk ghetto was officially created on July 25, 1941, one month before the first meeting of the underground took place. At the first meeting of the underground in August, the group created its primary function: to get as many Jews as possible out of the ghetto and into a partisan unit. Some of the first activities of the underground included creating an organizational network, creating contact with the non-Jewish parts of the city outside of the ghetto, setting up a printing press, and distributing information and news throughout the ghetto. Additionally, the underground set up a radio (radios were banned at the time) to counteract German propaganda within the ghetto. They hid the receiver in the chimney of one of the ghetto houses, and they twisted the antennae to look like a clothesline. Bulletins were issued sometimes on a daily basis, with news from monitored radio broadcasts.

The underground grew quickly to an estimated 300 members after six months. These members, divided into groups of ten, began collecting arms and storing them in various hiding places within the ghetto. Some of the weapons were acquired from underground members smuggling them out of German arms factories. Sabotage in the workplace was also committed by these groups. One documented example was the chemical contamination of an entire transport of alcoholic beverages shipped to the Eastern Front (Suhl, 1989, p.91).

The Minsk ghetto itself organized seven partisan units, six of which later became mixed by including other Belorussian partisans. One of the major reasons the Minsk ghetto was so successful in assisting with the escapes and formations of partisan units is that the Belorussian population was fairly supportive of the Jews. Once an escape was made, the Belorussians helped the Jews meet up with a partisan unit. Most of the Jews would make the journey on foot, but at least 500 made it by hiding on trains. The Belorussian underground would hide Jews in the coal compartment of trains and drop them off near their destination. From there, a prearranged guide would escort the Jews to the partisan units.

Another contributor to the success of the Minsk partisans was the Judenrat of the ghetto being extremely supportive of the underground. Often, the Judenrat actually took orders from the underground itself. When the Germans became aware of the Judenrat's activities, all of the members except one were arrested and publicly hanged (Suhl, 1989, p. 94).

\*

Treblinka was another death camp located in the northeastern part of the territory, referred to at that time as the Generalgouvernement in German-occupied Poland. First opening as a penal camp in 1941, the execution chambers were completed in July 1942, constructed largely by Jewish prisoners.

Escape constituted a major portion of strategy amongst prisoners at Treblinka. Hundreds of inmates, while under deportation from other areas, attempted to escape from trains heading to the camp. Many of these people were killed as a result of jumping from the trains, and others were murdered on the spot by the escort guards for attempting to flee. An additional number of prisoners who made it off the trains were captured by railway guards or were turned into the police by local residents in the area who would find them.

At the camp itself, many prisoners tried to break out, especially in the first part of its existence. The attempted escapes usually occurred at night and involved either breaking through the fence or hiding in railway cars full of prisoners' clothing that were about to leave. Although unsuccessful, many of the inmates at Treblinka also attempted to dig an underground escape out of the camp.

At the beginning of 1943, the first underground resistance group was formed at Treblinka. One of the first aims set by the group was to acquire weapons. They first attempted unsuccessfully to obtain arms with the assistance of Ukrainians. With this failing, the group devised a plan to steal weapons from the SS armory, with the eventual goal in mind of seizing control of the entire camp. After gaining control, the resistance fighters would then destroy the camp and escape to the forests to join the partisans. An estimated fifty to seventy men were involved in the resistance.

As it became clear that the liquidation of the camp may have been coming, the group set a date of August 2, 1943 for revolt. With this day in mind, all work went into preparing for the resistance. The fighters successfully copied a key to the SS armory and weapons were removed and given to the resistance members. Fearing that an SS guard knew that weapons were being stolen, the resistance members shot him. This death alerted the SS, and consequently the resistance was unable to continue acquiring weapons from the armory. As a result of having too few weapons and of the increasing suspicion of the SS into their activities, the resistance decided to call off attempting to seize the camp.

Instead, the resistance members immediately opened fire on SS men and set many camp buildings on fire. The majority of the prisoners simultaneously stormed the fence to escape, and most were shot by the SS. Approximately 750 inmates attempted to escape during this action, but only seventy survived to see liberation and the end of the war.

*

At Sobibor, notable resistance and uprisings also occurred. Located near the Sobibor village in the eastern part of the Lublin district in Poland, the death camp was built in March 1942. From October 1942 to June 1943 an estimated 70,000 to 80,000 Jews were brought to Sobibor from Lublin and other eastern areas (Arad, 1990, p. 1377).

The transporting procedure was similar to that used in other camps. Deception and immediate murder met the masses of Jews upon first arrival to Sobibor. Yitzhak Arad has written on the subject with horrifying description:

> The procedure for the reception of incoming transports was based entirely on misleading the victims and concealing from them the fate that was in store for them. When a train arrived, the deportees on board were ordered to disembark and were told that they had arrived at a transit camp from which they would be sent to labor camps; before leaving for the labor camps, they were to take showers, and at the same time their clothes would be disinfected. Following this announcement, the men and women were separated (children were assigned to the women), on the pretext that the sexes had to be separated for their showers. The victims were ordered to take off their clothes and hand over any money or valuables in their

possession; anyone who was caught trying to conceal any item was shot. There followed the march to the gas chambers, which had been made to resemble shower rooms... The victims were in a state of shock and did not grasp what was happening to them. When the gas chambers were jammed full of people, they were closed and sealed and the gas was piped in. Within twenty to thirty minutes, everyone inside was dead (Arad, 1990, p. 1376).

In July and August of 1943, the first resistance group was formed in Sobibor. Created by Jewish prisoners, the resistance maintained a goal of trying to organize an uprising and massive escape. A rough plan was established that involved killing SS men, taking their weapons and fighting to escape out of the camp.

On October 14, 1943 the uprising occurred, and eleven SS men and several Ukrainians were killed. Approximately 300 prisoners escaped during this revolt, many of whom were captured and killed shortly thereafter. Those who had stayed behind at the camp and did not attempt the escape met the same fate as those who escaped and were caught. Only an estimated fifty Jews out of the 300 who escaped during the uprising survived the war (Arad, 1990, p. 1377).

∗

In Lutsk, a city in Ukrainian SSR, Jews were moved into the ghetto on December 11 and 12, 1941. The liquidation of the ghetto began shortly thereafter. Between August 20-23, 1942, 17,500 Lutsk Jews were taken outside the city and shot to death alongside massive pits (Spector, 1990, p. 924). Another 2,000 Jews were murdered in this same method on September 3, 1942. Jews inside the labor camp were all who remained inside the ghetto at that time.

On December 11, 1942, the Jewish camp elder learned that all the remaining Jews were going to be put to death the next day. After hearing this news, Jews within the camp organized a resistance. They prepared axes, knives, iron rods, bricks, and acid for use during the revolt. In addition, the Jews acquired several revolvers and sawed-off shotguns.

On December 12, the Germans entered the camp and were met with massive armed resistance. Several Germans were wounded, and a German commander had his face burned with acid. In response, the Germans brought in their armored cars and began firing. After a few hours, most of the resistance fighters had been killed, and the Germans entered the area and murdered the remaining visible Jews. A small number did, however, manage to escape and/or hide from the Germans.

\*

The ghetto in Krakow was sealed on March 20, 1941, and by the end of that year some 18,000 Jews were placed inside. Located in southern Poland, Krakow became occupied by the Germans on September 6, 1939. On October 26, 1939, Krakow was declared the capital city of the Generalgouvernement, the territory inside German-occupied Poland. Due to this declaration, Jews within Krakow received perhaps some of the harshest treatment.

Resistance units were in operation since the initial formation of Krakow. Consisting of the *Akiva* and *Ha-Shomer ha-Tsa'ir* Zionist youth movements, the initial stages of the resistance focused on educating and providing assistance to ghetto residents. The underground also produced a paper entitled *He-Haluts ha-Lohem* ("The Fighting Pioneer").

The first armed resistance group, the *Zydowska Organizacja Bojowa* (Jewish Fighting Organization), was created in October 1942. Its primary function was to provide armed resistance against the Nazis. Feeling that the space inside the ghetto was too restricted, the group decided not to prepare for an uprising within the ghetto. Instead, the resistance wanted to move the fighting to the "Aryan" side of Krakow.

Throughout its existence, some ten operations were carried out in the Krakow area. The most famous was the attack in the center of the city on the Cyganeria Café, which was frequented by German officers. Eleven Germans were killed and thirteen others wounded in this siege (Krakowski, 1984, p. 832).

Like other ghettos and camps, the underground in Krakow attempted to create partisan units outside the ghetto. For the most part, this was unsuccessful, because the Polish Army was somewhat opposed to Jewish partisan units and therefore provided little, if any, assistance.

Inside German-occupied Eastern Europe, scattered uprisings and forms of resistance were present in many of the other ghettos and camps. In the LVOV ghetto, located in the western Ukrainian SSR, prisoners also fought back when Germans and Ukrainian police entered the ghetto for the final liquidation. Members of the resistance threw molotovs and hand grenades, killing at least nine people, a combination of Germans and Ukrainians. Approximately twenty more Germans and Ukrainians were severely wounded.

Nearby, in the suburbs of LVOV, the Janowska labor and death camp also had its share of uprisings. As the liquidation of the camp began in November 1943, there were a few scattered attempts at armed battle by the underground. Then on November 19, a Sonderkommando uprising began, ending with the deaths of several Nazi guards (Weiss, 1990, p. 735). Several members of the uprising were also able to escape. Those left behind were killed.

Buchenwald, situated within Germany itself, was one of the earliest camps, opening on July 16, 1937. Resistance cells were organized since the very first years of its existence. At first these were primarily focused on planting resistance members into key posts available to inmates to enable Jews to have input on various developments within the camp.

In 1943, the *International Underground Committee* was formed, primarily as an armed resistance group. It carried out sabotage in various German arms factories that employed Buchenwald inmates and also smuggled arms and ammunition into the camp. In the final days of the camp, the resistance members sabotaged the SS evacuation orders by slowing the pace down. As a result, the Nazis were unable to completely liquidate the camp before they themselves pulled out. On April 11, 1945, after nearly all the SS men had left the camp, the resistance members seized control from the remaining SS personnel and liberated the camp.

Nonviolent resistance took on various forms throughout Eastern Europe. Hiding became one of the primary strategies of this category. An estimated 20,000 to 30,000 Jews survived by hiding inside ghettos in Poland, which was less than one percent of all the Polish Jews under Nazi rule by 1941 (Powers, 1997, p. 276). Jews who were fortunate enough to survive were hiding in the ghettos that were some of the last to be destroyed—Vilna, Kovno, and others. A small number of people also survived by hiding their Jewish identities.

By far the main practice used by Jews in response to the sheer genocidal situation was attempting to maintain a "business-as-usual" policy. This constituted attempting to maintain a familiar economic, cultural, political, and religious life. Many identified this response as resistance, feeling that one of the Nazi's main aims was to destroy the morale of the Jews (Powers, 1997, p. 276). Raul Hilberg, in an essay entitled *The Destruction of the European Jews*, argued Jews had faith that their survival was certain, and therefore they tended to live their lives as normally as possible. He writes, "so long as the Jews thought they would survive the Nazi rule and the war they could see an incentive to re-enact the modes of passive conduct that in the past had tended to ensure the survival of the community" (Hilberg, 1961, p. 37).

This belief described by Hilberg directly relates to the religious history and beliefs of Jewish culture. Philip Friedman comments on this issue in an essay entitled *Jewish Resistance to Nazism: Its Various Forms and Aspects*:

> It was a resistance stemming from religious inspiration and it contained a deeply rooted ancestral heritage epitomised by the saying 'not by force but by the strength of the spirit'... the true weapon is the weapon of conscience, prayer, religious meditation and devotion and not armed resistance. The Orthodox Jew did not believe that it was possible or even desirable to resist the Nazis in any other way (Friedman, 1981, pp. 201-202).

Furthermore, heroism within Orthodox Jewry is closely associated with the concept of spiritual courage, and religious sacrifice referred to in Hebrew as *Kiddush Hashem* (Sanctification of God's name) (p. 201).

This concept was further explored in Isaiah Trunk's *Judenrat: The Jewish Councils in Eastern Europe Under Nazi Occupation*. Trunk writes:

> The Orthodox population of non-Soviet eastern Europe (constituting perhaps half the inmates of the ghettos) grew up amid the age-old Jewish tradition of spiritual heroism and martyrdom in times of oppression and was therefore historically and mentally unprepared and mostly opposed to the concept of physical resistance...These people were armed with quite different weapons: prayers and faith that the Almighty would have mercy on His oppressed people —that a miracle would happen in the end (1972, p. 453).

The relationship of religion to resistance was so prominent that in Warsaw, approximately 600 illegal minyanim groups (groups of Jews praying together) formed after religious observance was outlawed (Hilberg, 1961, p. 43).

Other forms of Jewish nonviolent resistance included smuggling food to stop the attempted starvation deliberately inflicted by the Nazis. In some areas this took on an organized form. For instance, in the Warsaw ghetto the Judenrat aided in the process of supplying food to the inhabitants. Germans had allocated a mere 336 calories daily to be distributed by the Judenrat in 1941 (Marrus, 1989, p. 42). By smuggling food into the ghetto the Jews were able to obtain approximately 1125 calories a day, at least for a short time. Likewise, similar operations were conducted in Kovno, where the smuggling was orchestrated by both the Judenrat and the Jewish police (pp. 42-43).

As education became outlawed by the Nazis in most of the camps and ghettos, another type of resistance arose in the form of teaching. In Warsaw, education continued in violation of the law, conducted in *complets*, where small groups of children would gather either in the home of the teacher or in the soup kitchen (Marrus, 1989, p. 43). Secret high schools were also formed in Warsaw, funded in part by the illegal *Jewish Joint Distribution Committee* (JDC). After newspapers were also outlawed, an estimated fifty newspaper titles are said to have existed in Warsaw itself (Hilberg, 1961, p.43).

The JDC was a United States-based, Jewish philanthropic agency that provided various kinds of assistance to Jews in Poland. In addition to the funding of the high schools in Warsaw, the JDC assisted with food supply and distribution. Approximately 260,000 Jews in the Generalgouvernement were fed by the JDC in 1941. Some 42,000 of these were children (Marrus, 1989, p. 44).

*House Committees* were also supported in various ways by the JDC. The *House Committees* consisted of groups of people living in apartment buildings, organizing together to create education, cultural activities, and aid. These were usually formed outside of the Judenrat. In the Warsaw ghetto alone, it is estimated that approximately 1,000 house committees existed.

One of the most famous directors of the JDC, Emmanuel Ringelblum, organized an underground archive called *Oneg Shabbat*. Contained within this archive were thousands of pages of testimonials from across Poland regarding the atrocities committed by the Nazis against Jews. Yehuda Bauer, in her essay *Jewish Resistance to the Holocaust*, writes, "this effort to preserve evidence of what the Nazis were doing to the Jews was a major manifestation of unarmed resistance" (1997, p. 277).

Even healthcare became an item of resistance for the Jews under these conditions. The hospital in Vilna had to hide an entire wing of the building from the Germans so they could attempt to treat cases of Typhoid in Jews. In Shavli, pregnant women were secretly given abortions or they were hidden, as pregnant women would be immediately killed by the Nazis (Bauer, 1997, p. 276).

Jews additionally were drawn to industry as a means for preserving this attempted normality of daily life. Trunk writes, "Industry in the ghetto was important not only for purely economic reasons, but because it also had weighty aspects in connection with the idea that the Jews could be rescued from their fate" (1972, p. 400). This phenomenon was based on the assumption that Jews, working both within and outside of the ghettos directly benefiting the German war industry, would be able to survive. These various attempts at survival have been seen by most historians as the chief activity utilized among the masses of Jews during this time.

Furthermore, on many isolated occasions within both ghettos and camps, there were people who outright disobeyed German orders and suffered the consequences. In October 1941, Dr. Joseph Parnas, the chairman of the first Jewish council at Lwow, was arrested and killed for refusing to comply with an order to deliver a few thousand Jews who were to be used for forced labor (Trunk, 1972, p. 437). Another example of this refusal to comply is cited by Trunk:

> In 1941 the Germans demanded that the chairman of the Council at Sandomierz (Lublin district), Leib Goldberg, deliver within a few hours a well-to-do Jew whom they accused of concealing personal property. Although Goldberg knew where the man had been hiding, he did not betray him. When the hidden person did not report at the appointed time, the German police shot Goldberg to death on the staircase of the Council building. Later on, SS men came to arrest the vice chairman of the Council, Apelbaum, for the same crime. Not finding him, they threatened to shoot 20 Jews. Apelbaum then reported to the police and was shot (p. 439).

Whether Jews in German-occupied Europe consciously carried out any sort of conspired and organized nonviolence is doubtful. Yet, various forms of resistance that can be placed within the nonviolence category did indeed exist. Why this was done was touched upon a bit in this segment and will be further explored in upcoming portions, as will the controversial analysis of the effectiveness of the Jewish response. As for nonviolent tactics performed by Jews within Eastern Europe, the above-mentioned survey constitutes the bulk of activity.

# WESTERN EUROPE

Due to the massive deportations of Jews to the ghettos and camps of Eastern Europe, the primary Jewish resistance can be seen in the East. However, the western portion of the continent under German occupation was not without its share of revolts and actions.

On May 9-10, 1940, Germans invaded the Netherlands and were successful in seizing the country four days later on May 14. In the Jewish section, both Jews and non-Jews organized to resist the Nazis. When a march was organized by the Dutch Nazis through the Netherlands, a small battle erupted, killing one Nazi. The Germans responded to this attack by completely enclosing and sealing off the Jewish quarter.

As the anti-Nazi sentiment was justifiably running high especially among the Jews, a group of German police was attacked inside a Jewish-owned cafe. On February 19, 1941, as they walked into the cafe they were sprayed with ammonium gas by the Jewish owner, who mistook the regular German police for Dutch Nazis (Gutman, 1990, p. 1048). The response that came from the Nazis was to further barricade the Jewish quarter and hunt down young Jewish men. In this particular action, an estimated 389 Jewish men were captured and deported to Buchenwald.

The arrests of these men and the general treatment of prisoners by the German police created widespread anger within the Amsterdam population. Communists in the region used this anger and opportunity to call for a massive strike, hoping to weigh down the German resolve for cruelty. On February 25, 1941 the strike occurred in Amsterdam and quickly spread to other nearby cities:

> The strike soon encompassed all sectors of the population, and the entire transportation system, the large fac-

tories, and the public services came to a standstill... The Germans were taken by surprise and put large forces into the field to suppress it, which they succeeded in doing by the third day...The Dutch realized that it had not led to any tangible results, since the Germans refused to make any concession regarding their treatment of the Jews (Gutman, 1990, p. 1048).

As the Nazis continued the deportations from the Netherlands, many Jews refused to appear at their summons and went into hiding. Because many Jews had non-Jewish contacts within the area, they were able to receive some assistance from supporters. A number of other organizations and individuals also began helping Jews with hiding places, ration coupons, forged papers, and moving from hiding place to hiding place. Some individuals and groups conducted these acts for a small fee, and others actually profited off the assistance (Gutman, 1990, p. 1055).

In 1944, a group called the *National Underground Organization* set up a special section to assist Jews financially in their hiding. An estimated 25,000 Jews went into hiding during this time period in the Netherlands (p. 1055). A good portion of these people benefited from assistance provided by the *National Underground Organization* and other such groups.

Approximately 4,500 children also were hidden in this area during the War, with very few ever being discovered by the Germans. In 1942, students began to organize specifically to rescue Jewish children and create safe hideaways. Later on, at least three other groups were created, devoted to hiding children from the Nazis.

Many people also attempted to escape the Netherlands during the German occupation, but most were not successful. Some tried to cross to Britain and were killed along the way. A few Jews did manage to reach the Swiss border, traveling through Belgium and France. Though at the border, even fewer were allowed to remain until after the war. Most were simply turned back.

Finally, there are reports that a small number of Jews were able to escape and join the armed Dutch underground. This underground did succeed in launching attacks on Dutch Nazi leaders before the underground themselves were killed. Exact numbers on the Jews involved in the armed resistance are unknown (Gutman, 1990, p. 1056).

\*

When Germany invaded France in May 1940, Jews and other Frenchmen headed south for the unoccupied zone. Approximately 100,000 Jews attempted to make this journey south, 30,000 of them returning north on June 22 after trusting an agreement signed between the French and Germans (Cohen, 1990, p. 513). At this time of early German occupation, the Jewish population in northern France was near 150,000 (p. 513).

In August 1940, an underground Jewish organization called *Solidarite* was formed. When approximately 4,000 Jews in Paris went through internment in May 1941, *Solidarite* conducted fairly widespread industrial sabotage. Attempting to receive aid from non-Jewish sources, the group formed a splinter organization in January 1942 called the *Movement National contre le Racism* (National Movement against Racism). *Solidarite* was also quite active in the formation of partisan units, especially prior to massive deportations that began in France in June 1942.

After these deportations, *Solidarite* began asking Jews to hide and to refuse working for the German war industry. Additionally, Jews were asked to join the active resistance against the Nazis. Owing to political and strategic differences between *Solidarite* and other more mainstream relief organizations, few Jews in France heard or acted upon the call.

The *Union des Juifs pour la Resistance et l'Entraide* (Union of Jews for Resistance and Mutual Aid; UJRE), was created by *Solidarite* in the summer of 1943. One of the main aims of the UJRE was to assist in hiding and saving children. When France became liberated, the UJRE claimed to have saved some 900 children (Gutman, 1990, p. 1535). Unfortunately, 120 UJRE partisans were killed during the war and another 400 UJRE members were deported to death camps (p. 1535).

Other relief organizations began very soon after the German invasion. A group called *Amelot* was created during the time period after the initial occupation, when thousands of Jews were migrating south to reach the unoccupied zone. *Amelot*, which was founded in Paris, had a main goal of trying to provide relief to Jews in the community. Owing to divisions between native French Jews and immigrant Jews, *Amelot* was unable to accomplish much (Cohen, 1990, p. 514).

In January 1941 various Jewish leaders came together in France to form an umbrella organization known as the *Comite de Coordination des Oeuvres Israelites de Bienfaisance* (Coordinating Committee of the

Jewish Welfare Societies). Nearly all of the relief and aid organizations in France were working with this group except for the more radical *Solidarite*. The *Joint Distribution Committee*, also active in other countries during this time, provided financial aid to the Coordinating Committee. Unlike *Solidarite*, the Committee itself, which represented the more "established" sections of the native Jewish-French community, "continued to bide for time, adhered to the legalistic approach, and counted on the French authorities for support" (Cohen, 1990, p. 514).

As a result of the massive move made by thousands of Jews during the initial phases of German occupation, relief in various forms was also needed in southern France. An umbrella organization was established in October 1940 called the *Centrale des Organisations Juives d'Assistance* (Central Commission of Jewish Relief Organizations; CCOJA). Similar to the Coordinating Committee in northern France, CCOJA sought to unite all the relief efforts in the area. The organization existed until 1942, but due to the same divisions among native and immigrant Jews, the CCOJA was largely ineffective (Cohen, 1990, p. 515).

Resulting from the deportations beginning in March 1942, when approximately 27,000 Jews were caught and shipped away, resistance began to be stepped up a bit, particularly in the northern region. Armed resistance became increasingly prominent in Paris not only from *Solidarite*, but also from a group called *Armee Juive*. This organization was an armed unit consisting of Jewish members of several youth movements. It not only assisted with many border crossings, helping Jews to attempt to escape to Spain, but also took part in military operations against the German occupation in France (Cohen, 1990, p. 517). In the end, an estimated 78,000 Jews from France lost their lives in the War (p. 517).

\*

Belgium was invaded by German forces on May 10, 1940 and surrendered to the Nazis on May 28. At the time of the invasion, an estimated 65,696 Jews existed in the country (Michman, 1990, p. 161). Deportations of Jews from Belgium began in the summer of 1942 and continued to September 1943. The vast majority of these Jews deported during this time ended up in Auschwitz. It is estimated that 34,801 Jews from Belgium were either imprisoned or deported, and 28,902 of these died (p. 161).

Jewish resistance in Belgium first came to be known during the latter part of 1941. The Jewish underground press was actively manufacturing newspapers, including a Yiddish paper, one in Dutch and another in French. Nearly all the newspapers universally objected to the AJB (*Asssociation des Juifs en Belgique*), a forced Jewish segregation association. The AJB, established on November 25, 1941, required every Jew to belong and to work in forced labor and attend segregated schools.

In July 1942, the *Comite de Defense des Juifs* (Jewish Defense Committee; CDJ) was formed. Its major function was to find hiding places, particularly for children. From 1942 to 1944, an estimated 4,000 children were successfully hidden by the CDJ and many adult Jews benefited as well (Michman, 1990, p. 167).

Other Jewish armed resistance groups were also active in Belgium, most having no direct association with the CDJ. Some of the revolts included seizing the card index of Jews that the AJB maintained in its office, as well as targeting Robert Holcinger, who was the official in charge of calling people out for the deportations.

The most famous and perhaps most successful example of Jewish resistance in Belgium came on April 19-20, 1943. Jewish underground members attacked a train that was transporting Jews from the Mechelen camp to Auschwitz. During the attack, some 231 Jews escaped from the train. Twenty-three of these were shot to death by train guards. This is one of the only known attacks on a train transporting Jews to their deaths in Europe (Michman, 1990, p. 167).

Escaping in general was a common goal shared by Jews in Belgium. Literally hundreds of Jews attempted to escape and make it to Spain by way of Switzerland and southern France. Many of those who succeeded were members of the Zionist youth movements (p. 168).

Overall, in Western Europe there was even less resistance offered by Jews than in the eastern section. As stated before, this perhaps is fitting since the ghettos and camps were located in the east. Tactics within the west centered around escape and hiding and still, as in the east, maintaining as much of a normal life as possible. According to Yehuda Bauer, an estimated two-thirds of the Jewish population in France, over one-half in Belgium, at least 11% in the Netherlands, and up to 83% in Italy survived the war by hiding (1997, p. 276). The acts of armed resistance and more substantial revolt were few and far between.

*

# SO WHAT DOES IT ALL MEAN?

So what *does* it all mean? What can the various wealthy accounts of Jewish resistance offered above tell us? What did these attempts at resistance mean for the fate of the Jews in World War II? What parallels can be drawn to current pursuits against genocide, murder, exploitation (*how many more terms must I use*)? Was Gandhi correct in his assumption that his Satyagraha nonviolence principles could successfully defeat the Nazis? Answering all these questions involves perhaps some of the most difficult realizations, controversial proclamations, and soul-searching missions. Yet, the answers are important—crucial, I would suggest—to understanding the human condition in times of severity and in endlessly trying to come to terms with the age-old questions of *what makes one act* and *which actions are effective?*

The objective here is not to be condemning or condoning the Jewish reaction to the genocide committed in World War II, but rather to understand where and how effective resistance was and was not practiced. It is an exercise in learning, if for no other reason than the fact that if we fail to learn from lessons taught in historical experience, we are doomed to repeat the same incidents and outcomes. By understanding what history has to teach us, we will be considerably better off in facing what may lie ahead in future years.

It is very apparent from evidence provided in this chapter that further Jewish resistance was prevented, by and large, from occurring due to the *business-as-usual* policies purposely followed by the Jews themselves. Jews did not want to believe and arguably could not foresee any such extreme inhumanity and therefore refused to acknowledge the need for any type of resistance. This was a reality for many up until it was arguably too late for resistance to have had much effect. Trunk writes:

> Even during the most difficult times, the Jews were confident that the world was not lawless. It was unthinkable that a government in the very heart of civilized Europe, even a Nazi one, should openly hold as its main political goal the physical elimination of an entire people; and it was unthinkable that the world would let it happen. This is one of the reasons why people did not believe in the terrible truth until the very end, when it was too late to plan or undertake anything (1972, p. 453).

Hilberg adds:

> The Jews entered into the phase of practical preparations
> for armed action only after the first so-called Aktion, i.e.,
> mass murder operation by the Nazis. Ghetto rebellions
> never took place when a hope of survival could be enter-
> tained - only when the realization finally struck that all
> Jews were going to be killed anyway (1989, p. 37).

In his book, *Pacifism As Pathology*, Churchill briefly discusses the business-as-usual policy:

> Manifested in the irrational belief that in remaining 'rea-
> sonable and responsible,' unobtrusively resisting by con-
> tinuing 'normal' day-to-day activities proscribed by the
> nazis through the Nuremberg Laws and other infamous
> legislation, and 'not alienating anyone,' this attitude im-
> plied that a more-or-less humane Jewish policy might be
> morally imposed upon the nazi state by the Jewish paci-
> fism itself (1998, p. 36).

Churchill is one of many historians who have argued that the Jewish response was ineffective and perhaps inherently wrong, ending in the
massive genocide of well over 5 million people (Churchill, 1998, p. 34).
Is this analysis well founded? Certainly, after reviewing the vast array of
documented examples of Jewish resistance listed within this work alone,
one may very well question the logic of such an assertion. As the majority
of resistance that did occur was in the nature of passivity and nonviolence,
it would be fitting to analyze the effectiveness of such tactics.

Earlier I made the assumption that it is doubtful that much, if any,
organized nonviolent resistance occurred in the Jewish response. Most
of the passive and nonviolent acts that did occur(i.e. hiding, escaping,
disobeying orders, schooling, various forms of aid, media, etc.) seemed to
stem more out of the sense of Jews wanting to continue the normality in
their lives rather than a conscious decision to create and employ a nonviolent strategy. Aside from the various relief organizations that formed and
operated in and outside many of the ghettos, most of the nonviolent acts
occurred more from an individual desire to prolong his or her life, while

at the same time refusing to acknowledge the severity of the genocidal problem.

Indeed, critics of the Jewish response have even proclaimed that the passivity and nonviolence employed by the Jews not only was ineffective but aided the Nazis in their work to bring about the *Final Solution* to the Jewish dilemma. Bruno Bettelheim wrote in 1960:

> The persecution of the Jews was aggravated, slow step by slow step, when no violent fighting back occurred. It may have been Jewish acceptance, without retaliatory fight, of ever harsher discrimination and degradation that first gave the SS the idea that they could be gotten to the point where they would walk into the gas chambers on their own... In the deepest sense the walk to the gas chamber was only the last consequence of the philosophy of business as usual (Miklos, p. x).

It is excruciatingly difficult to imagine people willingly walking into the gas chambers, to their deaths with minimal resistance, at best. Another depressing example of this can be found by reading the writings of Vera Laska, a survivor of Auschwitz:

> To prevent resistance, entire blocks were told that volunteers were needed for factory work in Germany. Most of the volunteers ended up in the gas chambers. So did the Czech transport from Terezin that had been kept alive for half a year in the exceptional family blocks. The SS used them for propaganda, or just loved to play cat and mouse games. These unfortunate people were packed off on Masaryk's birthday, March 7, and were told that they were being moved to another work camp. The following night they were all gassed. They entered the gas chambers singing the national anthem. Their postcards, an especially cruel Nazi custom, were postdated March 25, and arrived at Terezin postmarked from Dachau, stating that all was well. This was supposed to keep further transports from Terezin calm (Laska, 1983, p. 82).

Sure, the chambers were disguised as shower units. Yes, there involved a great amount of deception, psychological, and physical force against the Jewish victims. Of course, the camps and Jews were isolated from news and reports of the intentions and practices of the SS. But realistically, there is compelling evidence that when the massive killing began, even after the plans for the *Final Solution* were revealed, and also after news began to reach ghettos and camps throughout Eastern Europe, still there was little if any resistance. Ringelblum himself writes in his diary, "The Jews did not rise up against the slaughter anywhere; they went to their deaths without resisting" (Yahil, 1968, p. 61).

So what factors played a role in this phenomenon that Kovner described in 1941 as *like lambs to the slaughter*? Interestingly enough, many reasons have been given as to why the Jews did not offer more effective forms of resistance. It is useful to examine these with some discussion.

The first overall reality that should be acknowledged is that among an enormous number of Jews themselves, passive resistance was a deliberate choice as opposed to more radical forms of armed action. As mentioned earlier, religious beliefs played a crucial role in forming of these decisions. Additionally though, pressure came (again at least partially due to religious beliefs and the belief in business as usual) also from key figures within the Jewish society. While some Judenrats in ghettos secretly supported the need for armed resistance, others fully cooperated with the Nazis, condemning any sort of opposition to the functioning of the day-to-day life. Trunk writes, "It is clear from available sources that the majority of the Councils were against the idea of organized resistance. There were councils that actively opposed the underground groups and denounced them to the Germans" (1972, p. 455).

Another opposing force that increased difficulty for the Jewish response was the reality of fear instilled in the Jews. There was an overwhelming feeling of helplessness in the sense that if any resistance were offered, the repression would be far too great from the Nazis. Hilberg writes, "One major deterrent to nonviolent resistance was the Nazis group punishment strategy. If one individual or a few disobeyed, the Nazis would punish, usually kill an entire group of people" (1989, p. 38). Trunk adds, "The majority of ghetto inmates maintained that resistance was not a real alternative to their desperate situation. They feared that it might even speed up the liquidation process by giving the Germans an excuse to implement bloody repressions" (1972, p. 454).

In addition to the problems with the Judenrats, there was not unilateral support for armed resistance offered in German-occupied Europe.

Interestingly enough, key figures even within some of the undergrounds denounced the use of armed struggle. Hilberg states:

> Resistance would have been met with disapproval among Polish population and even Polish Underground. A leader of the Polish Underground, Stefan Rowecki, issued an order on November 10, 1942 stating 'the time of our uprising has not come' (1989, p. 37).

One final and important reason given as to the lack of further armed resistance by the Jews was the difficulty existing in obtaining weapons. Trunk argues, "Because of complete isolation, it was next to impossible to get arms from the outside world, even if they had been offered" (1972, p. 451). While all evidence points to the fact that Jews did not have an easy access to a full arsenal of weaponry, they were successful in obtaining arms in the few revolts that did occur. Whether it was smuggling them out of the German war factories, buying them from the local population or from black markets, or even from taking them directly off of the SS guards themselves, individuals and even groups of Jews were successful in obtaining arms when they so desired. Bettelheim argues:

> There is little doubt that the [Jews], who were able to provide themselves with so much, could have provided themselves with a gun or two had they wished. They could have shot down one or two of the SS men who came for them. The loss of an SS with every Jew arrested would have noticeably hindered the functioning of the police state (Miklos, 1960, p. xi).

With at least 5.1 million Jews perishing in the Holocaust, it is fair to boldly state that the resistance employed by the Jews was too little and too late (Hilberg, 1961, pp. 1047-1048). Could it have been worse? Could the absence of certain forms of resistance employed have resulted in the full success of the *Final Solution*? Arguably so.

The few acts of armed uprisings did in fact, in a minute manner, act to slow the pace of the holocaust. Shortly after the revolt of the twelfth Sonderkommando unit at Auschwitz, the chambers were closed, as the cover-up procedure became instituted into Nazi policy. Rebellions such as this famous one served to throw a major wrench into the genocidal engine, resulting in numerous lives being saved. Of course, the only problem was not enough of the armed rebellions occurred, and when they did, the Nazis were able to just rip the wrench from the engine and allow the genocidal operations to run smoothly.

At first glance, the same could be said for some of the passive forms of action that occurred, with respect to them perhaps slowing down the genocide. Yet, there is a crucial difference between the passive activities such as hiding or providing aid and the more direct and confrontational method of armed physical resistance. Where in the end the passive means could not have had the ability to defeat the Nazi program due to the avoidance of confrontation, the armed rebellion could have provided success in slowing down the murder and saving numerous lives.

It can be further argued, like others including Churchill have, that the passive action mixed with the business-as-usual policy *did* in fact *allow* so many Jews to be executed by the Germans. As a direct result of the inability of passive means to confront the Germans, the Nazi forces were able to carry out their liquidation of camps and ghettos with a horrifying institutionalism. The passive actions overall actually aided not the Jews, but the Nazi agenda by promoting a passive expectancy of the public. The concept of the good Jew, who sticks to the business-as-usual policy, was nearly demanded by the majority in ghettos and camps. This, along with the continuing denouncements of armed struggle and physical revolt, worked to strongly hinder the ability for armed resistance to grow and prosper.

So what about the question of organized nonviolence? While I have argued that for the most part it did not exist, could such a strategy as Gandhi's Satyagraha have proved to be successful against the Germans? Could the confrontational aspect of Satyagraha worked to slow the speed of the executions? No.

It became apparent early in the 1930s what fate was slowly coming to the Jews in Germany. In 1933 alone, Germany organized the first boycotts against Jewish-owned businesses; created quotas restricting the number of Jews in higher education; established Dachau—the first concentration camp; removed Jews from literature, art, broadcasting theater, and the press; and restricted Jews from working in the government, among other atrocities (Gutman, 1990, p. 1759). With the introduction of the Nuremberg Laws in September 1935, Jews were further victimized by having their German citizenship removed, and it was becoming increasingly obvious what may have lied ahead for them.

Buchenwald was established in 1937, and by 1938 approximately 1,500 Jews were put into concentration camps. These 1,500 imprisoned by Germany were some of the first Jews to enter the concentration camps in this time period. As the atrocities continued to pile up, it became obvious that the Germans under Hitler's rule had one thing in mind for the Jews: their extermination. This became official with the declaration of the *Final Solution.*

Gandhi's nonviolence principles, which contain a strict reliance upon the possibility of change within the opponent's heart and conscience, would have failed miserably against Hitler's Germany. The Nazis had proved—through their countless anti-Jewish policies adopted through the 1930s and through their increasingly severe and repressive, genocidal tactics—to have no respect, no love, no feeling at all toward the Jew. Rather, the Nazis considered the Jews to be subhuman, often comparing them to rats in propaganda.

In Satyagraha—Gandhi's soul force—the belief and practice relies upon the opponent's ability to see the evil in his or her own actions and to voluntarily change. This change is supposed to be able to be brought on by the nonviolent activist who engages in organized confrontation with the opponent, practicing the act of self suffering. By not striking back and accepting blows and physical and mental punishment from the opponent, the nonviolent activist is expected to win over the opponent's heart and mind.

In the case of Hitler's Germany, the Nazis early on made it quite clear that their beliefs and militaristic means of instituting policies contained no sense of decency, no traits of a working, healthy conscience. This working and healthy conscience is again required in the nonviolence application in order for the opponent to see his or her own evils and voluntarily change. There is a massive amount of evidence suggesting that similar to the passive resistance that was scarcely employed, organized nonviolence in the Gandhian tradition would have only served to speed up the liquidation and execution process.

How can this be certain? How can we be sure that Hitler's forces could not have been won over with love, respect, and decency? The atrocities carried out by the SS should be an abundant amount of proof on their own. Nazis, in addition to the mass executions which were carried out in gas chambers later in the war, routinely murdered Jews at random, many times for the thrill of it. This occurred even at the early formation of the ghettos, if not arguably before. Any confrontational and organized nonviolence (Gandhi's Satyagraha by its own methodology is confrontational) used against the Nazi forces would have immediately resulted in those involved, in addition to others, being executed.

In addition to this seemingly obvious reality, Gandhi's Satyagraha does not allow (for effectiveness reasons) for its own existence and that of armed resistance simultaneously. Therefore, as the Judenrats and other key figures in World War II Europe did with passive resistance, the Gandhian nonviolence followers would have ended up arguing for, and coercing others to abide by, a strict adherence to nonviolence. Not only would this directly reduce the amount of armed resistance, but as a result there would be even less resistance to the liquidations and executions of the Nazi policy. On these grounds, it is safe to state that if the Jews themselves had wished to speed up the executions and success of the *Final Solution*, the best method they could have used would be maximum adherence to organized and confrontational nonviolence. Arguably, they were not far off in their passive resistance.

This harsh critique of the Jewish response is by no means to be mistaken for the least bit of anti-Semitism. On the contrary, those historians who have argued that Jews were merely helpless victims with no possibility of a successful revolt are actually guilty of reducing and downplaying the capabilities of the Jewish people.

No one in their right mind can deny the outcome of the Nazi holocaust was horrific. Leni Yahil, in a paper presented at the *Conference on Manifestations of Jewish Resistance* held in Jerusalem in 1968, writes:

> In the lands taken by the Germans, not counting Russia, between 80 and 85 percent of the Jews perished. The point of departure in any discussion of Jewish resistance during the Holocaust must be the basic fact that the Jewish people did not succeed in defending these lives (1984, p. 36).

The goal of this analysis is to understand as much as possible why this outcome occurred, in order to aid people in current and future situations.

To me, one of the most striking and chilling similarities that can be drawn between the Jewish response and today's global struggles for justice is the phenomenon of the business-as-usual policy. Particularly in the westernized, post-industrial societies that have gained a certain amount of internal security for their people (largely at the expense of other nations), the business-as-usual policy has been quite prevalent in political and social causes. Here in the United States especially, citizens for the most part have rarely concerned themselves with issues of justice until they are personally affected (i.e., smokers who take up promoting non-smoking only after they become ill or one of their loved ones dies from cancer, citizens who begin to be concerned with air pollution only after they develop respiratory illness, law-abiding persons who believe whole-heartedly in our law enforcement only until they are mistakenly jailed or shot, etc.). Up until the point of acknowledging individual connectedness to a particular matter, as a nation we have been and continue to be consciously or subconsciously more than content with going about our everyday lives in a business-as-usual manner. Often, this is even true after we have become aware of our relationship to the cause of problems and our role in solutions.

Crucial to understanding how we as a global society can fully engage in a positive revolutionary transformation toward justice for all, is our ability to understand this phenomenon of why, in times of extreme evidence of injustice, we blindly turn our back in search of normality, in search of security, and in a conscious effort to maintain ignorance. For until we instill the value of personal responsibility and of confronting injustice head on into the concept of business-as-usual politics, we are doomed to continue to repeat lessons that should have been learned in the Holocaust of World War II.

# CHAPTER TWO

# The Civil Rights Movement in the United States

The modern African American civil rights movement in the United States made great strides forward toward equality using primarily nonviolent tactics. In perhaps one of the best examples of the potentiality nonviolent strategies have to accomplish social and political change, the civil rights movement challenged white morals and practices of discrimination stemming from the earliest years of black slavery in America. By mass mobilization and using the nonviolent technique of self suffering, citizens forced the federal government to give in to an increasingly uncompromising black population who demanded better living and working conditions, education, political opportunities and an overall sense of equal opportunity. However, because of the reformist nature of the struggle, the civil rights movement was unable to obtain true equality for African Americans.

So at what point did the modern civil rights movement begin? Did it begin officially with the famous bus boycott in Montgomery or with the landmark ruling in *Brown v. Topeka Board of Education*? Although historians, to this day, continue to argue over the exact starting point of the movement, the importance lies not so much in identifying key markers of origin as it does in understanding the chain of events that preempted the struggle. Therefore, it is crucial to at least briefly explore the history of African Americans in the United States prior to the 1950s and 1960s. The following is by no means meant to be a comprehensive historical survey, but rather a means by which the stage can be set to discuss the modern civil rights movement.

Black slaves first arrived in 1619 at Jamestown, Virginia, marking the beginning of a largely unaltered growth of slavery until the War of Independence (Verney, 2000, p. 1). During the war (1776-1783) the middle and northern colonies, which had become states, abolished slavery. After the 1776 Declaration of Independence, all men were thought to be created equal, even as slavery would continue and even grow in the South.

In the South, slaves were the principle labor force in growing tobacco, sugar and especially cotton. Although the importation of slaves into America was banned in 1808, illegal slave immigration continued, catering to the growing slave market in the South. By 1860, an estimated four million slaves lived and worked in the southern region of the country (Verney, 2000, p. 1).

During the same time period in the North, an increasing opposition to slavery led to the creation of *The Liberator* in 1831. Founded by William Lloyd Garrison in Massachusetts, this anti-slavery journal signaled the start of the abolitionist movement.

Growing tensions between the North and South led to the Civil War, from 1861 to 1865. Kevern Verney, in his book *Black Civil Rights In America*, writes that the Civil War "was not a northern attempt to abolish slavery but the refusal of the North to accept the right of the Southern states to secede, or withdraw, from the Union" (2000, p. 2).

President Lincoln finally committed the North to abolish slavery with the 1863 Emancipation Proclamation, which was confirmed by the passage of the Thirteenth Amendment to the Constitution in 1865. After the Civil Rights Act of 1866 and the Fourteenth and Fifteenth Amendments to the Constitution (ratified in 1869 and 1870), blacks—at least on paper—were supposed to have had full citizenship and voting rights. But this by no means translated into equality, as few whites initially changed their treatment of African Americans.

After this theoretical, newfound freedom for blacks, most had extreme difficulties trying to adjust to the new circumstances. Most blacks were extremely poor with no land, and the federal government provided no aid to assist in adjusting to these new rights. Most free men were forced into labor agreements with their former masters or other nearby planters. This brought on the sharecropping phenomenon.

In sharecropping, black families were provided with plots of land by white land owners, to work as their own. At the time of the harvest, though, the black planters were only repaid with one-third to one-half share of the crops (Verney, 2000, p. 3). Sharecropping became the most common form of agriculture in the South after 1865, continuing until the 1930s.

At best, sharecropping was barely a step up from slavery. Not only were blacks repaid little for their work in growing crops, most were forced to buy overpriced items from plantation stores. As a result, most sharecropper families accumulated large debts and many were forced into financial dependence on the white plantation owners.

An attempt was made in 1889 by Oliver Cromwell to provide for at least some security for black farmers. Cromwell formed the Colored Farmers Alliance, a group willing to engage in armed self defense to protect their rights. The Farmers Alliance was suppressed shortly thereafter by three companies of the state militia (Payne, 1995, p. 46).

Blacks were excluded from all political activity in the South, and in *Williams V. Mississippi* in 1898, the Supreme Court ruled these measures were constitutional. The exclusion from politics included restrictions, such as laws requiring applicants for voter registration to pass literacy tests or demonstrate an understanding of select passages from the Constitution. This obviously narrowed down the pool of "acceptable" voters as most Southern blacks had not been provided the necessary education to pass such tests.

Another famous historical case came in 1896 with *Plessy V. Ferguson*, when the Supreme Court ruled racial segregation to be constitutional. This began the "separate but equal" policy, which on paper inferred that segregation was not discrimination. Yet the black side of the policy saw little equality with the white. This practice of separate but equal segregation would not be overturned until the 1954 *Brown V. Topeka Board of*

*Education* case.

Frederick Douglass became a leading spokesperson for black rights in the nineteenth century. Escaping from slavery in September 1838, Douglas fled to New York and then on to New Bedford, where he began to publicly speak out for blacks, having been largely influenced by *The Liberator* (Douglass, 1845, pp. 105-110). Douglass died in 1895, and Booker T. Washington took his place as the leading black advocate.

Realizing the hardships that ex-slaves faced in trying to exercise their new rights, Washington started his own college, the Tuskegee Institute in Alabama. Specifically designed to cater to the educational needs of ex-slaves, the Institute attempted to differentiate itself from schools in the North that placed their major emphasis on higher education. Washington felt that what ex-slaves needed was not initial higher education but immediate education for survival. W.E.B. DuBois, who became Washington's primary critic, argued that Washington was preparing blacks for second-class citizenship only, by not giving them higher education. DuBois became a founder and member of the National Association for the Advancement of Colored People (NAACP) in 1909.

Before World War I, at least 90 percent of African Americans lived in the South (Verney, 2000, p. 12). Cotton was the main industry there, which created a growing economy until the war. Blacks in the North, prior to the War, had to compete with European immigrants for employment. During the War, as European immigration slowed, Northern employers began to increasingly solicit blacks for work. This led to the "Great Migration" between 1915 and 1925, during which some 1.25 million blacks left the South for employment in the North.

There were a few different reasons for the migration north. In the early 1900s, over 90 percent of the lynching took place in the South (Verney, 2000, p. 12). Verney writes that "on average at least 60 blacks a year were lynched in the Southern states between 1900 and 1914" (p. 12). The economy in the South also went downhill as a result of the War. With the booming war economy in the North, blacks found an easier time locating employment while at the same time enjoying voting rights and better education.

As increasing numbers of blacks migrated to the North, race relations became increasingly hostile. During the summer of 1919, there were over twenty-five race riots in various U.S. cities (Verney, 2000, p. 16). That time period became known as the "Red Summer."

In 1917, the NAACP won a victory with the outcome of *Buchan-*

*an V. Warley*. In this case, the Supreme Court held that city ordinances enforcing racial segregation were unconstitutional.

Booker T. Washington died in 1915 and was succeeded by Marcus Garvey, who took on the position of a leading black spokesperson. Garvey rejected Washington's integrated principles and strongly felt that blacks should develop their own institutions and minimize contacts with whites. Garvey would serve as a later influence for Black Power proponents such as Malcolm X. Harvard Sitkoff, in his book *The Struggle for Black Equality*, writes in reference to Garvey, "the Jamaican leader convinced masses of Negroes that white racism and not black failings explained their lowly status" (1981, pp. 9-10).

In the Depression of the 1930s, African Americans suffered worst of all. For the most part, they were the last hired and first fired in the employment world. Asa Philip Randolph, who became one of the foremost African American leaders of the 1930s, became a co-founder and president of the National Negro Congress (NNC) in 1935. The NNC was an umbrella organization formed to unite black groups to confront problems associated with the Depression. Various "Don't Buy Where You Can't Work" campaigns were organized by the NNC between 1935 and1940.

President Roosevelt, elected in 1932, came into office on promises of his "New Deal." The purpose of the New Deal was to achieve relief, recovery, and reform for the people and economy damaged by the Depression. Roosevelt's Deal established a number of aid programs, some of which benefited African Americans. The Deal also began the process of desegregating public bathrooms, secretarial pools, and cafeterias. Yet, the overall quality of life for blacks still didn't improve much.

As a result of the Depression, lynching patterns, particularly in the South, altered. The number of lynchings actually declined, which was uncommon during times of economic hardship. This is due to poor white people, who usually made up the bulk of mobs conducting the lynching, being better off financially as a result of the New Deal programs (Payne, 1995, p 20). Wealthier whites also began to see lynching as counterproductive, concerned largely about their image, as they attempted to lure big business to the South.

In 1935, the Congress of Industrial Organizations (CIO) was formed as an umbrella trade union group for unskilled, blue collar workers. The CIO made an effort to attract black members and work with civil rights groups. Formed as a more radical alternative to the American Federation of Labor (AFL), established in the 1890s, the CIO helped to raise the political consciousness of black workers. This growing political consciousness led to the growth in membership of the NAACP (Verney, 2000, p. 33). Black memberships in labor unions would grow to 1,250,000 by 1945 (Sitkoff, 1981, p. 12).

Contrary to World War I, most African Americans supported the U.S. involvement in World War II (Verney, 2000, p. 34). Not only did the War help to boost the economy with the growth of the defense industries, thus allowing more blacks to find employment up North, but African Americans were also enjoying at least a few more rights than previous generations. But of course, the discrimination continued.

In January 1941, Asa Philip Randolph launched the March on Washington Movement (MOWM). Randolph's plan was to make this a mass mobilization in protest of discrimination against black workers in defense industries. After Randolph threatened to have 100,000 demonstrators at a mass rally in Washington, D.C., President Roosevelt responded by issuing Executive Order number 8802, which established a Fair Employment Practices Committee (FEPC) to monitor hiring procedures (Verney, 2000, p. 34). This act by Randolph was one of the earliest demonstrations of the political power and capabilities of organized mass black protest.

Both black and white students at the University of Chicago formed the Congress On Racial Equality (CORE) in 1942. CORE members committed themselves to the use of nonviolent direct action to oppose discrimination and segregation. The group would become a major force in the upcoming civil rights movement.

Perhaps one of the most important factors in galvanizing the birth of the civil rights movement was the growing black consciousness. Certainly, minute changes had been made on the U.S. home front for blacks, including increasing political realizations brought about by exposure to more forms of media, but World War II added tremendously to this awareness. From 1941 to 1945, over one million blacks served in the U.S. Armed Forces (Verney, 2000, p. 35). Some 132,000 black U.S. servicemen were stationed in the United Kingdom by May 1944 (p. 35). As race relations were much better in England, African Americans enjoyed an atmosphere of greater freedom and equality. Returning home after the War, black servicemen had greater expectations for life inside the U.S. and less of a tolerance for the slow pace of change.

Many blacks, including Metgar Evers, were motivated and greatly influenced by the rebellions against colonialism in Africa. There was a major concern that blacks in Africa would achieve success in destroying colonialism before African Americans in the U.S. even gained any resemblance of equal rights and opportunities.

A 1944 NAACP victory also further added a spark to help ignite the movement. In *Smith V. Allwright*, the Supreme Court held it was unconstitutional for black voters to be excluded from Democratic Party primary elections. This was important, as the white primary had been the most effective means of keeping blacks from voting (Payne, 1995, p. 24).

During the 1940s, attitudes held especially within Mississippi blacks, began to transform into political action. A chapter of the National Progressive Voters League was formed in Jackson by T.B. Wilson to assist in gaining voting rights for blacks. The initial response was not great, but it did improve after the 1944 verdict.

After the decision, many blacks began attempting to register. Charles Payne, in his book *I've Got the Light of Freedom*, documents how the black registration improved as a result of the 1944 decision. He writes, "In 1940, only three percent of Southern Blacks were registered, a figure that had not changed much since the turn of the century. By 1947, twelve percent were registered; by 1952, twenty percent" (1995, p. 24).

Southern states, in particular, continued to resist positive changes for African Americans. These states came up with many tactics to minimize voting by blacks. Some of these included requiring one or more white character witnesses, making black applicants show their property receipts, strictly enforcing the literacy tests given to black applicants, rejecting blacks on the grounds they made technical mistakes, and evasion techniques such as claiming it was time to close, the cards for registration had run out, etc. Mississippi was the state most notorious for using these tactics (Payne, 1995, p. 26).

It can be sufficiently argued that the civil rights movement could not be fully started or realized until the completion of World War II. While discrimination on the U.S. domestic home front continued to be a reality for African Americans, an increasing emphasis by most was made on winning the war. Sitkoff writes:

> While discrimination in defense employment and in the armed services had stimulated militancy early in the war, the prolonged involvement of the United States in what it viewed as a war for survival dampened that militancy... Winning the war as speedily as possible with the least possible loss of American lives overrode all other con-

cerns. Few took kindly to anything that threatened that goal, such as a war against racism at home. Accordingly few black leaders after 1942 flirted with any tactic or strategy that might remotely be considered to harm the war effort, and the belligerence of blacks dramatically decreased (1981, p. 12).

For these reasons, mixed with the previously mentioned growing black consciousness, I feel justified in arguing that the end of World War II signaled the birth of the modern civil rights movement. This atmosphere, created by the above conditions, allowed for the beginnings of the mass mobilization of blacks arguing for their civil rights unlike ever before.

As the beginning of the Cold War with the Soviet Union became realized by 1947, conflicts arose on various levels between the U.S. and the Soviets. Aside from the obvious military determent issues at stake between both countries, the U.S. began to care more and more about its image to the rest of the world. The U.S. government did not want to be seen as a country practicing open discrimination against blacks, while simultaneously trying to prove its system superior to the communist model. President Truman therefore in 1948 issued Executive Order number 9981, which ordered an end to segregation in the military.

Of course the move made by Truman, although seemingly significant, did not change much in the reality of U.S. domestic relations between blacks and whites, particularly in the South. Verney writes, "Southern national and state leaders were all too successful in using anti-communism as a justification for the official prosecution and oppression of civil rights groups" (2000, p. 42). Indeed, any domestic group deemed in opposition to U.S. governmental policies during this time period fell victim to allegations of communist motives and allegations. White supremacist groups used this reality as an opportunity to discredit and attempt to destroy civil rights groups (Sitkoff, 1981, p. 17).

In 1947, CORE and a group called the Fellowship for Reconciliation organized the Journey of Reconciliation. This Journey went through the upper South to test the compliance of a Supreme Court ruling against segregation in interstate travel. Owing to the involvement of CORE, many civil rights leaders at the time shunned and attempted to ignore the effort due to the use and promotion of militant nonviolent tactics such as civil disobedience. Similarly, when Asa Philip Randolph called for civil disobedience against segregation in the military in 1948, civil rights leaders opposed the call (Sitkoff, 1981, p. 18).

In June 1953, one of the first major battles of the modern civil rights movement occurred in Baton Rouge, Louisiana. There African Americans successfully conducted a mass boycott against the city's segregated bus system. Owing to the pressure from protesters and the resulting financial loss to the bus system, authorities were forced to give in to the demands from blacks to desegregate the buses (Morris, 1984, p. x). This first bus boycott at least partially influenced the more famous campaign in Montgomery that occurred in 1955.

The famous *Brown V. Topeka Board of Education* ruling came next on May 17, 1954. Ruling against school segregation, the Supreme Court, with help from an earlier ruling in 1950, reversed the separate-but-equal policy. But the implementation of this decision would not be immediate. The Supreme Court allowed local federal judges to determine the pace of desegregation and refused to set a deadline for compliance.

Immediately, southern states began refusing to cooperate with any desegregation. On March 12, 1956, 101 members of Congress from the South signed a "Declaration of Constitutional Principles," which asked their states to refuse to obey the desegregation order (Sitkoff, 1981, p. 26). Where desegregation did slowly begin, blacks were hit with stones, yelled at with insults, and physically and mentally harassed as they came near white schools.

Various attempts at legislation were made by those opposing desegregation who sought to delay or stop the process. The opposition was successful in this attempt with the pupil placement law. On face value, the law said that authorities could not consider race when assigning kids to schools. They could, however, accept or reject transfer applications based on "the psychological qualification of the pupil" as in Georgia, "the psychological effect upon the pupil of attendance at a particular school" and "the morals, conduct, health and personal standards of the pupil" (Sitkoff, 1981, p. 28). This law resulted in blacks and whites being assigned to different schools. Remarkably, the Supreme Court upheld the constitutionality of the pupil placement laws in 1958.

Back in 1955, December 1st in Montgomery, Alabama marked the continuation of the desegregation efforts started earlier in Baton Rouge. When Rosa Parks refused to give up her seat on the bus so a white man could sit down, she unknowingly signaled a massive movement. Parks, who then served as Secretary of State for the NAACP, was arrested for demonstrating the injustice of the segregated bus system. News of Park's arrest quickly spread through Montgomery, making many people feel the need for action.

Both E.D. Nixon, who was then the president of the Alabama NAACP, and JoAnn Robinson, the head of the Women's Political Council, agreed that Park's case was one worthy of mobilization. The two organized a one-day bus boycott on December 5th to coincide with Park's trial date. On that day, over 90 percent of blacks who would have normally ridden the bus refused to board. This officially began the Montgomery bus boycott, which would last 381 days.

Prominent black ministers in Montgomery, including E.D. Nixon, felt the boycott needed a leader to keep momentum, to keep inspiration, and to keep on track. They thought it would be best to find someone from out of town who would not already have stigmas against him. Martin Luther King Jr. was agreed upon. King, who had come to Montgomery a year before to serve as pastor of the Dexter Avenue Baptist Church, was nominated to the position and accepted the role.

The group of ministers also agreed on an organizing committee they named the Montgomery Improvement Association (MIA). This committee was to lead the boycott until the city met the demands proposed by Nixon and the NAACP regarding desegregation of the buses.

Prior to King's election, he seldom discussed current racial matters in his sermons (Sitkoff, 1981, p. 48). The extent of his advocacy had been limited to giving some support for blacks registering to vote and for people to support the NAACP. Although King had been interested in the possibilities of nonviolent resistance, having been exposed to Gandhi, he had not come to any conclusions on what exactly to do (p. 48).

On the night of Park's trial, thousands of blacks turned up at King's church to hear him speak about the campaign. King preached that love was the means for protest arguing in the Gandhian ethic that nonviolence was the only way for a meaningful and lasting change. This sermon was received with widespread support, energizing and mobilizing African Americans to act.

After just three days of the boycott, King met with the Mayor, his commissioners, and attorneys for the bus company to discuss the campaign. City officials refused to meet any demands of the MIA nor would do anything that could be perceived as giving in to a black victory. The Mayor went as far as threatening legal action on black cabs who had been transporting blacks at bus fare prices. As a result, black cab drivers were forced into raising their prices back up.

74

Determined to keep the campaign going, the MIA organized carpools to assist those in need of transportation due to the boycott. This was met with almost immediate pressure and harassment from the city. At the end of January, 1956, the Mayor announced a "get tough" policy against those involved in the boycott. Carpool drivers were routinely pulled over and charged with bogus traffic violations. Many drivers also were threatened with losing their licenses and insurance. Blacks who appeared to be prominent within the boycott lost their jobs (Sitkoff, 1981, p. 53).

When people began to be arrested on false charges, many of those involved in the boycott became increasingly fearful. As a result, some drivers left the carpool, while a small number of other blacks resumed riding the buses. All this came after only four days of retaliation by whites.

King was then pulled over and arrested for speeding, an event that actually re-energized the campaign. After hundreds of people showed up at the jail to protest, King was released on bond. A few days later, as King was speaking at a rally elsewhere, a bomb went off, destroying the front of his house. Immediately, hundreds of blacks with weapons surrounded his house for protection. King told the crowd of nearly 1,000 people, "Get rid of your weapons. We are not advocating violence. We want to love our enemies. We must love our white brothers no matter what they do to us" (Sitkoff, 1981, p. 53). News of this incident and King's response calling for love spread throughout the nation.

But the pressure and harassment from the city continued against those involved in the boycott. On February 21, 1956, city officials obtained indictments against King and 100 other leading boycott participants on the charge of violating a 1921 law forbidding hindrance to a business without just cause or legal excuse. All of the people indicted immediately turned themselves in, creating widespread news stories. Hearing the news, support in the form of letters and donations came from people all over the country and world. King was found guilty after a trial the next month, and the news of the verdict again was covered by national and international media.

During this same time period, the harassment also targeted the NAACP and the MIA. Montgomery outlawed the NAACP on the basis that it failed to register and that it caused "irreparable injury to the property and civil rights of residents," and the city imposed a fine of $100,000 for refusing to hand over its membership lists (Sitkoff, 1981, pp. 56-57). The MIA was indicted on charges of conducting the carpool without a business license.

But owing to the resolve of the protesters and the work of the MIA organizing group, the effort prevailed. On November 13, 1956 the U.S. Supreme Court affirmed the decision of three U.S. District Court judges declaring segregation on buses unconstitutional. In a display of success and power, King and his aides boarded a bus on December 21, 1956 and sat down in front.

Before blacks in Montgomery were to resume riding on the buses, King conducted nonviolence trainings, attempting to prepare people for any resistance they may encounter. Contained within a leaflet distributed in every black church in the area was a passage asking blacks to "read, study, and memorize" seventeen rules:

> Pray for guidance and commit yourself to complete non-violence in word and action as you enter the bus... Be loving enough to absorb evil and understanding enough to turn an enemy into a friend... If cursed, do not curse back. If pushed, do not push back. If struck, do not strike back, but evidence love and goodwill at all times... If another person is being molested, do not arise to go to his defense, but pray for the oppressor and use moral and spiritual force to carry on the struggle for justice... Do not be afraid to experiment with new and creative techniques for achieving reconciliation and social change... If you feel you cannot take it, walk for another week or two (Sitkoff, 1981, pp. 59-60).

King's view on and belief in nonviolence stemmed from his Christianity and from his studies of the Gandhi's work in South Africa and India. Both men believed and taught the powerful potential that non-violence application can have in social change. King, like Gandhi, emphasized the crucial role self suffering plays in winning over an opponent with love and respect. The two men differed, though, in their thoughts on coercion. Gandhi, throughout his social change activities, denounced the use of coercion and insisted that his Satyagraha nonviolence method was free of this pressure he deemed as counterproductive. King, on the other hand, recognized that coercion was a necessary component of the nonviolent strategy. By taking part in a nonviolent campaign, the opponent is pressured without violence into a reaction. Once the pressure becomes too great, the opponent—through the effects of coercion—chooses to give in to the protesters.

The Montgomery Bus Boycott is a superb example of how organized, mass nonviolent action can have a direct impact on changing unjust laws. The boycott would not have had the power, or arguably worked at all, if there hadn't have been such a high percentage of blacks within the city participating. One of the most difficult aspects of a campaign of any length is the ability to sustain the interest, participation, and effectiveness of the people involved. In the Montgomery case, a main factor that determined its successful outcome was the MIA's ability to see the wisdom in asking people to sacrifice only after the group made every effort to secure a replacement for people's needs. Upon the beginning of the boycott, the thousands of participants would immediately need transportation for work and other activities. Realizing this, the MIA first organized low-cost cabs to run at the same rate as the buses. After city officials cracked down on this, the MIA came back and set up a network of carpooling, which also provided some relief for the participants.

Even before the Montgomery boycott was finished, the efforts galvanized black ministers in other cities to begin planning actions. After visiting King, Reverend Charles K. Steele organized a successful bus boycott in Tallahassee. Similar bus desegregation efforts occurred in Atlanta and Savannah and in other cities in Alabama.

Shortly after the Montgomery court ruling, King called on civil rights clergymen to convene in Atlanta on January 10-11, 1957 for organizing purposes. Some sixty blacks from ten states attended and named themselves the Southern Conference on Transportation and Nonviolent Integration. At a more formal organization meeting of the conference in New Orleans in February, King was elected president and the name was changed to the Southern Christian Leadership Conference (SCLC).

King's nonviolence principles had an immediate effect on the SCLC organization. The group called upon blacks "to understand that nonviolence is not a symbol of weakness or cowardice, but as Jesus demonstrated, nonviolent resistance transforms weakness into strength and breeds courage in the face of danger" (Sitkoff, 1981, p. 65). SCLC, largely due to the Southern white backlash that grew tremendously in the late 1950s, was unable to accomplish much. Sitkoff writes, "the SCLC accomplished little and failed to spark the mass direct action movement needed to alter the South" (p. 65).

In a growing response of opposition to the *Brown V. Topeka Board of Education* ruling, Southern whites continued to employ various techniques to delay integration or prevent it altogether. After 1956, it would take seven more years to desegregate the University of Alabama. Governor Faubus in Little Rock, rather than give in to the Supreme Court decision, decided to close the schools completely at one point. Likewise, Virginia closed all the educational facilities in Prince Edwards County rather than comply with desegregation. Additionally, black homes and churches were torched and crosses were burned as white racial rage struck the South.

The Little Rock case is a prime example of the difficulties faced by blacks attempting integration. On September 2, 1957, Governor Faubus ordered a National Guard contingent to guard Central High School and not let any blacks in. This was in direct response to a federal court ruling ordering that nine blacks be admitted to the high school. Realizing they were going to be faced with the National Guard and would be refused entry to school, the nine black students stayed at home the first day. Another court order came from an Arkansas federal district court stating that desegregation must begin immediately. But the next day, the National Guard was back in front of the school, guarding it from the black students. On September 20, an additional order for desegregation was given by a federal district court. Under pressure, Faubus withdrew the National Guard and left the town. In his place came 1,000 angry white protesters who still refused to let the blacks inside the school. The mayor stepped in after three days of massive white protests, ordering the backs not to attempt to go in, out of fear of violent outbreaks.

As news of the situation in Little Rock continued to spread across the country and internationally, President Eisenhower was forced to act. He had previously refused to take a supportive role of the desegregation, fearing the loss of Southern support. But concern over how his government was viewed internationally as well as domestically pressured Eisenhower to move. He federalized the Arkansas National Guard and ordered 1,000 troops of the 101st Airborne Division to Little Rock to guard the high school and permit the entry of the nine black students (Sitkoff, 1981, p. 32). Still, by 1964 only 123 black children out of approximately 7,000 students in Little Rock were able to attend desegregated schools (p. 37).

Owing to increasing pressure from African Americans and the resulting violence and opposition from whites in response, Congress was also pressured into acting. In 1957, Congress enacted civil rights legislation for the first time since the Reconstruction period. The legislation came in the form of a voting rights bill that authorized the Justice Department to seek injunctions against those responsible for interfering with the right to vote.

As the growing repression continued to take a mental and physical toll on African Americans, many began to question King's logic in regards to nonviolence. In 1959, Robert Williams, then head of the Monroe, North Carolina NAACP, was dismissed for, according to Sitkoff, "publicly advocating defensive guerilla warfare by blacks and calling for the formation of rifle clubs through the South" (1981, p. 66). Earlier in 1959, Williams had organized a gun club of approximately fifty blacks. They, at least on one occasion, successfully repelled with gunfire a group of Klansmen who were threatening the home of an NAACP official (p. 66).

Near the end of the 1950s, a surge in activity by blacks signaled the continued growth and potential of the movement. After attending a nonviolence workshop given in 1958, Barbara Ann Posey organized a sit-in to desegregate stores in her area. Posey, a member of the Oklahoma City NAACP Youth Council, successfully desegregated five stores with her organizing efforts. The idea quickly spread to other cities in Oklahoma and Kansas.

Also in 1958, King helped organize the Youth March for Integrated Schools, in which 9,000 young blacks marched in Washington, D.C. The following year some 20,000 people would take part in this event. Many other protests and actions against segregation took place in 1959 in Virginia, North Carolina, South Carolina and Florida, among other locations, but they all failed to spark a national movement.

Then came the famous case of the four students from Greensboro, North Carolina in 1960. On February 1, these four students conducted a sit-in at the Woolworth's store, asking to be served. After being denied service the students sat there through the rest of the day until the store closed. News quickly spread of this action, and the four met with fifty other students that same evening. They decided to form the Student Executive Committee for Justice and voted to continue the sit-in at Woolworth's until they were served.

The next day, twenty-three A & T students and four black women from Bennett College joined the original four at the lunch counter. Once again, the store refused to serve them. By the following day, students occupied nearly all of the seats in the lunch area. Even a few white students began joining in the protest and, as the total number of demonstrators continued to rise, the effort spread to other stores in the area.

After two rallies within the same week attracted 300 and then

1,600 students respectively, city officials expressed their desire to negotiate. Protesters agreed to cease the demonstrations to allow for an agreement to be reached. The only problem was that the city officials were unwilling to compromise at all. Therefore, the sit-ins resumed on April 1, 1960. Six months after the four students originally sat down at the lunch counter, the city was forced to give in.

The Greensboro case inspired many others who organized sit-ins and other actions against segregation. On February 8, 1960, sit-ins began in Durham and Winston-Salem. The very next day, a sit-in began in Charlotte. Sitkoff documents that the sit-in technique was adopted by many after hearing of Greensboro. He writes, "By April 1960, the tactic had spread to seventy-eight Southern and border communities; some two thousand students had been arrested" (Sitkoff, 1981, p. 72). Students even began a new tactic on March 18, known as the jail-in. This simply referred to the purposeful decision to choose to go to jail rather than pay a fine. This technique was adopted not only as a refusal to give the unjust city and courts money from the protesters, but also to place direct pressure on the courts and jails and thus the city, to take positive action.

Other similar desegregation efforts were conducted in various cities. Some of them included kneel-ins at churches, sleep-ins at motel lobbies, swim-ins in pools, wade-ins on restricted beaches, read-ins at public libraries, play-ins at public parks and watch-ins at movie theaters (Sitkoff, 1981, p. 81).

Prior to the Greensboro case there were, at least in the planning stages, similar actions which were to be conducted in Nashville. Some historians, including Clayborne Carson in the book, *In Struggle: SNCC and the Black Awakening of the 1960s*, argue that the role of the Nashville attempts is often underrated. Carson writes:

> In fact a few black students in Nashville had not only engaged in such planning, but also had schooled themselves in the philosophical doctrines of the Gandhian passive resistance movement in India. It was these Nashville activists, rather than the four Greensboro students, who had an enduring impact on the subsequent development of the southern movement (1981, p. 16).

Regardless of which actual group had the most influence, they both played crucial parts in laying the groundwork for the mass movement of the

1960s.

Ella Baker, then executive director of the SCLC, decided to organize a youth leadership meeting, which convened on April 15, 1960. Observing the power and dedication of the young activists involved in the sit-ins, Baker allowed the meeting to be largely controlled by the youth rather than be taken over by outsiders. The meeting ended with students organizing a temporary coordinating committee and declaring civil disobedience as the primary, strategic tool necessary for change.

In May, the group made the decision not to be directly affiliated with other existing organizations such as SCLC, but rather to be independent. They named themselves the Temporary Student Nonviolent Coordinating Committee. The group established its headquarters in Atlanta and voted Marion Barry as chairman, who would be followed by Charles McDew. In October, at a meeting in Atlanta, the group dropped the Temporary from its name and was from then on known as the Student Nonviolent Coordinating Committee (SNCC). Believing nonviolence to be the most effective weapon, preferred over legal battles in court, SNCC's main goal was a quick end to Jim Crow practices of segregation and discrimination.

CORE's national director, James Farmer, issued a call on March 13, 1961 for volunteers to conduct freedom rides through the South. Just prior to this call, the Supreme Court had extended a 1946 prohibition against segregation in vehicles used in interstate travel to include interstate terminals. Farmer states, "Our intention was to provoke the Southern authorities into arresting us and thereby prod the Justice Department into enforcing the law of the land" (Sitkoff, 1981, p. 98). This Freedom Ride was to be modeled after the 1947 Journey of Reconciliation.

Just like the Journey of Reconciliation, the Freedom Ride in 1961 would begin with nonviolence training in Washington, D.C. A main goal of the ride was to challenge discrimination in terminal restaurants, waiting rooms, and restrooms in the deep South. Before leaving in April, CORE wrote to the FBI, Justice Department, President John F. Kennedy, and to the bus companies involved, informing them of CORE's campaign and proposed civil disobedience. There was no reply.

This display of respect and the honest attempt at negotiating first was shared among CORE, King, and Gandhi. Gandhi stressed the importance of relating to the opponent in a compassionate, respectful and loving manner. Before one of his most famous campaigns—the Salt March in India—began, Gandhi contacted the English viceroy to inform him of the plan. Feeling that "any secrecy hinders the real spirit of democracy," Gandhi openly communicated in a friendly manner his objections and his plans for civil disobedience (Fischer, 1954, pp. 96-97). This methodology makes sense, since if the problem could be solved initially by negotiating with the opponent, there would be no need for further, more extreme action. Additionally, the initial attempt at negotiation, if successful, also provides a more secure grounding for the justification of further extreme action.

On May 4, 1961, thirteen people, including seven blacks and six whites separated into interracial groups, left Washington, D.C. on two separate buses. Immediately, the ride was hit with horrendous white anger and violence. The pressure was so enormous that CORE's Freedom Ride was forced to disband on May 17 due to massive violence in Alabama.

Wanting to ensure that the effort would not be a failure, SNCC resumed the Ride in Birmingham. SNCC felt that the Freedom Ride "must continue to prove to the world that violence could not overcome nonviolence" (Sitkoff, 1981, p. 102). From Birmingham and then on to Montgomery, the mob violence became stronger and increasingly fierce. As a result, the ride consistently made the headlines of newspapers across the country.

Mounting pressure from public outrage over the treatment of these youth forced President Kennedy to act. He previously had refused to act on the entire civil rights issue and had refused to provide for the protection of the Freedom Riders. Growing concerned over the view foreign nations would have of the situation, Kennedy ordered 350 to 400 U.S. Marshals to Montgomery to assist state authorities in protecting people and property.

Martin Luther King, Jr. also expressed concern over the necessity for the Ride to continue. He held a mass rally on May 21 in Montgomery, in which some 1,200 people attended (Sitkoff, 1981, p. 108). Many white people in mobs showed up also and began inflicting violence on the attendees. U.S. Marshals ended up having to surround the church to protect it. It was decided the next day that the Ride would continue.

From that point on, various groups including CORE, SNCC, SCLC, and the Nashville Christian Leadership Committee, formed the Freedom Ride Coordinating Committee. They worked together to help insure the completion and success of the Ride that had come into so much conflict. From the formation of this coalition came many new recruits to join the Riders. They came from places such as Atlanta, New York, New Orleans, and Washington, D.C., and on May 24, a total of twenty-seven people continued the Freedom Ride.

The federal and state protection continued en route from Montgomery to Jackson, Mississippi. Sitkoff writes, "Three airplanes and two helicopters flew reconnaissance overhead while motorized National Guard units scouted the road ahead and patrol cars escorted the shiny red and white buses" (1981, p. 109). Unfortunately, when they reached Jackson the protection stopped.

All twenty-seven Riders were arrested in Jackson after they attempted to enter the white cafeteria restrooms. They were all found guilty, fined, and given two-month, suspended sentences. In a show of solidarity to one another and the cause, they decided to go to jail rather than pay the fines. Others quickly came to continue the work in the South.

Sitkoff documents that the participation in the rides became so great that "by the end of the summer (1961), over a thousand persons of every age and faith, from every section of the country had participated in Freedom Rides" (1981, p. 110). In Jackson alone, some 300 people were jailed in just a few months (p. 110). People in other states began to be involved, and the movement spread to attempt the desegregation of railroad and airport facilities as well.

The Freedom Rides, due to the mounting public pressure and concerns over the image of the U.S. internationally, forced the government to act. The U.S. Attorney General asked the Interstate Commerce Commission to issue rules against racial discrimination in interstate facilities. CORE claimed the campaign was a success in desegregating interstate travel by the end of 1962.

One of the most interesting aspects of the Freedom Rides was the means by which the ride continued to mobilize people into action. Momentum is a key determinant in the success of a social movement. It must always continue to build, even if slowly, if the movement is to progress. This entails energizing more people to get involved continuously to provide for more action and pressure. How to inspire, energize, and get people mobilized to act is one of the pertinent mysteries to organizers. The Freedom Rides had this momentum, and they played a major role in desegregating the interstate travel facilities.

Upon completion of the Freedom Rides, many of the major civil rights groups decided to next concentrate on registering African Americans to vote. The Voter Education Project (VEP) was formed as a joint project of CORE, SNCC, SCLC, and the Urban League. VEP began its voter registration campaign in 1962 and estimated that it would be completed after two and a half years.

On August 7, a Voter Registration School opened up in Pike County, Mississippi. This immediately was met with anger from local whites who opposed the right of blacks to register. One of the first blacks in Pike County to register to vote was shot by a white person on August 10.

Having more success in the upper South than in the lower, VEP had a direct impact on the registration numbers of black citizens. Sitkoff documents that the group:

> recorded 688,800 blacks qualifying to vote for the first time in the South between April 11, 1962 and November 1, 1964, a jump from 26.8 to 38 percent of the potential black registrants. Almost all the increase, however, came from the urban and upper South. In Mississippi, the pro-portion of black voters rose from 5.3 percent to just 6.7 percent (Sitkoff, 1981, p. 121).

Resulting from the extreme hostility from whites in the South and the poor registration success rate, the VEP decided in 1963 to not fund anymore voter work in the deep South.

Sitkoff writes about the impact white violence had on the civil rights efforts in the South during this time:

> The violence against the effort to enfranchise blacks, largely unnoticed by the nation and unhindered by the federal government, continued until the Mississippi Free-dom Summer of 1964, when at least thirty homes were bombed, thirty-five churches burned, eighty persons were beaten, and there were more than thirty shooting inci-dents, and six known murders (1981, p. 123).

In Georgia, beginning in November 1961, thousands of blacks engaged in boycotts, marches, and sit-ins to gain enfranchisement. This movement in Georgia failed not because there were too few participants, but rather due to sheer strategy issues. Instead of being exceedingly re-actionary, as had been the case with the majority of Southern police, the local police departments in Georgia tried out somewhat different tactics. They purposely sought to minimize their harsh treatment of the black protesters, in order to keep the public from sympathizing with the protestors. By minimizing mob violence, filling the jails with blacks, and minimizing police brutality, the police felt they could still defy federal law without forcing the President to send in troops in to ensure compliance.

This strategy worked for the police, and they avoided the massive public sympathy that had arisen for the protesters in other campaigns. A necessary strategy in nonviolent civil disobedience is that participants constantly provoke a confrontation where the opponent is continually forced to deal with them. The Georgia campaign was not successful because the intended confrontation was less effective than predicted. The Georgia organizers had figured there would be a typical violent response from the police, which would be captured in the national news media. Exposure to this violent reaction was supposed to anger, energize, and galvanize the nation into support and action. However, the police departments' modified response tactics neutralized the protestors' efforts.

The Freedom Rides were successful as they continuously confronted and challenged Southern white racism. As the numbers of participants grew and the media exposure of the violent, reactionary police increased, rising and intense pressure forced the government into action. But it was mainly a result of constantly challenging white racism in a way that led to some of the largest and most controversial confrontations.

King became further convinced of the importance of confrontation, and along with the rest of the SCLC, he wanted to create a crisis so big that President Kennedy would have to act. After he was invited by Reverend Fred Lee Shuttlesworth, then the head of an SCLC affiliate group, to come to Birmingham to conduct nonviolent demonstrations, King agreed and set out for what was considered to be the most segregated big city in America at that time.

Along with his task force, King then began preparing for "Project C," the C standing for Confrontation. Project C began with small groups of protesters staging sit-ins at segregated, downtown lunch counters. As the campaign continued, increasing numbers of people were arrested. This, along with gaining the interest of the Kennedy administration and the national news media, comprised stage one of the project.

On April 6, stage two of Project C began. This involved daily marches to city hall, where each participant would be arrested. From its beginning, this stage in the project received massive media coverage. On April 10, within four days, city officials obtained an injunction banning racial demonstrations. On April 12, King immediately announced he would violate this injunction. On that day King, along with fifty others, once again marched on city hall. Some 1,000 blacks came out to line the parade route and demonstrate support. The marchers all were arrested, and while in jail King composed his famous *Letter from a Birmingham Jail*.

King's letter was meant to be directed towards those who opposed his tactics of civil disobedience and nonviolent confrontation. It was met with great interest, as national periodicals published the letter in its entirety. The widespread publication of the letter further gained support for the effort.

As the marches on city hall continued, the police response involved greater degrees of violence. Protestors responded to these violent outbreaks by the police with even larger marches and demonstrations (Sitkoff, 1981, p. 135).

Looking back on the situation now, it is interesting to note that King's efforts in Birmingham would not have been as successful if the police did not succumb to the tactics of violence and intimidation. If the police would have chosen tactics similar to that used in Albany, Georgia—one of restraint to avoid losing public support—the Birmingham movement could also have been weakened considerably. But because Birmingham was known for its extreme segregation and discrimination, it was a prime location for King's effort.

The individual bravery of African Americans throughout the civil rights struggle has to be admired. They faced daily mental and physical violence while attempting to assert their right to equal opportunities and freedoms shared by whites. Another incredible example of this bravery is the case of William L. Moore. A member of CORE, Moore set out April 21 on what he called a "Freedom Walk" from Chattanooga to Mississippi. He wore a sandwich board that stated "Equal Rights for All - Mississippi or Bust" and intended to walk to Jackson to deliver a letter to Mississippi Governor Ross Barnett stating his objections to Southern segregation. Just two days later, Moore was last seen alive walking through Gadsden, Alabama. He was found that night shot in the neck and head, left dead on a road about ten miles outside the city (Sitkoff, 1981, p. 135).

The murder of William L. Moore further angered an already scarred black nation, who vowed to continue the Freedom Walk. Shortly after the murder, Diane Nash Bevel took a group of eight Birmingham blacks to Gadsden to continue the Walk. All of them were quickly arrested. Staff members from CORE and SNCC then set out from Chattanooga on May 1st to continue the attempt. Like Bevel's previous effort, all of the participants were arrested and subjected to further violence. Even after being shocked repeatedly with cattle prods by the police, the CORE and SNCC activists refused to accept bail and spent a month in a jail. Demonstrating the great resolve to make this Walk successful, another CORE group continued two weeks later. A mixture of six black and five white activists were arrested as the police refused to allow the Walk.

In Birmingham upon his release, King held a meeting for youth on May 2nd at the Sixteenth Street Baptist Church. After the meeting, an estimated 1,000 black children emerged from the church demonstrating against segregation. They were all arrested, and the story was thoroughly broadcast in the national news media (Sitkoff,1981, p. 136). The next day 1,000 more black children repeated the same action and were met with a violent police reaction. In these two days some 1,300 children were arrested and 200 more were added on May 4. The shocking scenes of children being subjected to police brutality shown in the national media further angered black America and began to increasingly spark the interest of whites. As a result, King immediately had an overwhelming amount of public support.

King purposely chose to involve the children in these actions to create the most extreme display of white oppression and confrontation. He realized that the images of children being beaten and hurt by white police would tug at the public's heartstrings. Although his strategy did indeed produce the desired results, King was heavily criticized by other black leaders for allowing such young children to be exposed to violence.

The public pressure brought on by the youths in Birmingham forced the federal government into action. Behind closed doors, the Kennedy Administration pressured business leaders in Birmingham to meet and negotiate with King and the SCLC (Sitkoff, 1981, pp. 138-139). Both sides began talks, but within a short time neither would agree to compromise and the meetings resulted in a deadlock.

King ordered the protests to continue, and on Monday, May 6, an even larger protest began with students once again coming out of the Sixteenth Street Baptist Church. Over 1,000 of these students were arrested, and during the process the police force unleashed an attack on a large group of people in a nearby park. With national media standing by, the public witnessed further massive bloodshed in Birmingham.

Public pressure again increased on the federal government, and talks resumed between the white business leaders and civil rights proponents. As still no ground was made in the meetings, protestors held the largest demonstration yet in the campaign on May 7th. Over 2,000 young blacks met in the Birmingham downtown area at noon and engaged in sit-ins and picketed major stores (Sitkoff, 1981, p. 140). While the police attacked the protesters, a secret meeting was held, in which white business leaders asked their negotiators to come to an agreement with the SCLC. After three days of negotiation, an agreement was reached.

King and the SCLC had won the desegregation of lunch counters, restrooms, fitting rooms and drinking fountains. Furthermore, business leaders agreed to a more unbiased hiring policy in various Birmingham industries. A biracial committee was also established to voice concerns of blacks and monitor progress of the agreements. The SCLC did, however, give in to their demand of immediacy and agreed the new regulations would be implemented in stages. All those who were jailed during the campaign were released on bond, but they still faced charges.

Like the Montgomery Bus Boycott and the Freedom Rides, the Birmingham campaign continually increased the momentum level necessary for success. By operating in the South's most segregated big city and by using children, King and the SCLC were able to create the most extreme confrontation that pressured—and really coerced—the federal government to intervene.

This latest victory had far-reaching effects, and increasing numbers of black uprisings occurred in cities nationwide in late 1963. Sitkoff estimates that "nearly eight hundred boycotts, marches, and sit-ins in some two hundred cities and towns across the South occurred in the three months after the Birmingham accord... More racial change came in these few months than had occurred in three quarters of a century" (1981, p. 149). During the spring and summer of 1963, it is estimated that over 15,000 demonstrators were arrested in the deep South.

The successful campaigns, particularly the case in Birmingham, led to a dramatic rise in the violent reaction of Southern whites. On June 11, 1963, Medgar Evers, who had been the NAACP field secretary in Jackson, was murdered. This added fuel to the fire, forcing the federal government to increasingly act on behalf of civil rights. Business leaders also realized that the confrontations resulted in massive economic losses. Sitkoff writes:

> The threat of black insurrection, and even of more Birminghams, and the intensification of black economic boycotts, especially touched the national corporate com-

munity. Businessmen saw no profit in turbulence, and many concluded in mid-1963 that meeting the reasonable aims of the civil-rights movement was the best way to lay to rest the specter of increasing racial violence and disorder (1981, p. 155).

Amazingly enough, many chairmen of corporations and foundations agreed to give a combined $1 million to the five main civil rights groups in support of their work (Sitkoff, 1981, p. 155).

Yet, regardless of the successes of 1963 and before, many blacks increasingly questioned the nonviolent code preached and adhered to by the main civil rights organizations. In the atmosphere of extreme, often violent, white southern resistance, a growing number of African Americans looked toward more militant tactics. The emergence of black power advocates such as Malcolm X, with his support of armed self defense and his outright public criticisms of the nonviolent methodology, added to this situation. This perceived threat posed by Malcolm had a direct, powerful effect on whites. Sitkoff states, "the more Malcolm loomed as the alternative that whites would have to confront if CORE, SNCC, and SCLC failed, the more white officials acceded to the stipulations posed by the established leadership of the campaign for racial equality" (1981, p. 155). In other words, increasing numbers of people believed that if whites did not deal effectively with the nonviolent civil rights groups, they would be faced with the less tolerant and armed, angry blacks.

As the pressure in 1963 continued to build, President Kennedy was forced into proposing the most extensive and comprehensive civil rights legislation in U.S. history. Created in June, this measure called for:

> provisions for desegregating public accommodations; granting authority to the Attorney General to initiate school-desegregation suits; establishing a community relations service to prevent racial conflict; improving the economic status of blacks; and empowering the government to withhold funds from federally supported programs and facilities in which discrimination occurred (Sitkoff, 1981, p. 158).

Over 200,000 blacks and whites from all across the United States met at the Capitol on August 28, 1963 to urge Congress to pass the legislation.

At this gathering, King delivered his *I Have A Dream* speech to an enormous crowd who supported the move by Kennedy. Yet others, including Malcolm X, refused and felt it a mistake to rely on the government to give blacks their rights. Referring to this march on Washington as the "Farce on Washington," Malcolm denounced the event to the public (Sitkoff, 1981, p. 165).

After President Kennedy was assassinated in Dallas in November, even more public pressure mounted for Congress to pass the bill. Finally, after both the House and Senate signed the bill, President Lyndon Johnson signed the act and made it into law on July 2, 1964.

The passage of this legislation resulted only after years of increasing pressure, mostly from the nonviolent civil disobedience campaigns performed by blacks and some whites. Even though many whites, particularly in the South, were so opposed to granting blacks even the most minute civil rights, the nonviolent campaigns worked to produce the needed pressure for the federal government to act.

After the 1963 March on Washington, CORE and SNCC decided to return to the South to work on voter drives. Bob Moses of SNCC, states that "no other battle on the civil rights front posed greater risks than voter registration in Mississippi" (Sitkoff, 1981, p. 169). He decided to take on the task and reformed the Council of Federated Organizations (COFO), which had originally formed to help secure the release of the jailed Freedom Riders in 1961, to unite various civil rights groups to the voter registration cause.

Just before the November 1963 elections, Moses and COFO conducted a "Freedom Election" to demonstrate the desire blacks truly had to vote. An estimated 80,000 disenfranchised blacks participated, casting their votes for Lieutenant Governor and Governor (Sitkoff, 1981, p. 170). COFO and Moses also were assisted in this effort by a group of white students from Yale, who brought with them national media attention and increased protection.

A controversy had begun to erupt within the civil rights movement regarding the participation of whites. While black power advocates such as Malcolm X felt, as Marcus Garvey did, that blacks needed to run their own campaigns and control their own lives, many in the movement saw benefits to white participation. For one, the racist nation (and therefore the media) was much more prone to care about the subjection of whites to extreme cruelty than blacks. Secondly, due to the nation's dominant concern for the protection of whites first, white involvement in the civil rights movement meant added protection from law enforcement. It wasn't a coincidence that in the areas where white activists showed up to protest police usually provided greater security. Since a goal of various campaigns was to create a large, direct confrontation to white racism that would be documented by the media, white participation helped make that goal possible.

For these reasons COFO planned a "Mississippi Freedom Summer" that would purposely involve whites. The planned project involved the creation of schools and various institutions to assist in providing blacks the necessary education to register. Additionally, COFO established a new political party that would be open to all people. Referred to as the Mississippi Freedom Democratic Party (MFDP), its enrollment quickly exceeded 60,000 blacks (Sitkoff, 1981, p. 179).

COFO's Mississippi Freedom Summer was a continuation of an earlier effort by the Highlander Folk School, which had worked to establish Citizen Schools in the South back in the 1950s. Septima Clark, who worked for Highlander beginning in 1956, was a driving force behind the Citizen Schools, which were set up to teach blacks how to read and to prepare them for voting.

As with every other campaign in the civil rights movement, the Freedom Summer created a violent response from racist whites. As a result, many civil rights advocates, including those who previously preached and practiced strict nonviolence, armed themselves. According to Sitkoff, "by the end of the summer, most SNCC workers in Mississippi carried a gun" (1981, p. 177). At the end of the year SNCC publicly defended the right of its field workers to carry weapons for protection. CORE, in Louisiana, also became increasingly convinced of the necessity for armed protection. The group accepted the protection of the Deacons for Defense and Justice, an armed black organization that offered to assist with CORE's efforts.

The controversy regarding involvement of white people became extremely heated around the time of the Democratic National Convention. The Mississippi Freedom Democratic Party attempted to get seated at the Convention but failed because they were unwilling to compromise with President Johnson. This refusal by Johnson to seat the MFDP created further doubts among the black movement regarding the true intentions of white liberals. Sitkoff argues that the situation:

> proved to SNCC and CORE's southern organizers that white liberals could not be counted on, that they would compromise black needs whenever it suited them, and that real change would come only when blacks possessed the independent power to remain a threat to the power structure (1981, p. 184).

The SNCC felt like certain leaders, including King, had been co-opted into ineffectiveness by white liberals who cared more for their own political power than the rights of blacks.

King and the SCLC knew they had to create a strategy to force the government to act more on behalf of blacks. SCLC then changed its nonviolent approach from Satyagraha to Duragraha. This is an important difference to note. In Satyagraha, a practical nonviolence philosophy established by Gandhi, there is an insistence that coercion not play a part in the social change process. Gandhi felt that the opponent must see the evils in his/her own actions and voluntarily change if lasting results are desired. He stated, "The Satyagrahi's object is to convert, not to coerce" (Burrowes, 1996, p. 199). Gandhi equated coercion as a relative of force in manipulating one's opponent to change where he or she might otherwise not. The Duragraha adopted by King and the SCLC admittantly contained the use of coercion. In King's view, the nonviolent coercion of various actions of civil disobedience and self suffering is the very component that pressures the opponent into changing.

Of course, the argument can be made that Satyagraha, whether Gandhi admitted to it or not, did contain at least a partial element of coercion. An opponent who chooses to give in to the requests of the nonviolent activists only after they have conducted a rigorous, pressuring campaign, did so only as a result of outside influences. The opponent did not decide on his or her own, but rather was pressured into this decision. If the opponent were pressured into a decision that would have not been made before, that constitutes coercion.

King was aware of the role coercion must play in nonviolent campaigns. The Montgomery Bus Boycott was ultimately successful due to the increasing momentum and pressure that forced the buses to desegregate. In Birmingham, the case was much the same, as action by the federal government and business leaders of that area came only after a tremendous campaign was waged by the nonviolent civil rights activists.

Admitting that coercion was a necessary strategy for change, King and the SCLC in late 1964 set a goal of pushing a strong voting rights law. King then outlined "Project Alabama," which consisted of the following:

> 1) nonviolent demonstrators go into the streets to exercise their Constitutional rights; 2) racists resist by unleashing violence against them; 3) Americans of conscience in the name of decency demand federal intervention and legislation; 4) the Administration under mass pressure, initiates measures of immediate intervention and remedial legislation (Sitkoff, 1981, p. 187).

Choosing Selma as the focal point of this campaign, King stated, "We will dramatize the situation to arouse the federal government by marching by the thousands to the places of registration" (Sitkoff, 1981, p. 188). Kicking off the campaign, King led first dozens and, after a short time, hundreds of blacks on daily marches to attempt to get their names on voter lists. An estimated 2,000 blacks were arrested by the end of January 1965.

As a result of Project Alabama, the news spotlight continued to shine on Selma. All across the nation people witnessed extreme police brutality, white mob violence and anger directed at blacks for trying to vote. After two attempts by the civil rights activists to march from Selma to Montgomery ended in extreme violence against the participants, President Johnson delivered a televised address on March 15, 1965 to a joint session of Congress requesting the passage of a voting rights bill.

Additionally, after the televised address, Johnson ordered prevailing Judge Johnson to issue a permit for a march from Selma to Montgomery. He also phoned Governor Wallace in Alabama, making it clear that this time the marchers would be protected. Sure enough, the march went on as scheduled, with over 3,000 black and white participants on March 21, 1965. Just five months later, in August 1965, President Johnson signed the 1965 Voting Rights Act.

Despite the success of the Voting Rights Act and the previous desegregation victories, an increasing number of blacks did not feel change was coming quickly enough. There was a growing criticism of the lack of enforcement of laws once they were passed. In the second half of the 1960s, blacks became increasingly drawn toward militancy as a result.

On August 11, 1965, Watts, a poverty-stricken ghetto area in Los Angeles, erupted in a massive riot. After six days, thirty-four people had been killed and another 900 injured. Nearly 4,000 people were arrested during the riot, an uprising that caused $30 million in property damages (Sitkoff, 1981, p 211). This event sparked further black rioting and unrest in cities across the United States. Sitkoff describes the effect Watts had on the late 1960s: "That explosion of bitterness over unmet demands for black dignity and a stop to racial oppression sparked a succession of 'long hot summers' and proclaimed an end to the era of nonviolence" (1981, p. 200). By the end of 1968 the police reported over 50,000 arrests and over 8,000 casualties in the approximately 300 race riots that had occurred since 1965 (p. 200).

In this atmosphere of both black unrest and continued white violence in the South, both CORE and SNCC adopted a growing militancy. Both groups came out and denounced nonviolence and reversed their opinions on the involvement of whites in the black movement. Like Garvey and Malcolm X, the organizations now believed that blacks themselves must be responsible for their own liberation without the help of whites. Additionally, both the SNCC and CORE identified liberals as being a major part of the problem hindering black advancement (Sitkoff, 1981, p. 211).

As the U.S. involvement in the Vietnam War became increasingly controversial, SNCC, CORE and SCLC all began to focus on not only civil rights or black power, but also on the anti-war effort. King became the leader of the Spring Mobilization Against the War and urged all Americans to become conscientious objectors. Unfortunately for him, by this time he had lost a considerable amount of public support due to the belief held by many that he was too liberal and cooperated too much with whites (Sitkoff, 1981, p. 219). In March 1968, he began organizing what was referred to as the Poor People's Campaign, which was to go to Memphis to provide support for striking sanitation workers. A month later, on April 4, 1968, King was shot and killed.

Upon King's death, riots again flared up in major cities across the country. Likewise, in response to the growing anger demonstrated by blacks, white violence against blacks also increased. The modern civil rights movement would then come to an end due to the anti-war movement becoming prominent, the assassinations of both Malcolm X and Martin Luther King, Jr., and black power groups such as the Black Panther Party becoming successfully targeted for extreme repression and neutralization. While the application of nonviolent struggle produced amazing results for blacks, particularly during the 1940s, 1950s, and 1960s, it arguably stopped short of providing for the full equality of rights and opportunities for African Americans.

There is overwhelming evidence today of continued white dominance and racism against blacks. Even a quick glance at the federal government, and the racial profiles of its executive positions, indicates that as a nation we are still far from practicing any semblance of equality between races. Walking into a jail one can immediately notice, as I have on many occasions in cities across the country, there is also an obvious discrepancy between the numbers of white inmates versus inmates of color. The prison industrial complex in the United States has boomed in recent history at the expense of massive populations of African Americans. The *Sentencing Project*, based in Washington, D.C., estimates that African Americans are "7.8 times more likely to be imprisoned than whites when convicted of the same crime" (IGC, WWW, 2001). Racial profiling conducted by law enforcement continues to be a reality in areas across the country. Police brutality, connected to racial profiling, also has been a persistent aspect of life for black Americans. Fortunately, a small number of these unjust incidents do get publicized, as in the cases of the Los Angeles police beating Rodney King and the New York police murdering Amadou Diallo. But the majority of the racism and oppression dealt to blacks by white America is hidden.

At least a partial factor that enabled the growth of the modern civil rights movement was that the discrimination and racism was so open and obvious. The government, from the federal down to the state and local levels, publicly supported and enforced segregation, disenfranchisement, and discrimination for years. It was not a far stretch for people to observe the injustice towards blacks during these times. This made the mobilization of campaigns more successful, as people could see their oppression firsthand and rebel against it.

In more modern times, as blacks began to enjoy new rights as a result of the civil rights movement, the overt repression has transformed into a more covert and hidden racist policy. As blacks have increasingly made strides toward freedom and respect, many have become caught up in the cycle of consumerism, at the expense of a continued awareness of racial politics. While the majority of blacks are poor, there is a minority who have enjoyed lives comprised of more material wealth and power. For the wealthy, there is a certain sense of security that comes with wealth. With comfort and security also comes a certain possibility of ignorance, a state in which it is much easier to enjoy the comfortable life than to sacrifice security for a higher cause. At the same time, the poor have continuously been fed material from mass media, schooling, employment and the government telling them in a sense that success, freedom and happiness come from taking part as much as possible in consumer culture. Those buying into this most powerful propaganda effort are left little choice but to work endlessly to provide for their families' needs and desires. This consists not only of food, clothing, shelter, and items for survival, but also of items desired—those learned about in the movies, on television, and advertisements—that to a certain extent are unnecessary. There is this myth pushed on to African Americans in the United States that if they wear the white man's clothes, buy his cars, vote for his politicians, and help his economy, freedom will be finally granted to blacks. Unfortunately, believing in this lie has only served to cloud the mind, making it less able to notice and object to the everyday underlying racism that continues to thrive in the United States.

The nonviolent tactics employed by the civil rights movement were successful in pressuring the federal government to act on numerous occasions. This success was due, at least in part, to the movement seeking to only modify the existing social and political framework already in place in the United States. Civil rights advocates, prior to the beginnings of the black power movement, sought not to overthrow or destroy the government per se, but rather to work on fixing its unjust policies. The application of nonviolence was therefore successful as, for all realistic purposes, it did not demand or expect the opponent to give up all its power, privilege and wealth. Whites who opposed civil rights had a much easier time being convinced to give in to a few minor allocations of rights for blacks, than if all of white power and wealth were being challenged.

There is sufficient reason to believe that nonviolent tactics, on their own, would not have worked if the civil rights movement had primarily set out to overthrow and destroy the U.S. government. Rather than asking for an incredibly minute piece of the pie, as ended up being the case in the civil rights movement, this other option would have demanded the full pie, thus forcefully seeking a new form of governing that would be more open to an honest democracy and equality. The response from whites, knowingly being threatened with losing their power, privilege and wealth, would have been to violently stop the effort by any means necessary. Whites would not have given up complete power merely due to the same factors being put into action that the nonviolent civil rights movement relied so heavily upon.

The whole idea of the benefits of confrontation would have been vastly different. For one, threatened with giving up their security, whites observing brutalities against black protesters would have been far less sympathetic. As a result, the nonviolent confrontations could not serve the purpose of galvanizing massive public support needed to overthrow the government. Secondly, faced with losing its power and identity, the federal government would have been more than willing to use extreme military force to kill the black protesters, regardless of the media presence.

Another interesting question is whether or not the nonviolent movement, in a pursuit of overthrowing the government, could maintain and build participation and momentum. As the dynamics of the confrontation would be altered in such a manner as stated above, the extreme violence applied by the government, mixed in with little direct white support, would have arguably turned possible participants away out of fear and intelligence. Those still seeking to be involved in the efforts most likely would be drawn closer to armed rebellion. This was somewhat the case later in the 1960s, with the growth of the black power movement. Noticing that the white man still held control of the entire pie, a growing movement emerged refusing to believe in the nonviolence strategy.

So, in a sense, the application of nonviolence—the theoretical strategy King, SCLC, SNCC, CORE, and others gained from Gandhi and Christianity—only worked for purposes of domestic reform and could not work for complete revolution. Even though tremendous steps were accomplished in this reformist effort, the reality of racism still existing today over thirty years later suggests that reform may not be the answer for black liberation. If, and when, African Americans mobilize, not to change just one aspect of the government but rather to overthrow it completely, an adherence to the *Five Rules for Social and Political Change* will have to be abandoned.

# CHAPTER THREE

# *The Movement in the United States Against the Vietnam War*

In the early 1990s, while pursuing my undergraduate degree at Portland State University, I enrolled in a class specifically on the U.S. Vietnam War protest era. The professor had lived through that time period and had been active in the anti-war protests, so I felt he had a decent amount of credibility. During the second class session, he walked into the room, stared at everyone and bluntly stated that no matter how much progress was achieved in the way of social justice during the 1960s and early 1970s, real social change was never accomplished. After taking a lengthy pause to further stare at the class and allow for reflection on his comments, he explained his statement. He said that although various groups, both within and outside the anti-war movement, were crying out for peace and justice, they were not crying out together. Rather, according to this professor, the 1960s marked a definitive increase in the growth of the single-issue phenomenon. The results, in his view, of this phenomenon were single-issue groups working individually, concentrating solely on their own issues.

Now, I will admit that prior to this class, I had little knowledge of the entire 1960s movements, let alone the anti-war movement. The limited knowledge I did have was gained primarily from the scarce historical teachings I had in high school and that of popular media. In my mind I truthfully believed that the 1960s were a time of revolution and social change, when peace and justice became known to various struggles. I vividly recall hearing the professor in that University class state that real social change never occurred. I remember being shocked literally speechless as I pondered what he actually meant by his bold proclamation. Even after his explanation, it would be a number of years before I would fully grasp the intelligence of his words.

The U.S. anti-war movement of the 1960s and early 1970s, like other social and political movements, was full of its share of internal conflicts. The more conservative end of the spectrum for years dealt with exclusionary politics, fearing the movement would be linked with communism. On the other end of the paradigm, more radical groups preached inclusion, and some went as far as linking the U.S. presence in Vietnam to other forms of problematic imperialism.

In the current time of the U.S.-led "War on Terrorism," studying the topic of the Vietnam era anti-war protests is extremely important and applicable. It is also quite interesting to hear the various opinions today on the 1960s movement and its effectiveness. I have found that many people who lived through, and perhaps participated in, the anti-war events of this time period still hold a true belief that social change really was accomplished. Yet younger people, particularly those on the more radical fringe, tend to sneer at even the remotest mention of the 1960s as having any true and lasting political effect on U.S.-based injustice.

So in the above-mentioned views of the anti-war movement, where does the truth actually sit? How effective actually was the 1960s anti-war movement? How was effectiveness judged then, during that time period, versus today? If it *was* effective or successful, in what ways? What were the determining factors that made the progress possible? If it was not successful, why? What can be learned from this time period to aid in current struggles for peace and justice? These are all pressing questions that I will examine in this chapter.

# U.S. MOVEMENT AGAINST THE VIETNAM WAR

The following is not meant to be a thorough examination of the entire anti-war movement or its activities in the 1960s and 1970s. Rather, my main focus will be on surveying the various types of actions that did occur, the politics within the movement, as well as an examination of the effects of the protests on the country's political body.

\*

One of the earliest acts against the United States presence in Vietnam came in April 1963, with an Easter Peace Walk in New York. The main focus of the event was to have a "ban the bomb" march, which would concentrate efforts on persuading the U.S. and USSR to sign a treaty banning nuclear testing. Approximately 7,000 people attended the march, some of whom held signs against the U.S. presence in Vietnam.

This was one, if not the, earliest-known acts of U.S. public defiance against the Vietnam situation (Zaroulis, 1984, p. 8). Yet, it did not go over well. Organizers of the rally demanded that the signs against U.S. presence in Vietnam be removed, feeling they were too controversial and might negatively influence their efforts to get a test ban treaty signed. Two individuals at the rally, David Dellinger and Fred Halstead, insisted that the signs remain. Dellinger, who spoke out against the U.S. presence in Vietnam at the rally, was later warned by the organizers. Members of the National Committee for a Sane Nuclear Policy (SANE), one of the sponsoring groups, told Dellinger that he would never speak at another one of their events again (p. 8).

The first organized protests directly against U.S. involvement in Vietnam occurred in August 1963. They took place in various locations in the country during the annual commemorations of the Hiroshima-Nagasaki atomic bombings. In Philadelphia, members of the Student Peace Union marched in front of the Federal Building with signs criticizing U.S. action in Vietnam. In New York, Thomas Cornell and Christopher Kearns from the Catholic Worker movement picketed in front of the residence of Vietnam's permanent observer to the United Nations. The two carried signs that read "WE DEMAND AN END TO U.S. MILITARY SUPPORT OF DIEM'S REGIME." For nine days straight, these two picketed alone in front of the residence, and on the tenth day, as was planned, 250 people joined them. The American Broadcasting Company filmed the event and showed it on their evening news, one of the first protests covered by news media against the Vietnam War.

By 1963, the war in Vietnam had been going on for eighteen years, and the United States had been involved since the beginning. In 1941, the Viet Minh (Vietnam Doc Lap Dong Minh—Vietnam Independence League) was formed to fight for a free, independent and united Vietnam. On September 2, 1945 before a crowd in Hanoi, Viet Minh leader Ho Chi Minh proclaimed the independence of Vietnam. The country had been dominated by China for over 1,000 years and more recently for sixty years as part of the French colony of Indochina. Within three weeks of Ho's declaration, France attempted to retake its former colony.

The United States, fearful of communism and the domino theory (which avers that once one country fell to communism they all would) supported the French action. The U.S. government was fully aware of Ho Chi Minh being a communist, which made their support of the French that much easier. By 1954, the U.S. had spent over $2 billion supporting the French.

That same year, 1954, the French suffered a major defeat at Dien Bien Phu. In July at a major powers meeting in Geneva, the Viet Minh were forced to accept the division of Vietnam by a military line separating the North and South. As part of this agreement, elections were promised to be held in 1956. While the Vietnamese people were allowed to settle in either of the two zones, the United States recognized only the puppet government created by France in Saigon. There Ngo Dinh Diem was put into power as the premiere. When 1956 finally arrived, Diem refused to have the election, a decision supported by the Eisenhower Administration (Zaroulis, 1984, p.14). Yet, he was later elected President of South Vietnam in a fixed election (p. 14).

By the end of 1960, the United States had 900 military advisors in Vietnam. Even with the growing assistance from the U.S., Diem steadily lost territory and influence to insurgents in the South known then as the Viet Cong. One year before, in 1959, the U.S. suffered its first casualties of war when two military advisors were killed in a Viet Cong raid on the Bien Hoa military base near Saigon.

In December 1960, the National Liberation Front (NLF) was formed in South Vietnam as a political wing of the Viet Cong. The group endorsed the call for the overthrow of the Diem puppet regime. Yet, the U.S. government continued to support Diem.

By 1963, there were over 16,000 United States military personnel in Vietnam, still acting only officially as "advisors." Between 1961 and 1963, 109 of these military advisors died in Vietnam. The conflict continued to spiral out of control.

Back in the United States, Mme Nhu, the wife of Ngo Dinh Nhu (the chief of South Vietnam's secret police and brother of Diem) spoke at Harvard Law School on October 14, 1963. She was on a speaking tour of the United States, attempting to build American support for Diem's regime. As she spoke at Harvard, she was booed by an estimated one hundred students, mostly from the Students for a Democratic Society (SDS) (Zaroulis, 1984, p. 15). As Nhu was still on tour in the United States, her husband, along with Diem, was assassinated in Saigon by leaders of a military coup who had been encouraged by U.S. officials (p. 15). When Lyndon Johnson took office on November 24, 1963, after President Kennedy's assassination, he reaffirmed America's commitment to South Vietnam.

On April 7, 1964, two hundred fifty members of the Women's International League for Peace and Freedom went to Washington, D.C. to lobby against U.S. involvement in Vietnam. This marked one of the earliest direct political attempts to influence the political body into pulling out of Vietnam. Much more of the lobbying efforts would come.

*The National Guardian*, a leftist weekly publication, ran an ad on April 7, 1964 signed by eighty-seven youths stating they would refuse to fight in South Vietnam. This was also one of the earliest public examples of young men declaring their full opposition to participating in the U.S. military action in Vietnam. A similar ad appeared in the New York *Herald Tribune* in late May, signed by 149 men of draft age stating they would not fight in Vietnam. This marked the first time one of these ads was allowed to appear in a non-activist-related, more mainstream paper. Throughout years ahead, the movement would be filled with accounts of conscientious resisters, draft dodgers, draft card burners and more.

The next month, on May 2, 1964, nearly 400 college students marched to Times Square and to the United Nations in New York. Calling themselves the May 2 Movement, they demanded the withdrawal of U.S. troops from Vietnam and the end of U.S. military aid to the South Vietnamese Government.

On July 3, 1964, the same day that President Johnson signed the Civil Rights Act, David Dellinger called a protest against the Vietnam War to be held in Lafayette Square in Washington, D.C., across from the White House. The demonstration was in support of the "Declaration of Conscience," which consisted of statements supporting draft resistance. Just days later, the announcement came from Washington that the U.S. was sending more troops to Vietnam, to then total 21,000.

Perhaps one—if not the—most important occurrence of the entire war came on August 2, 1964, with the Gulf of Tonkin incident. The United States reported that three North Vietnamese PT boats had fired on a U.S. destroyer in the Gulf of Tonkin. The U.S. reportedly returned fire and then went on to bomb bases and other targets allegedly involved in attacking the U.S. ships. The very next day, President Johnson asked Congress to pass a joint resolution giving him support for "all necessary action" to protect U.S. forces in the area. Johnson signed what was known as the Gulf of Tonkin Resolution on August 10. This marked a major escalation period in the war, as Congress then had given the go ahead for any and all necessary action to protect U.S. troops.

Howard Zinn, in his book *You Can't Be Neutral on a Moving Train*, was among the many people who questioned and criticized the Gulf of Tonkin incident. He writes:

> The president, the secretary of state, and the secretary of defense were lying to the American public - there was no evidence of any attack, and the American destroyers were not on 'routine patrol' but on spying missions. However, Congress and all the major newspapers and television networks accepted the story without question. Congress immediately passed the Gulf of Tonkin Resolution, giving President Johnson a blank check for massive intervention in Vietnam (1994, p. 104).

On August 6, 1964, approximately 1,000 people gathered for a rally in Washington Square in New York City. The attendees listened to speakers denounce the war as evidence began to show in the crowd relating the civil rights movement to the anti-war movement. At least one of the protest signs that day read "United States troops belong in Mississippi, Not Vietnam." The civil rights movement was perhaps first connected to the anti-war movement during this time in August, when people made the connection between the Gulf of Tonkin Resolution and the killing of three civil rights workers in Mississippi.

Some of the first protesters arrested during an anti-war protest were taken into custody during a demonstration on August 8, 1964. Organized by the May 2 Movement, the rally in New York City called on the World's Fair visitors to help stop the war in Vietnam. Some seventeen people were arrested for refusing to leave when asked (Zaroulis, 1984, p. 24). Similar protests occurred in New York City on October 3 and December 19, 1964, as protesters attempted to keep the Vietnam issue before the American public and federal government.

Early in 1965, two demonstrations occurred on the same day in New York City and Washington, D.C. In New York, fourteen people were arrested at the U.S. Mission to the United Nations for blocking entrances. Organizations that took part included the Committee for Nonviolent Action, the War Resisters League, the Student Peace Union, and the Catholic Worker. In Washington, approximately three hundred members of the Women's International League for Peace and Freedom and of Women Strike for Peace picketed the White House, calling for negotiated peace and a dignified U.S. withdrawal from Vietnam.

The first teach-in on the Vietnam conflict occurred on March 24, 1965, at the University of Michigan at Ann Arbor. It was organized by forty-nine faculty members and attracted over 3,000 students. As the University wouldn't allow the teach-in during regular hours, the faculty held the event all night long. Afterward, other teach-ins began at universities across the country.

In response to the growth of teach-ins on campuses throughout the United States, the federal government sent around a "truth team" from the State Department to counter the results of the alternative education. The team was met with hostility and protests at most locations.

During the next month, both SANE and SDS organized noteworthy actions. On April 10, 1965, some 3,000 people took part in a rally and march from Columbus Circle to the United Nations in New York. The protest was led by Dr. Benjamin Spock, who was the co-chairman of SANE. At the rally Spock called for an immediate cease fire on Vietnam. SDS held the first national protest against the war in Washington D.C. on April 17. An estimated 20,000 people took part in the demonstration. SDS took what was at the time a controversial stance at the protest, by declaring a policy of nonexclusion, meaning no one would be excluded even if he or she were from a communist group. Many older activists were quite wary of this decision, remembering the severity of the anti-communist war led by McCarthy in previous years. These skeptics feared they would lose support if they did not firmly exclude communists and exonerate themselves of communist sympathy. As simple as this disagreement may seem today, it became a major fuel for internal conflicts within the early anti-war movement.

One of the largest teach-ins to occur during the Vietnam War protest era came on May 21-22, 1965 in Berkeley. The event, held at the UC Berkeley campus, attracted as many as 30,000 people and became known as Vietnam Day. Berkeley's Vietnam Day Committee was established at this teach-in, which would later be responsible for many actions on the West Coast.

In June, protests occurred both in New York city and at the Pentagon in Washington D.C. On June 8, 1965, SANE organized a rally at Madison Square Garden in New York, attracting over 17,000 participants. Eight days later in front of the Pentagon, the Student Nonviolent Coordinating Committee (SNCC) and the Committee for Nonviolent Action (CNVA) held a speak-out against the war. SNCC, a group that was created during the student protests of the civil rights movement, took a bold and needed step in this action, further publicly linking the civil rights movement to the anti-war struggle.

Also in June, from the 9th to the 13th, 1965, SDS held a convention in Michigan. At the meeting, SDS decided not to take a leading role in the anti-war movement. Nancy Zaroulis and Gerald Sullivan, in their 1984 book *Who Spoke Up: American Protest Against the War in Vietnam*, state in reference to this SDS decision:

> It was agreed to leave actions and projects entirely up to
> local chapters, with no direction from the National Office;
> to not build a strong, nationwide campus organization; to
> not organize a nationwide antidraft campaign (p. 47).

Instead, SDS tried to concentrate on changing the whole of American society. The national SDS office held the view that if the group abandoned its work in the inner cities helping the poor and people of color to fight against the war, it would not be addressing the overall problem. This overall problem they would later refer to as U.S. imperialism. This decision made at the conference in Michigan would have lasting repercussions for the group throughout the rest of the 1960s.

Four hundred people from the Committee for Nonviolent Action and the Workshop in Nonviolence marched from City Hall Park to an Army recruiting building in New York City on July 29, 1965. When the crowd reached the recruiting building, several men burned their draft cards. This increasingly popular tactic amongst anti-war protesters signified the refusal of a growing number of men to participate in the Vietnam

War. The image is also quite reminiscent of the passbooks that were burned by Indian protesters in South Africa during the time Gandhi had traveled there to practice law. In both cases, although the direct threat caused by the burning of government property was extremely small, the symbolic meaning was of utmost importance and demonstrated a bold resistance.

On August 6th through 9th, 1965, a meeting sponsored by groups including the Catholic Worker and Committee for Nonviolent Action took place in Washington, D.C. Calling itself the Assembly of Unrepresented People, the meeting had two purposes: to hold workshops on domestic issues and Vietnam, and to stage a protest and march to Congress to present a "Declaration of Peace with the People of Vietnam" (Zaroulis, 1984, p.52). On August 6, nearly 1,000 people picketed the White House, and many stayed there for a few days around the clock. Thirty-six protesters were arrested for blocking an entrance two days later on August 8. On the last day of the meeting, August 9, over 800 protesters marched down the Mall in Washington and attempted to pressure Congress into adopting their declaration of peace. On this particular day, over 350 people were arrested.

Perhaps one of the most important results of this meeting was the formation of the National Coordinating Committee to End the War in Vietnam. Comprised of thirty-three organizations, this Coordinating Committee was the first of several umbrella groups that would organize nationwide protests against the war.

Faced with a growing number of men burning their draft cards in protest of the Vietnam War, President Johnson decided to act. On August 30, he signed a bill into law that called for a five-year jail sentence and $10,000 fine for willful destruction of a draft card.

The very same month on the West Coast, people attempted to halt and board trains destined for the Oakland Army Terminal, the site where the troops would leave for Vietnam. On three separate occasions, some 300 people took part in these actions that were organized by the Oakland SDS, among other groups.

The first International Days of Protest took place on October 15-16, 1965. In the United States, protests occurred on both the East and West Coasts. In Berkeley, 10,000 people marched and staged a teach-in at a vacant lot across the street from the Oakland Army Base. A massive police response, turned back the crowd, which ended up having the teach-in on the UC Berkeley campus. Meanwhile, in New York City, an estimated

20,000-25,000 people participated in a march on October 16. Zaroulis and Sullivan summarize the events of these two days by stating, "estimates were that as many as one-hundred thousand people participated in rallies in fifty cities across the United States" (1984, p. 56).

That same weekend another protest of far smaller magnitude would take place. Yet, the symbolism of this one particular act would be just as widespread and important. David Miller, a twenty-two year old Catholic Worker, burned his draft card during a small protest at the Army Induction Center in Manhattan. While there had been draft cards burned before, Miller on this day was the first person to do so after President Johnson signed the felony bill against it. Perhaps unknown to Miller at the time, his action would prompt others to follow his lead.

It is of particular interest from an organizing standpoint how these individual acts of courage, like the one taken by Miller, can have a domino effect provoking a mass movement or they can simultaneously go absolutely unnoticed. Was it a prerequisite for Miller, before burning his draft card, to know for certain that others would also defy Johnson's law? Did his action rely upon this highly uncertainly outcome? No. Miller, like many others throughout history, most likely burned his card out of a personal desire to make a statement in protest of the U.S. involvement in Vietnam. The same can be said for the four African American students who first sat down at a whites-only lunch counter inside the Greensboro, North Carolina Woolworth's store. The action was conducted, not so much with the direct goal of starting a massive sit-in movement (in addition to the many other 'in' tactics that took place), but rather out of a personal desire to take a stand against injustice. Like Miller, the four students in Greensboro had little idea that their few hour sit-in would actively work to energize and engage much of the black nation into action.

It is of great interest to organizers to understand how one particular individual act can spark a movement into action while another will do little. While it does seem difficult or even impossible for an individual to know the outcome of his or her actions in advance, historically some leaders of political and social movements have obtained that gift. It is not absurd to suggest that understanding the strategies of these past individuals is one of the keys to unlocking the potential of social and political progress today.

Mahatma Gandhi, for example, studied this topic thoroughly and incorporated his beliefs into his Satyagraha nonviolence principles. He nearly perfected the art of directly challenging the opponent in such a manner as to achieve optimum results with each individual or mass act. What can readily be referred to as active nonviolence, Gandhi's Satyagraha rejected passivity and worked to force the opposition into one of two responses: Either the opponent would give in and agree to the demands of the Satyagrahi, or they would choose to try to ignore the Satyagrahi and quash the protest. But the key to success in Satyagraha is to constantly be challenging the opponent in such a way as to force them to make that response, while simultaneously increasing the odds or pressure in favor of the Satyagrahi.

In his famous march to the sea to make salt, Gandhi gave us a fine example of his grasp of successful nonviolent strategies, in addition to the power one individual can have to promote social change. He knew well ahead of time that the Salt March could not and would not physically challenge the British Government. Rather, it was a symbolic gesture specifically designed to signify a mass of people defiant to colonial rule. Gandhi also knew full well beforehand that his march, by something as seemingly minute as making salt, might well spark a nation into revolt. Since the British had a monopoly on the manufacture and selling of salt, this act demonstrated to the international community that the Indian people were at least then mentally independent of Britain. Sure enough, after Gandhi walked out onto the beach and made salt in his hands, the Indian people responded en masse, making and selling their own salt.

Martin Luther King, Jr. also had a firm understanding of the strategic needs of nonviolent activity. Witnessing the power one individual can have, as with the case of Rosa Parks sparking the successful Montgomery Bus Boycott, King realized that a key to progress lies in direct confrontation. Holding the same belief as Gandhi in the necessity for provoking a response from the opponent, King increasingly attempted to heighten confrontations at demonstrations for best results. In 1963, King created "Project C," a strategy for change used he used in Birmingham. With the 'C' standing for Confrontation, King structured a successful desegregation campaign in what was considered the most segregated big city in America.

So it is possible to grasp the effects that one individual or mass action can have beforehand. Yet, this can perhaps only be accomplished by fully understanding the political atmosphere of the area at the given time, in addition to being aware and knowledgeable of the climate of the particular movement for change. Yet, without any deserved criticism, most individual acts of nonviolence taken in movements for change are engaged in more out of a personal objection to injustice rather than a realistic expectation of sparking a massive mobilization.

Two weeks after Miller burned his draft card, 200 people gathered in front of the U.S. Courthouse in New York City's Foley Square to protest the war. As two men, Tom Cornell and Marc Paul Edelmen, attempted to burn their draft cards they were prevented by a rush of police and news people. Members of the public then began attacking some of the protesters, and the demonstration was resultantly called off.

Five young men did succeed in burning their draft cards on November 6, 1965 during an anti-war rally in New York City's Union Square. Sponsored by the Committee for Nonviolent Action, the five men followed Miller's lead in signaling a growing opposition to the draft.

Just four days before, on November 2, 1965, another individual act of conscience would have far-reaching results. Norman Morrison, a thirty-two year old Quaker, doused himself in kerosene and set himself on fire. He had walked to within 100 yards of Secretary of Defense Robert McNamara's office and was in full view of its windows. After news of Morrison's death reached Vietnam, the North Vietnamese understood what had happened. The North Vietnamese Government issued a stamp in his honor and named a street after him in Hanoi, and songs about Morrison were sung most cultural performances (Zaroulis, 1984, p. 3).

On November 9, 1965, Roger Laporte, a twenty-one year old member of the Catholic Worker movement, burned himself in front of the United Nations library in New York. While dying he stated, "I'm a Catholic Worker. I'm against war, all wars. I did this as a religious action" (Zaroulis, 1984, p.3). Both Laporte and Morrison were two of the eight people that burned themselves to death in the United States in protest of the Vietnam War from 1965 to 1970.

Alice Hertz was the first person to die in the U.S. in protest of the war by burning herself. In March 1965, when she was eighty-two years old, Herz burned herself on a Detroit street corner after the U.S. had begun bombing North Vietnam. She said that she did it "to protest the arms race all over the world" (Zaroulis, 1984, p. 3). A member of the Women's International League for Peace and Freedom and of Women Strike for Peace, Herz had mailed a note to her daughter to explain her action. She wrote, "I do this not out of despair but out of hope. I choose the illuminating death of a Buddhist to protest against a great country trying to wipe out a small country for no reason" (p. 3).

It is difficult to imagine how some people could choose to take their own lives by burning themselves for any cause. Many within the status quo in the U.S. most likely would dismiss this sort of action as one only the insane lunatic or suicidal fringe would engage in. But is that so? Certainly there have been people throughout history who have willingly given up their lives for a particular cause. Even today, headlines in the news are full of accounts of suicide bombers in the Israeli/Palestinian conflict. There lies within the belief system of participants of these actions some devotion and drive to do whatever it takes to either make a personal stand, to spark a mass movement, or both. Whether this belief comes out of differing interpretations of religious doctrines or just out of a personal desire to demonstrate resistance, each individual who has died in this manner likely holds his or her own individual reasoning. Even so, the drive that gets the perfectly sane individual to the point of committing suicide for a political or social cause is worthy of much attention. For understanding that which prompts such devotion is an important asset to social and political change movements.

The last major protest of 1965 came on Thanksgiving weekend. Approximately 25,000 people participated in a SANE-sponsored march in Washington on November 27.

Early in 1966, the anti-war struggle would be further linked to the civil rights movement after a tragic incident. On January 3, Samuel Younge, a black SNCC worker was murdered in Tuskegee, Alabama for trying to use a whites-only restroom. Within three days SNCC released a statement directly associating Younge's murder with America's involvement in Vietnam. Included in the statement, SNCC wrote:

> The murder of Samuel Younge in Tuskegee, Alabama, is no different from the murder of people in Vietnam, for both Younge and the Vietnamese sought and are seeking to secure the rights guaranteed them by law. In each case the U.S. government bears a great part of the responsibility for these deaths (Zaroulis, 1984, p. 69).

January 28, 1966 marked the beginning of the famous Fulbright hearings in Washington D.C. Senator J. William Fulbright, chairman of the Senate Foreign Relations Committee, held meetings for a three-week period on the U.S. involvement in Vietnam. Zaroulis and Sullivan state, "The argument, as time progressed and those in attendance proved to the already persuaded, tended to lapse into simple harangue: the United States was woefully, sinfully wrong and should get out of Vietnam now" (1984, p. 72). The outcome of the hearings had a crucial impact on the anti-war movement. The two write:

> "The importance of the 1966 Fulbright hearings cannot be overstated, for it was while watching them that millions of Americans learned for the first time there was a 'respectable' basis for opposing the policies of their own government, that sons and daughters caught up passionately in campus movements were not indulging in a newer, more pernicious form of collegiate high jinks" (p. 75).

The Fulbright hearings had legitimized the anti-war movement.

On March 25-26, 1966 the National Coordinating Committee to End the War in Vietnam organized another International Days of Protest. Seven hundred people marched in Boston the day after eleven were arrested outside an induction center at the Boston Army Base. Two days later, a few of these eleven tried to burn their draft cards on the steps of the South Boston Courthouse. They were beaten bloody by a mob of South Boston high school students (Zaroulis, 1984, p. 76).

During the International Days of Action in the U.S., 3,500 people marched in San Francisco, 26,000 marched in New York City, and 200 or so picketed in front of the Capitol in Washington. Other, smaller protests occurred in cities across the country.

In late April 1966, it was announced in the media that over 300 people were refusing to pay the federal income tax in protest of the war. The famous folk singer Joan Baez was one of them. Hearing this news, the Internal Revenue Service promised to prosecute.

The deliberate decision to stop paying the federal income tax is one of the most direct methods that could affect the policies of the federal government. Since it is the very taxpayer dollars that make up the federal government's budget, the failure of the American public to pay would mean less or no monetary resources. Such a large amount of the federal budget is usually allocated for defense purposes, especially in times of military action or full-fledged war, that if enough members of the public refused to pay federal taxes, it could directly affect the outcome of the conflict. Of course, the difficulty lies with the individual being able to face the possibility of lengthy jail sentences. Furthermore, no one wants to be the first one, or among the first 10, 100, 1000, or even 100,000 to refuse to pay the tax. So the greatest difficulty with this tactic lies in creating a mass mobilization to simultaneously stop paying. The more people who refused to pay at once, the less likely the IRS would be to prosecute due to a lack of resources.

The tactics of the anti-war movement continued to escalate. In late Spring 1966, Barry Bondhus, a draft eligible man from Big Lake, Minnesota, broke into his local draft board and destroyed draft records. He poured two large buckets of human feces over the records.

On the sixteenth of May 1966, SANE, Women Strike for Peace, and other moderate groups in the movement gathered in Washington, D.C. This group of 8,000 people announced they had 73,000 voter pledges to support congressional candidates who agreed to scale down the war. Others in the movement saw this action as proof that the more moderate element of the movement had sold out and was merely giving in to the system.

Also in May, 400 students at the University of Chicago took over the administration building for three days. This was in direct response to the Selective Service holding qualification tests for high school seniors, college undergraduates and graduate students. The test grades were to be used to determine which students would get drafted if the draft were expanded. A few weeks later, both SNCC and SDS issued a joint call for the end of the draft.

One month later, on June 30, 1966, the Fifth Avenue Peace Parade Committee introduced the Fort Hood 3 at a press conference. The Fort Hood 3 was comprised of privates in the Army stationed at Fort Hood, Texas who decided they would refuse to serve in Vietnam. This landmark decision resulted in the three men being imprisoned for two years. Yet, it was this very sort of disloyalty and breaking of ranks that the federal government feared. The very symbolism involved in this act, not to mention the others who would do the same and those veterans who would come back to join the anti-war movement, struck a direct blow to the U.S. government in its attempts to control morale. It was one thing for civilians to disagree with the U.S. government and armed forces, and quite another for actual, enlisted soldiers to openly refuse to fight when the government called upon them.

In August, SNCC held demonstrations in front of the Atlanta Selective Service Office chanting, "Hell No, We Won't Go!" (Zaroulis, 1984, p. 86). Many people were arrested during these protests, and six received three and one-half year prison sentences. The same month, thousands of people in cities across the U.S. protested the war on the twenty-first anniversary of the Hiroshima bombing.

During November in Cambridge, Massachusetts, a group of Harvard SDS greeted Secretary of Defense Robert McNamara as he came for a lecture. As he tried to leave students surrounded his car and forced it to stop. McNamara climbed onto the hood of the car with a bullhorn and agreed to talk to the crowd for five minutes or, more realistically, until the police arrived. Moments later, the police did arrive and led McNamara out of the area. He would not offer himself publicly for discussion or questions about Vietnam again.

Toward the end of the month, on November 26, 1966, a coalition of groups gathered in Cleveland for the third of three meetings. At this meeting the various organizations from the peace and anti-war movements formed the Spring Mobilization to End the War in Vietnam. They set a date for a massive protest to be held on April 15, 1967.

In December, over 200 students from across the country met at the University of Chicago to consider a proposal for a national student strike. Out of this meeting came a new organization called the Student Mobilization Committee to End the War in Vietnam. On the 15th of that month, sixty people were arrested for blocking the entrance to the Whitehall Street Army Induction Center in Manhattan. Before the year would be over, the number of American troops in Vietnam would grow to 389,000 (Zaroulis, 1984, p. 98).

The year 1967 brought an increase in momentum for the anti-war movement. In January, during a protest at St. Patrick's Cathedral in New York, protesters displayed posters of wounded Vietnamese children. The incident, which occurred on the 22nd of the month during 10:00 a.m. high mass, resulted in twenty-three people being arrested. On the 31st of January, 2,000 members of Clergy and Laymen Concerned about Vietnam protested in front of the White House. At the end of their three-day gathering in Washington, the group announced a nationwide Fast for Peace in February. Over one million people would take part in this action.

In mid-February, shortly after the February 11 death of anti-war leader Reverend A.J. Muste, 2,500 members of Women Strike for Peace gathered at the Pentagon, demanding to see the generals who sent their sons to Vietnam. Women took off their shoes and banged on the doors of the Pentagon with the heels (Zaroulis, 1984, p. 103). Eventually the women were let in (amazingly enough) to present their demands to an aide of McNamara. One Senator, Jacob Javits, also met with them.

During the third week in February, 100 students at the University of Wisconsin in Madison conducted a sit-in at the offices used by recruiters for the Dow Chemical Company. Dow manufactured and supplied not only napalm to the Defense Department, but also the plastic body bags used to ship home dead U.S. soldiers. During this particular action, nineteen students were arrested. Two students the following day blockaded the chancellor in his office to protest the arrests. The chancellor gave in and came up with the bail money for those arrested (Zaroulis, 1984, p. 106).

In late February 1967, Martin Luther King, Jr. began to take a firm public stand against the war. On February 25, King addressed a conference on Vietnam in Beverly Hills heavily criticizing the war. He spoke, "the promises of the Great Society have been shot down on the battlefield of Vietnam" (Zaroulis, 1984, p. 108). Shortly thereafter, King led 5,000 people in an Easter Peace March in Chicago.

Also in April, the Spring Mobilization to End the War in Vietnam held marches in New York and San Francisco. Over 100,000 people attended the march in New York and over 50,000 in San Francisco on April 15th. Prior to the New York march, an estimated 175 draft cards were burned (Zaroulis, 1984, p. 113).

The protests in the United States were beginning to have a serious effect on the U.S. armed forces in Vietnam. Owing to the rising concern over the message being sent by the anti-war protests, the U.S. government ordered the Air Force in late May 1967 to drop 1.75 million leaflets on North Vietnam. The leaflets warned the North Vietnamese "not to be misled by protests in the United States into thinking that America had lost its will to fight" (Zaroulis, 1984, p. 115). By the end of April 1967, 438,000 U.S. troops were in Vietnam (p. 115).

On June 23, 1967, the Los Angeles Peace Action Council announced an anti-war protest to coincide with a visit by President Johnson, who was to speak at a Democratic Party dinner in Los Angeles. At the protest, the police showed up in numbers and engaged in massive brutalities. Hundreds of protesters were injured, sixty were hospitalized, and over fifty were arrested (Zaroulis, 1984, p. 119).

In the fall of 1967, campus protests, which had quieted a bit during the spring and summer, sprung up again focused largely against Dow. Of the sixty large protests held during that time, twenty were directly against Dow (Zaroulis, 1984, p. 106). Most of these protests were led by SDS and consisted of obstructionist tactics. SDS, constantly full of internal conflicts pertaining to strategies and focus, had changed its strategy from protest to resistance, practically abandoning its previous strict nonviolent beliefs.

During an October 1967 demonstration in Madison involving 300 students, violence broke out after the Madison police used tear gas and mace in addition to dogs and riot cops to stop the protest. Protesters responded by throwing rocks and bricks. In the end, three policemen and sixty-five students had to be treated for injuries. Students at Madison immediately organized a fairly successful strike in response. Dow was, at least temporarily, banned from the campus while thirteen students were suspended and three faculty members fired for joining the strike.

The most famous protest against Dow came in 1969 when nine radical Catholics, mostly priests, broke into the Washington, D.C. office of Dow. They destroyed office equipment, poured blood, put up photos of children exposed to napalm and threw many documents onto the street. After being arrested, the participants fasted for a week before being released. The account of this particular action is amazing to read. The phenomenon behind what motivated this group of Catholics to take this extreme action is very powerful and should be uncovered and understood.

The major focus of many anti-war groups during 1967 was to influence the 1968 elections and to assist in obtaining alternative candidates. A new organization was specifically formed for these purposes. Created over Labor Day, the National Conference for New Politics (NCNP) hoped they could organize a third, alternative party for the 1968 elections. Unfortunately, this ended up failing, as various factions within the group could not work together (Zaroulis, 1984, p. 128).

In early October 1967, 158 professors, authors, clergy, and others signed and published *A Call to Resist Illegitimate Authority*. This call presented moral and legal objections to the war and supported resistance to it. Spokesmen for this group announced a plan for civil disobedience during the week of October 16th during what was known as "Stop the Draft Week."

On Monday, October 16, 1967, during the Stop the Draft Week, hundreds of draft cards were collected at various sites across the country. This same day in California, 125 people were arrested for civil disobedience while attempting to blockade the Northern California Draft Induction Center at Oakland. Some 3,000 people gathered there early the next morning and massive street battles with police ensued. Twenty-five people were arrested and over twenty were injured (Zaroulis, 1984, p. 135). On Wednesday and Thursday that week, more peaceful civil disobedience occurred, ending in ninety-seven arrests. When Friday came, 10,000 people showed up at the induction center, many of whom wore helmets and carried shields. They succeeded in blocking the entrance to the center for three hours before dispersing.

On October 21, 1967, some 50,000-100,000 people gathered at the Lincoln Memorial for a rally. It ended with a march on the Pentagon that faced a massive police presence. As the march reached the Pentagon, a large group of people broke away and attempted to storm the building. At least twenty-five of the group, mainly SDS members, managed to make it inside the building (Zaroulis, 1984, p. 137). Another group cut away from the main section of the march and stormed through a police fence to stage a sit-in on the Pentagon steps. Several hundred draft cards were burned, and protesters attempted to have a teach-in with the National Guard troops who were on hand to protect the building. The sit-in went on into the night, and some remained on the stairs the next day before being arrested. In the end, a total of 683 people were arrested during this march on the Pentagon (p. 137).

In New York City, a Stop the Draft Committee was organized after the Pentagon demonstrations. The group decided they would try to stop all activities at an armed forces induction center in Manhattan. On the first day, a sit-in took place by older, more moderate elements of the anti-war movement. An estimated 2,500 police showed up to meet them. The next day, 2,500 younger protesters tried unsuccessfully to break the police line, and forty of them were arrested (Zaroulis, 1984, p. 146).

On Thursday, December 7, 1967, demonstrators in New York continued their activities. Instead of going back to the induction center, demonstrators chose to go to the United Nations, where 300 were arrested (Zaroulis, 1984, p. 146). The next day, protesters marched to the Dow Chemical Company at Rockefeller Plaza. One hundred forty people were arrested on December 8 during this action, bringing the total arrests for the week in New York to 585 (p. 146).

Early the following year the federal government began to fight back more against the growing anti-war movement. In Boston, a federal grand jury indicted five anti-war leaders on a single count of conspiracy to "counsel, aid, aid and abet young men to violate the draft laws" (Zaroulis, 1984, p. 149).

As the second session of the Ninetieth Congress began, Jeanette Rankin, an 87- year-old former Congresswoman, led a group of over 5,000 women in a protest at Capitol Hill. The group wanted to present Congress with its petition, which demanded the withdrawal of all American troops from Vietnam. The group was not allowed to present its petition.

In April 1968, anti-war activity again increased across the nation. On April 3, anti-draft rallies were held in New Haven, Boston, and New York City. Then on April 23, an SDS chapter at Columbia University held a rally in protest of a disciplinary meeting in which six students were disciplined for taking part in a prior protest. Specifically, the act in question was one against the University's involvement with the Institute for Defense Analysis. Several hundred students attended this protest (Zaroulis, 1984, p. 165). In response to the disciplinary measures taken, students conducted sit-ins in various buildings, which lasted for seven days before the police moved in. On April 30, the police charged members of the group who were staging the sit-in, clubbing them and dragging them away. Of the 1,000 people who took part in the sit-ins, 711 of them were arrested and 148 received injuries (p. 166). In a dramatic show of their dedication, thousands of students at Columbia, responding to the police brutalities, went on strike. Several days later, the sit-ins resumed and more arrests were made.

Also that month, one million college and high school students across the country participated in a one-day boycott on April 26 in protest of the war. The next day in New York City, the National Mobilization Committee held a march in which over 100,000 people took part. In Chicago this same day, over 12,000 people marched against the war and were severely attacked by the police (Zaroulis, 1984, p. 169). On the opposite coast in San Francisco, over 10,000 people took part in an anti-war march.

On May 17, 1968, another bold draft board raid took place. Entering the office of the local Draft Board 333 in Catonsville, Md., a group of Catholics seized 378 files. They took them outside and burned them in front of the press in the parking lot across the street (Zaroulis, 1984, p. 229).

Organizations nationwide next began preparing for the famous 1968 Democratic National Convention held in Chicago in August. Groups such as the National Mobilization Committee, the Youth International Party (Yippies), SDS and others all played a role in organizing, and all had somewhat different plans for the protest. While the National Mobilization Committee had planned for another peaceful anti-war rally, groups such as the Yippies were preparing for something a bit more confrontational. The Yippies organized what they called the "Festival of Life." Zaroulis and

Sullivan describe what the Festival of Life was supposed to be:

> [. . .] hundreds fornicating in the city's parks and on
> Lake Michigan's beaches, releasing greased pigs all over
> the city; slashing tires along the freeways; floating ten
> thousand nude bodies on the lake; using Yippee girls as
> hookers to seduce and drug delegates; using Yippee men
> to seduce delegates' wives and daughters; having one
> hundred thousand people burn their draft cards with the
> fires spelling BEAT ARMY (1984, pp. 180-181).

The police response to the protests was quick and brutal, with
arrests being made almost immediately. On August 25, a major confrontation took place in a nearby Chicago park where protesters faced off with
over 400 police officers. This scene would be repeated for many days
during the Convention. These August 1968 protests in Chicago signaled
the end for many people in the movement of working within the system
to achieve change and end the war. Zaroulis and Sullivan argue that as a
result the anti-war movement became directly linked with violence in the
eyes of the public (1984, p. 199). According to these two, this important
change in the direction of the anti-war movement would signal the slow
decline of its effectiveness and, eventually, its very existence.

SDS, as previously stated, was a group stricken with constant
internal conflicts. In 1968, although the membership of the group was at
over 100,000 people, the group was more disorganized than ever (Zaroulis, 1984, p. 199). The group, throughout the anti-war movement to this
point, had never been able to come to a clear decision as to how to respond
to the war. While some within SDS felt like there should be a concentration primarily on anti-war efforts, perhaps even more members felt that
attempting to change the whole of American society was more important.
This primary conflict, in addition to growing disagreements over tactics
and strategies, would lead to the demise of SDS within the next year.

On June 18, 1969, the ninth and last annual SDS convention was
held in Chicago. A final, severe split in the group occurred between the
Progressive Labor (PL) representatives and others involved in SDS. A
few days after the convention, Bernardine Dohrn, then head of SDS, left
the group with many others to form the more radical Weathermen. Left in
the hands of the PL representatives, SDS quickly disappeared.

Richard Nixon was elected to the Presidency and came into office on January 20, 1969. He was expected by most people to be the one who would put an end to the situation in Vietnam. But the anti-war movement for the most part was not convinced. In reality, Nixon further escalated the war, especially the military actions conducted in secrecy. The National Mobilization Committee, then led by David Dellinger and Rennie Davis, organized a counter-inaugural demonstration to greet Nixon on his way into power. The protest was not well attended and was barely even covered in the news media (Zaroulis, 1984, p. 209-210).

The Nixon administration also increased its attempts to stop the various anti-war activities. COINTELPRO (Counter Intelligence Program - Started by Hoover in the 1940s) tactics were used to gain information on and to disrupt groups, not only in the anti-war movement but also in the civil rights and black power struggles during this time period. Additionally, a federal grand jury in Chicago on March 19, 1969 indicted eight people on charges of conspiracy to incite a riot during the 1968 Democratic National Convention. "The Chicago 8," as they were known, consisted of Tom Hayden, David Dellinger, Rennie Davis, Lee Weiner, Bobby Seale, John Froines, Jerry Rubin, and Abbie Hoffman. They represented groups such as SDS, the Black Panthers, the Yippies, and the National Mobilization Committee.

The National Mobilization Committee was experiencing problems of its own during this time. After the 1968 Chicago protests and the dismal 1969 counter-inaugural demonstration, the group was increasingly losing support from the public and therefore losing effectiveness. On July 4-5, the coalition decided to hold an organizing conference to restructure the group. Sponsored by the Cleveland Area Peace Action Council, the meeting was held on campus at Case Western Reserve University in Cleveland. Out of this conference, the New Mobilization was formed, which set out a few priorities for 1969. The group voted to support the call for the October 15 Vietnam Moratorium, to support November 15 demonstrations in Washington and San Francisco, and to organize the actions that were to take place around the Chicago 8 trial.

The Weathermen had put out a call for protests to take place in Chicago on October 8-11, 1969, referred to as the "Days of Rage." Determined to make the Days of Rage a militant display of opposition to U.S. policies, the Weathermen issued a provocative statement in August, which gave insight into their plans. They wrote, "Fuck hippie capitalism. Build culture in struggle... Events like the Woodstock gentleness freakout and the demonstration [at San Clemente] indicate that as long as militancy isn't a threat, pig and ruling class approval is forthcoming" (Zaroulis, 1984, p. 261). Referring to the Woodstock Music and Art Fair and Equarian Exposition held in Bethel, New York on the weekend of August 16 and a peaceful, uneventful protest held at the Nixon summer residence in San Clemente, the Weathermen were rejected anything they did not consider militant enough.

In preparations for the October 8-11 protests, representatives from the New Mobilization met with the Weathermen to attempt to come to some agreements regarding what would transpire during the Days of Rage. The meeting ended in perhaps one of the worst possible ways, with the New Mobilization pulling support for the action and the Weathermen calling them in print "the twice-yearly Sunday afternoon anti-war movement" (Zaroulis, 1984, p. 261).

Thousands and thousands of participants were expected by the Weathermen to take part in the Day of Rage. But when the days came, the crowd numbers would never exceed three hundred any time from the 8th to the 11th. Zaroulis and Sullivan describe the events of the first night:

> For sixty minutes the berzerk mob terrorized that neighborhood, breaking windows, smashing cars, assaulting unprotected civilians and police alike. Only sixty eight of the nearly three hundred arrests made during the Days of Rage occurred that night. But wherever the Weathermen congregated during the next few days the police moved in to continue the arrests. No one mourned the harsh treatment handed out by the police, who suffered twenty-eight injuries in the first night (1984, p. 262).

Todd Gitlin, in his book *The Sixties: Years of Hope, Days of Rage*, further described the confrontation:

> The police fought back in kind, shooting six of the Weather soldiers, arresting two hundred fifty (including forty on felony charges), beating most of them, sticking them with $2.3 million worth of bail bonds requiring $234,000 in cash bail. The fighters injured enough cops (seventy-five), damaged enough property, precipitated enough arrests and headlines ('SDS WOMEN FIGHT COPS,' 'RADICALS GO ON RAMPAGE'), and out-

lasted enough fear to talk themselves into a fevered sense of victory (1987, p. 394).

Just four days later, the well-organized Vietnam Moratorium Day would take place. The goal of this particular action was to have campus demonstrations on the 15th and then, one month later, to move into the surrounding communities for two days in November. Endorsements for the Moratorium came from Congresspersons, the United Automobile Workers, the United Shoe Workers of America, and other prominent figures and groups within the country. An estimated $700,000 was spent preparing for this particular day (Zaroulis, 1984, p. 266). Millions of Americans took part in protests on Vietnam Moratorium Day in thousands of cities, towns, and villages across the country.

Not only were students involved in campus demonstrations, but as Zaroulis and Sullivan document, other activities served to further legitimize the entire movement:

> What began as a day of student protest spilled out into the adult community. Fifty congressmen and other leaders from the world of politics and diplomacy set out on multiple speaking assignments. Clergy, doctors, and lawyers were caught up in the events. A crowd of twenty thousand gathered on Wall Street to hear Bill Moyers, once an assistant in the Johnson White House. An after-work rally in Bryant Park was jammed with people who left Times Square traffic hopelessly snarled as they marched to the site. Mayor Lindsay decreed the day a day of mourning and ordered the city's flags to be at half-staff. In Washington, as the day's light dwindled, Coretta Scott King addressed a crowd of thirty thousand before leading a candlelight procession past the White House gates. The soft refrain of 'Give Peace a Chance' was repeated over and over as the solemn marchers, three or four abreast, reached the Nixon abode. 'The whole world is watching. Why aren't you?' one marcher cried out. A presidential spokesperson declined comment on Mr. Nixon's mood (1984, pp. 269-270).

In response, Nixon immediately ordered Vice President Agnew to go before the news media to demand that the leaders and organizers of the Moratorium repudiate the support of a regime that "has on its hands the blood of forty thousand Americans" (p. 273).

During a November 3, 1969 speech to the nation, Nixon demonstrated, to a degree, the extent of the anti-war movement's effect on him. Trying to identify the anti-war movement as the enemy of the American people, he stated, "North Vietnam cannot defeat or humiliate the United States. Only Americans can do that" (Zaroulis, 1984, p. 279). He finished the speech with a direct appeal "to you, the great silent majority of my fellow Americans - I ask for your support" (p. 279).

On Thursday evening, November 13, 1969, a March Against Death took place from the Virginia side of the Potomac River, across the Arlington Memorial Bridge, passing in front of the White House and then down Pennsylvania avenue to the west side front of the Capitol. Every hour, 1,200 protesters began the march and crossed the Arlington Memorial Bridge on the four-mile walk. This hourly procession continued through two nights into Saturday morning with an estimated 45,000 marchers taking part. As each one of the marchers reached the White House, they paused opposite the main entrance to state out loud the name of a soldier who had died in Vietnam.

That Saturday, after the March Against Death concluded and a rally was held in Washington, a march was formed to go to the Justice Department. Upon reaching the Justice Department, the protesters engaged in a massive confrontation with police, all under the eyes of U.S. Attorney General John N. Mitchell, who was watching from his fifth-floor window. By the end of the day 200 people had either been arrested or hospitalized with injuries.

Also on Saturday, November 15, 1969, upwards of 250,000 people marched for peace in San Francisco. This was the largest gathering ever on the West Coast for peace (Zaroulis, 1984, p. 295). Organized by the New Mobilization, the San Francisco protest was far calmer than that which had occurred in Washington. These demonstrations during the late fall of 1969 marked perhaps one of the last climaxes of the anti-war movement.

On January 1, 1970, a stolen plane was used to drop three bombs on the Badger Army Ammunition Plant outside of Madison, Wisconsin. None of the bombs ended up going off, but this activity signaled a new trend in the anti-war movement. An anonymous caller (later identified as Karl Armstrong of the "Vanguard of the Revolution," better known as

"The New Years Gang") to the University of Wisconsin student newspaper stated that "Unfortunately, all the bombs were duds" (Zaroulis, 1984, p. 301). That same week, two of the campus buildings housing ROTC officers were firebombed, and an army reserve building in Madison was broken into and had its equipment destroyed (p. 301).

During the 1969-1970 school year, an amazing number of bombings occurred in the United States. Zaroulis and Sullivan document that "nearly 250 bombings occurred with at least six deaths and 247 cases of arson, including a $320,000 fire at the library on the Berkeley campus of the University of California" (1984, p. 301).

The trial of the Chicago 8 wrapped up in February 1970. By that time it was actually the Chicago 7, as Bobby Seale had been removed from the group to have a separate trial. Two of the seven, Froines and Weiner, were exonerated of the charges by the original trial jury. The other five were found guilty but won on appeal. Documented by national news media, the Chicago Conspiracy trial became a strong symbol of defiance against U.S. governmental policies.

In January 1970, the Vietnam Moratorium announced its plans for the spring. They consisted of organizing local actions in areas across the country on April 15 and then later aiding anti-war congressional candidates in the midterm elections. During the same time, the New Mobilization released its own plans for the spring. In February, the group decided it would work on civil rights and political repression, and then in March it would concentrate on the draft. In April, the New Mobilization would focus on Tax Day and the relationship between war and the economy.

The Student Mobilization Committee, then the only student group with a nationwide, campus network since SDS was gone, announced it would sponsor a week of anti-war demonstrations from April 13-18. It would also call for a nationwide student strike in high schools and colleges on April 15.

When mid-April rolled around, demonstrations took place in cities all across the country. In New York, Pittsburgh, Kansas City, Boston and Chicago, reenactments of the Boston Tea Party were staged. In Berkeley, students marching on the ROTC building were met with fierce police officers, who clubbed and sprayed tear gas on them. The confrontations there continued on into the next day, when the university was closed and declared to be in a state of emergency. The largest protest on April 15 occurred in Boston, where some 75,000 people gathered on the Common. A group broke off from the main demonstration, marched into Cambridge's

Harvard Square area and proceeded to smash windows and set fires (Zaroulis, 1984, p. 311).

A tragic event had occured a month prior, in March 1970, and showed how varied in tactics the movement had become. On the sixth day of the month, three Weathermen were killed in a townhouse explosion while trying to construct a bomb. Diana Oughton, Terry Robbins, and Ted Gold died that day in Greenwich Village as a result of misconnecting a wire on an antipersonnel device.

President Nixon announced on April 30, 1970 that American troops, supported by B52 strikes, had invaded Cambodia. Nixon previously had been successful in his policy of Vietnamization, which strategically sought to continue the Vietnam conflict while decreasing the opposition at home. This was done through small periodic troop withdrawals and lower draft calls, lowered American body counts (at least those publicly reported), and a public campaign suggesting Nixon was phasing out the war. After the April 30 announcement, students immediately took to the streets to protest in cities across the country.

Two days after Nixon's announcement, the protests continued and confrontations began. At Ohio State University, the National Guard was called out in response to a protest, and one student was shot by a Guardsman from 200 feet away. At Kent State, students burned down the ROTC building. Student strikes had been announced, and more than 100 colleges and universities pledged their support and participation within just one hour after the call (Zaroulis, 1984, p. 319). Zaroulis and Sullivan estimate that "over 80 percent of the nation's colleges and universities had announced some kind of strike action" within the next few weeks (p. 319). As the weekend finished up, on May 3 at Kent State, one girl was wounded by a National Guardsmen bayonet, and sixty-nine students were arrested as students were herded into their dormitories by police. (p. 319).

The next day at Kent State, Ohio National Guard troops killed four students and wounded nine. During a noontime protest called by the students against Nixon's Cambodia invasion, the commanding officer ordered the demonstrators to disperse. Tear gas canisters were fired at the students, who threw them back along with bricks, rocks, etc. After retreating to a nearby hillside, the National Guard opened fire on the students. A total of sixty-one shots were fired by the troops, whose officers later denied giving the order to fire. In his 1973 book, *The Truth About Kent State: A Challenge to the American Conscience*, Peter Davies states that the National Guardsmen were instructed to carry loaded weapons and were led by a commander who wanted to teach the students a lesson. He writes:

> At 11:55am guardsmen were selected to take part in carrying out the dispersal order and the men chosen were ordered to 'lock and load' their weapons. This calls for the guardsmen to insert clips of ammunition into their guns and place one round in the chamber ready for firing. It was at this moment that someone sought out [General] Canterbury and told him, ' You must not march against the students.' As the crowd was still relatively peaceful, this was sound advice. But, as reported by Michener [in his book Kent State: What Happened and Why], the general set the tone for what was to follow by replying, 'These students are going to have to find out what law and order is all about' (p. 33).

The response from the nation amounted to unprecedented numbers of protests on campuses and many schools closing their doors for the semester. Zaroulis and Sullivan state that "protest of some kind occurred at more than 50 percent of the nation's campuses; over four million students were involved" (1984, p. 320). Over 500 campuses canceled classes altogether, and fifty-one of them closed the schools for the duration of the semester (p. 320). The same week of the Kent State murders, thirty ROTC buildings were destroyed either by bombs or fire, and the National Guard was called out to twenty-one campuses (p. 320).

On Saturday, May 9, 1970, 130,000 people converged on Washington, D.C. for a protest organized by the New Mobilization. Over 20,000 of these people were prepared to confront the White House, with the President inside, in a civil disobedience action (Zaroulis, 1984, p. 327). Unfortunately, as a result of the extreme disorganization on the part of the Mobilization, the rally was uneventful, and the enormous crowd simply dispersed after the rally held at the Ellipse.

Although the May 9 protest in Washington left many participants disillusioned by its seeming ineffectiveness, the Nixon Administration was, largely out of the public eye, engaging in meetings with various anti-war groups. Nixon himself secretly met with a small group of protesters at the Lincoln Memorial early in the morning on May 9th before the massive gathering. Additionally, Kissinger and other aides in the White House

126

held multiple meetings with student groups.

During this time period, Congress proposed the Cooper-Church amendment, which would cut off all the funding for American forces in Cambodia after July 1, 1970. That is the date that Nixon had declared the U.S. would withdrawal from Cambodia. The Senate passed this amendment on June 30, but it failed in the House. A revision of the amendment was approved eight months later but only related directly to ground troops and not air raids in that country. Other similar attempts by Congress during this time also failed to stop the war.

Owing to tactical differences and the increased failure rate of the New Mobilization's actions, the group fell victim to internal disputes, ending with the abolition of the group by June 1970. Two groups rose out of the demise of the Mobilization: the National Peace Action Coalition (NPAC) and the National Coalition Against War, Racism, and Repression (NCAWRR). NPAC set a very direct goal for itself of organizing single-issue, single-tactic, legal and peaceful demonstrations against the war. NCAWRR, a group that by its very name attempted to categorically take on the big piece of the societal-problem pie, was largely ineffective and short lived for various reasons. Perhaps two of the most important, though, were that the group had no large student base and lost many of its knowledgeable and capable leaders that had previously been in the Mobilization. Furthermore, many of the coalition members had differing aims and beliefs on tactics and strategies.

In January 1971, NCAWRR met in Chicago to plan its next anti-war action. Yet, both because of the group's wide array of coalition members with differing views and because of the meeting's infiltration by undercover government agents, little was accomplished.

The next month, the group ended up changing their name to the People's Coalition for Peace and Justice (PCPJ). With a planned, mass civil disobedience action scheduled for May 1 in Washington, the PCPJ issued an ultimatum to the U.S. government. Either the government would agree to sign the People's Peace Treaty, or the group would invade and shut down the capitol (Zaroulis, 1984, p. 346). The People's Peace Treaty was created by a student delegation that traveled to meet with its counterparts in both North and South Vietnam. It was ratified by students both in the United States, in South Vietnam, and by North Vietnam professors. The provisions for the treaty called for a cease fire, the immediate withdrawal of U.S. troops from Vietnam, the release of prisoners of war, and free elections in South Vietnam (Zaroulis, 1984, p. 346).

After the expansion of the war into Laos on February 8, 1971, protests broke out in cities across the country on February 10. The largest protest of the day took place in Boston, where an estimated 4,000 people gathered for a rally and march. Fourteen people were arrested after many protesters began smashing windows, spray-painting, and fighting with the police (Zaroulis, 1984, p. 347).

NPAC had previously scheduled a mass march and rally in Washington, D.C. for April 24. After the invasion of Laos was announced, the PCPJ endorsed the April 24th action, which had the aims of demanding the withdrawal of U.S. forces from Vietnam, ending the draft, and obtaining a guaranteed annual income of $6,500.

On Monday, April 19, 1971, a group of 1,100 members of Vietnam Veterans Against the War marched in Washington. They went first to Arlington National Cemetery, where they paused at the Tomb of the Unknown Soldier and held a service for those killed on both sides of the war (Zaroulis, 1984, p. 356). The veterans next went to the Capitol, where they presented Congress with a list of demands and began lobbying. Some of them went to the Mall and began setting up camp, where they intended to stay for a week. The demonstrations by the veterans lasted throughout the week, as did the lobbying efforts. Some 100 of them were arrested later on in the week after going to the Supreme Court building and asking the Court to rule on the constitutionality of the war. The week was a great success, as the nation witnessed those against the war as not only students, youth, and radicals, but also now the very soldiers who had been fighting.

The day after the Veteran's Week finished, 500,000 people gathered in Washington to protest the war. Beginning at the Ellipse behind the White House, the protesters marched to the Capitol steps, where they had been given permission to hold a rally. After five hours of listening to speeches, the enormous crowd dispersed. Out of all those attending the march and rally, only ten were arrested that day for minor offenses (Zaroulis, 1984, p. 359).

One hundred fifty Quakers were arrested the next morning after attempting to move their peace vigil from Lafayette Square to the sidewalk in front of the White House. That night, an estimated 1,000 protesters on their way home stopped their cars on the New Jersey Turnpike, blocking traffic for four hours. After dancing, chanting slogans and starting a bonfire in the southbound lanes, 100 of them were arrested by the police.

Also on April 24, 150,000 people attended an anti-war protest in San Francisco. After a seven-mile march to Golden Gate Park, a rally was held that turned violent. Some representatives of more militant groups took possession of the microphone at the rally and condemned the peace movement, as one speaker put it, as "a conspiracy to quench the revolution" (Zaroulis, 1984, p. 360).

In early May, the disruption of Washington that one might have expected to occur on April 24 (but didn't) became a reality. Even before the protests officially began, the police had arrested 242 people (Zaroulis, 9184, p. 361). On May 2, 1971, the police moved in and revoked a permit for an all-night rock concert that was being held in Potomac Park. Attendees were arrested after the permit was revoked and people refused to leave the park.

On May 3, the first day of the protest, a group called the May Day Tribe began its attempted assault on the city. Just prior to 6:00 a.m. group members moved out onto the streets of Washington, D.C., attempting to stop traffic in places like DuPont, Thomas, and Scott circles and Mount Vernon Square. They were met by a massive coalition of federal forces from the metropolitan police, the National Park Police, National Guard, and other federal troops. Arrests immediately began as protesters engaged in street battles with the police, throwing whatever they could find at them (Zaroulis, 1984, p. 361). Hundreds of people were arrested that day, and most were either freed that night or bailed out at $10 a head (p. 362).

On Tuesday, May 4, nearly 3,000 protesters converged on Franklin Square in Washington, D.C. and marched to the Justice Department. Upon reaching the intended location, they held a two-hour rally, which was far less eventful than the activities of the previous day.

The next day, 2,000 May Day protesters gathered in front of the Capitol demanding that Congress adopt the People's Peace Treaty. While four Congresspersons spoke to the crowd, one protester began taking off his clothes. The police used that as a sign to move in, and 1,146 people were arrested. Those arrested on this day and throughout the week were taken either to the Washington Coliseum or to a practice field used by the Washington Redskins. Nearly all the demonstrators arrested up to this point were let out of jail within forty-eight hours (Zaroulis, 1984, p. 364). Although this week of protests in early May did not achieve the goals set beforehand by the organizers (that of stopping the war or getting the People's Peace Treaty signed), Washington clearly had its hands full for that period.

May 15, 1971 signaled a growing trend in the anti-war movement. On this day, known as Armed Forces Day, protests were held at nineteen military bases, including those of the navy and air force (Zaroulis, 1984, p. 365). Several hundred active duty personnel attended these actions. The importance of these actions cannot be understated, as this had to be an extreme embarrassment for the U.S. government.

The famous Pentagon Papers began to be published by the *New York Times* on June 13, 1971. These were a collection of documents detailing the history of the United States' involvement in Vietnam from 1945 to March 1968. Robert McNamara had ordered the Papers to be prepared in 1967 in secrecy, and they were finally completed some eighteen months later. Leaked to the *Times* by former Rand Corporation employee Daniel Ellsberg, the Pentagon Papers allowed the public to see for the first time the true motives of the U.S. government in Vietnam. Within the papers lay documented proof that the primary concern for the United States was not winning the war, but rather the avoidance of humiliation and defeat (Zaroulis, 1984, p. 368).

Disagreements between anti-war groups continued into 1971. During the NPAC and PCPJ conferences held in June and July that year, conflicts between the two groups on tactics and politics continued to be prominent. With the help of a mediator, the two groups did agree to work together to organize three actions during the rest of 1971. They would include the Hiroshima-Nagasaki commemorations on August 6-9, a national moratorium on October 13, and regional anti-war protests on November 6.

That fall, Women Strike for Peace, the Fellowship of Reconciliation, and the War Resisters League took part in what was called Project DDT (Daily Death Toll). On a daily basis, people from all across the country came to Washington, D.C. to stage a "die-in" in front of the White House. The act was meant to highlight the ongoing killing in Indochina.

The October 13 demonstrations went on in cities around the country with little notice. Participation numbers were low, and NPAC afterwards shifted all its efforts to the November 6 regional protests. On October 25-26, May Day Tribe members held an "Evict Nixon" day, which was to consist of a march and rally designed to shut down the White House. Unfortunately for them, it turned out to be largely a failure, as a mere 800 people showed up (Zaroulis, 1984, p. 370).

Attendance at the November 6 protests was a little better. In San Francisco, 40,000 people gathered for the action, 30,000 gathered in New York, and 15,000 in Denver. Many other cities took part in the day of actions across the United States. Zaroulis and Sullivan state that although tens of thousands of people participated in the November 6, 1971 protests, the public was clearly losing interest in the issue because of the perception that Nixon was on path to stopping the war. This is further proof that the President's Vietnamization campaign was working, at least enough to convince the mass body of the public that the war was being phased out.

In late 1971, a series of meetings were held by NPAC, PCPJ, and a group called the People's Party. For NPAC, the goal of its December meeting was to plan further anti-war actions in 1972. PCPJ decided its chief purpose at that point was to attempt to build a large American multi-issue coalition. The People's Party was primarily concerned with nominating stand-in candidates for President and Vice President. It sought to affect the outcome of the 1972 elections.

After the U.S. campaign "Operation Deep Proud Alpha" was launched on December 26, 1971, the anti-war groups struggled to create an effective response. The Operation consisted of the heaviest bombing of North Vietnam since 1968 (Zaroulis, 1984, p. 374). Perhaps the most effective demonstrations during this time were those carried out by the Vietnam Veterans Against the War.

On December 27, 1971, twenty-five VVAW entered the Betsy Ross House, where the first American flag was created. After flying an American flag upside down for an hour, they were removed by police. The next day 150 members of VVAW marched through Washington, D.C. and dropped bags filled with blood at the White House gates. They continued on to block the Lincoln Memorial and were arrested. At the Statue of Liberty on December 26-28, fifteen VVAW members entered and remained there after closing time, barricading themselves inside. The group proceeded to fly the American flag upside down from the Statue of Liberty's crown and then from her torch. After forty-two hours, the group left on the order of a federal judge (Zaroulis, 1984, p. 375).

During the Presidential election period of 1972, candidates frequently discussed the Vietnam issue during their campaigns. Senator Edmund S. Muskie, who announced his candidacy for the Presidency in January 1972, demanded the total withdrawal of U.S. troops from Vietnam. Another contender for the Presidency, Senator Hubert H. Humphrey, stated, "It has taken Mr. Nixon longer to withdraw our troops than it took us to defeat Hitler" (Zaroulis, 1984, p. 377).

During this time, President Nixon continued his Vietnamization policy, which included slow troop reduction, even as bombing raids continued and/or increased. It was announced on January 13 that 70,000 more troops would be withdrawn from Vietnam by May 1, 1972 leaving some 65,000 there. It was this sort of announcement that continued to hurt the anti-war movement in the eyes of the public. Nixon's Vietnamization removed the sense of urgency from the anti-war movement.

On April 1, 1972, 10,000 gathered in front of the Pennsylvania state capitol to protest the war in general and to specifically protest the conspiracy trial of the Harrisburg 7. The seven defendants-- Reverend Philip F. Berrigan, Sister Elizabeth McAlister, the Reverend Neil McLaughlin, Anthony Scoblick, Mary Cain Scoblick, the Reverend Joseph Wenderoth, and Eqbal Ahmad-- were on trial for allegedly conspiring to kidnap Henry Kissinger and hold him for ransom. On April 5th, after the jury was deadlocked, a mistrial was declared.

On April 15, U.S. air strikes against North Vietnam resumed, and PCPJ called an emergency protest in Washington. Some 800 people showed up to the action, and over 200 were arrested after refusing to obey a dispersal order given by the U.S. Park Police.

Student activity on campus, largely dead since the demise of SDS, also resumed. Two days after the bombing resumed, on April 17, the National Student Association put out a call for a nationwide student strike on April 21. The same day in Madison, 3,000 people at the University of Wisconsin engaged in a massive street battle with police. In San Francisco, 1,500 people surrounded a federal building and forty-one were arrested during a protest at the Alameda Naval Air Station.

Within the next few days, protests around the country intensified. On April 18, Harvard students broke into the Center for International Affairs, smashing windows and destroying offices. After police seized the building, the protesters took their action to the streets of Cambridge, smashing windows of stores and an IBM building. On April 21, during the nationwide student strike, students took over buildings on campuses across the country. Zaroulis and Sullivan summarize a good portion of the day's events:

> At Princeton 350 students seized the building of the Woodrow Wilson School for Public and International Affairs, demanding to know the identity of its donor... At Stanford over 100 students were arrested for blocking highways; previously they had attacked an electronics lab which, they said, did war-related research. At the University of Michigan students attacked an ROTC build-

ing, vandalizing its offices; later 1,500 of them roamed through Ann Arbor, tying up traffic for four hours. At Boston University 1,500 students attacked the administration building, smashing doors, taking files, ripping out telephones; the next day 40 students took over the office of the dean of students. At the University of Texas at Austin police dispersed demonstrators with tear gas and nightsticks. Twenty-seven students were arrested at Syracuse University while barricading the entrance to an air force recruiting office; 15 were arrested at Idaho's Boise State University (1984, p. 382).

Additionally, 800 National Guard troops were called out to the University of Maryland in College Park on April 20 to stop a student protest. Over 2,000 students had blocked U.S. Route 1. As police moved in to clear them, confrontations between the police and demonstrators flared up and continued for hours, ending in many arrests.

NPAC held an international Peace Action Day on April 22, 1972, consisting of protests in cities around the world. In New York, 35,000 people gathered for the event and 30,000 attended in San Francisco. Further protests were held in the United States, one on April 29 organized by NPAC and another on May 4, the second anniversary of the Kent State killings.

During the beginning of May 1972, the United States ordered the mining of all North Vietnamese ports and the bombing of all North Vietnamese rail lines leading to China. This was in response to a North Vietnamese offensive, which had pushed South Vietnamese soldiers back. The response from the U.S. anti-war movement was quick and confrontational. Massive battles with police erupted in cities all across the United States, with many demonstrations involving widespread property destruction. Of the anti-war groups still around, many got together and planned a major action in Washington, D.C. on May 21-22.

Meanwhile, on May 19, the Weathermen were making their own presence felt. The group successfully detonated a bomb inside the Pentagon, creating widespread damage in protest of the heightened military campaign by the United States. Ron Jacobs, in his book *The Way the Wind Blew: A History of the Weather Underground*, describes the impact of the action:

Weather lent a revolutionary credence of its own

to the protest when, on May 19, 1972 (Ho Chi Minh's birthday), the group exploded a bomb in the Air Force wing of the Pentagon. The bomb was placed in a women's restroom on the fourth floor. The blast devastated the rest room, blowing away a 30-foot section of the wall, breaking windows, and mangling the plumbing. The consequent flooding shut down a computer on the first floor which served as part of a military communications network spanning the globe. In addition, a computer tape archive containing highly classified information was severely damaged. The inner sanctum of the war machine had been attacked (1997, p. 142).

Organizers of the May 21-22 protests anticipated that attendance would be at over 50,000, but the actual numbers were closer to 15,000 (Zaroulis, 1984, p. 387). The May 21-22 organizers attributed the lack of attendance at their demonstrations to the Weathermen action.

On June 22, 1972, Coreta Scott King, Joan Baez and others staged a "Ring Around Congress" protest. Over 3,000 women showed up and circled the Pentagon, demanding that funding be cut for the war and used for domestic needs. The action ended with many of the women attempting to lobby their congressional representatives.

That year both the Democratic and Republican National Conventions were targeted with protests, the fiercer of the two occurring at the Republican event. There several thousand people, including Yippies, "Zippies," members of PL-SDS, Vietnam Veterans Against the War and others converged in Miami to confront the Republicans. By far the most impressive event during this week of action was staged by three Vietnam Veterans who had managed to get into the Convention. When Nixon appeared, the three Veterans held up a sign reading "STOP THE WAR" and immediately began screaming, "Stop the bombing," and "Stop the war," until Secret Service agents pushed them in their wheelchairs out of the building.

On August 12, 1972, the last U.S. ground troops left Vietnam. An estimated 43,500 air force and support personnel remained (Zaroulis, 1984, p. 392). President Nixon announced publicly on August 29 that by December 1972, only 27,000 U.S. troops would still be in South Vietnam. Nixon was elected to his second term as President on November 7, 1972, based largely upon the public perception that he was ending the war, among other alleged breakthroughs in peace with China and Russia.

Meanwhile, the anti-war movement continued to lose support and momentum. NPAC held nationwide demonstrations in twenty-one cities on November 18, but the attendance was quite small for the most part. The largest demonstration took place in New York where some 2,000 people attended.

Since October of 1972, Henry Kissinger had been in peace negotiations with North Vietnam, South Vietnam, and the Viet Cong troops for a cease fire. After the elections, the nation, including the anti-war movement, patiently waited to hear if Kissinger's promised peace would actually become a reality. On December 16, Kissinger stated publicly that the peace talks had broken off with the North Vietnamese due to disagreements over the proposed peace treaty. Just two days later, Nixon acknowledged that the U.S. resumed bombing in places such as Hanoi, Haiphong City and Haiphong Harbor, presumably to force the North Vietnam into an agreement. It didn't work, as the agreement signed in January 1973 was virtually the same as the one tentatively reached in October.

The bombings continued even over December 25th, creating widespread anger among the international community. In London, Rome, Berlin and other cities around the world, thousands of people protested against the U.S. war. In the United States, cities such as New York, Boston, Madison, Hartford, and Washington all witnessed anti-war demonstrations. Before 1972 ended, both NPAC and PCPJ issued a joint call for massive protests at Nixon's second inaugural on January 20, 1973.

When January 20 finally came, over 60,000 people—including 2,500 VVAW members—took part in the protest organized by NPAC and PCPJ (Zaroulis, p. 402). The same day in New York City, a six-hour prayer and vigil, calling for healing the wounds of war, was conducted in the Cathedral Church of St. John the Divine. In Central Park a group that boasted it was the "largest assembly of Jewish organizations ever to protest the Vietnam War" planted a tree symbolizing the rebuilding to take place after the war.

Finally, on January 23, Nixon announced to the nation that Kissinger had initialed an agreement to end the war. The agreement was formally signed in Paris on January 27, 1973. Within sixty days all of the remaining 23,700 U.S. troops were to be withdrawn from Vietnam. While the vast majority of Americans celebrated the long-awaited news, some in the anti-war movement continued their work.

Sidney Peck, Tom Hayden, and Jane Fonda held a press conference in Boston to announce their upcoming actions. They intended to seek support for the rebuilding of the Bach Mai Hospital, which the U.S. destroyed in the Christmas bombings of 1972. The group also wanted to create a committee to watch over and ensure the agreement signed in Paris would not be violated. Lastly, they sought to pressure the U.S. government into stopping all aid to the Thieu government and to conduct congressional inquiries on the thousands of prisoners held in South Vietnam.

Throughout the rest of the year, scattered prayer vigils and demonstrations occurred. On August 15, the bombing by the U.S. stopped, and in Washington, sixty anti-war protesters engaged in a prayer vigil at the White House. A separate protest along the fence on Pennsylvania Avenue, organized by various anti-war organizations, called for President Nixon's impeachment, particularly for his "illegal" bombing of Cambodia.

Throughout the rest of the year, on into 1974 and 1975, small protests continued, still targeting, among other issues, the U.S. aid to South Vietnam. For all intents and purposes, though, the movement had largely phased out. It had been a long, rough and windy road to the end of the war, but it was clear that the anti-war movement had an impact. What sort of impact is left to be examined.

*

Perhaps the most fitting question that should be asked at this point is *did the movement succeed?* The answer to this question truthfully depends on each individual view of success and effectiveness. To state that the anti-war movement did not play at least some role in ending the war would be a mistake. But to proclaim that the movement on its own did stop the war is also untrue. The ten years of protests had an impact on the political process in the United States, but the extent of that influence continues to be debated among movement participants, scholars, politicians, and activists today.

Looking back upon the anti-war movement one year after the Paris Peace Agreement was signed, the Weather Underground released its book, *Prairie Fire: The Politics of Revolutionary Anti-Imperialism.* In it, the group discusses its political ideology, which includes a reflection on the effectiveness of the anti-war movement. They write:

> The movement played a specific and important role. Without it, the Johnson-Nixon governments would

most likely have:
- launched a land invasion of North Vietnam
- waged tactical or full nuclear war
- started a war with China
- bombed the dikes of North Vietnam

These were all genocidal weapons in the ruling-class arsenal. Without a growing anti-war movement, without drastic escalation in the nature and militancy of our resistance, they might have been used. The political cost at home for each successive strategy became an important point in deterring the use of these weapons (1974, p. 35).

For certain, during the Nixon Administration, the President was clearly affected psychologically by the anti-war movement as Zaroulis, Sullivan, and Gitlin document in their books. Proof of this can be seen not only in Nixon's compulsion to discuss and condemn the protests on various occasions, but also in his early morning meeting with demonstrators just prior to the May 9, 1970 protest in Washington, D.C. Furthermore, Nixon's policy of Vietnamization, however brilliant, was a direct maneuver to ease the public pressure mounting against the war while at the same time allowing the conflict to continue for another five years.

With its attempts to lessen U.S. casualty rates, slowly pull out troops, and reduce draft calls while simultaneously continuing the conflict, Vietnamization was very similar to tactics used by the police in Georgia in combating black protests. Instead of being exceedingly reactionary, as had been the previous case with the majority of Southern police, the local police departments in Georgia tried out somewhat different tactics. They sought to minimize their harsh treatment of the black protesters in order to keep the public from gaining sympathy for them. By minimizing mob violence, filling the jails with blacks, and reducing their harsh treatment, the police effectively controlled the situation. Similarly, Vietnamization sought to reduce, as much as possible, public support for the anti-war movement. By lowering the U.S. casualty rates, a factor that had been a major catalyst for the anti-war movement, Nixon was able to slowly lessen the public participation in the struggle against the war.

During and just after the 1963-1973 anti-war movement, differing organizations held a wide range of views as to their own effectiveness. While groups such as SANE and the Mobilization (in any of its various incarnations) to some degree over the years felt as if they were having an impact, others including the Yippies and post-SDS/Weathermen groups were far more critical. The Weathermen, in particular, broke off from SDS to follow a path involving more radical tactics. They too became heavily criticized, charged with alienating and destroying the entire movement with their clandestine, exclusionary bombings and police confrontations.

Were the Weathermen to blame, as argued by Zaroulis and Sullivan, for the loss of public support and weakening of the movement during the time they were active in the very late 1960s and early 1970s? The same arguments against these sorts of actions have been heard in various movements globally, throughout modern history. In the abolitionist movement in the United States, there were blacks who argued strongly against slave uprisings, fearing an increased repression from and a rougher relationship with whites. Jews in the Nazi holocaust also argued amongst themselves over engaging in more extreme forms of resistance. Some in the ghettos and death camps argued that any resistance would just bring a quicker death and liquidation, while others felt that their only hope was to act by any means necessary.

Similarly, in the civil rights movement in the United States, leaders such as Martin Luther King, Jr., following a Christian and Gandhian based ethic of nonviolence, spoke out against more extreme forms of action. King felt that the main route towards success for blacks was to win over the hearts and minds of the white American public. Even today in the environmental movement in the U.S., groups (such as the Earth Liberation Front) that engage in underground property destruction are somewhat universally condemned by mainstream organizations. The common argument, just as it was heard against the Weathermen, is that those types of activities reduce public support and make it that much more difficult for "legitimate" groups to conduct their work. By legitimate, anti-violence proponents are usually referring to organizations that adhere to only those activities contained within the *Five Rules for Social and Political Change in the United States.*

Did the more confrontational tactics of late SDS and the Weathermen, in addition to the numerous unknown individuals and groups, really have a true negative effect on the entire anti-war movement? Anytime there are controversial tactics presented in a movement, there will be a time of confusion and often contempt for these measures. In the eyes of those committing the more controversial tactics, the police confrontations, the bombings and other property destruction were every bit as valid—and

many would say more effective than—the state-sanctioned, legal strategies employed by the mainstream.  The opposing opinion, of course, is
that these tactics only served to create a violent reputation for the anti-war
movement, thus reducing public support.  Yet, the primary problem did,
and still does today, lie in how the entire movement responds to such activity.  Will the movement as a whole allow the activity to divide it, to create
weakness, and thus force people to take sides?  Or will it embrace all tactics and concentrate on ensuring that public condemnation about differing
strategies is kept to a minimum?

One undeniable fact that directly pushed the U.S. into signing the
peace agreement in Paris in 1973 was the success of the Viet Cong.  These
guerilla fighters withstood an incredible amount of U.S. air and ground attacks and continued to have small victories over the U.S. into 1973.  The
reality that the Paris agreement had been largely unaltered from some of
the earliest requests from the North Vietnamese government demonstrated
that the United States had not succeeded in its military campaign.  This is
an amazing notion, since the U.S. had far greater resources available as
far as finances, weapons, and troops.  By not engaging in the conventional
warfare that the U.S. military was trained for and used to, the Viet Cong
held their ground against what was considered the most powerful country,
with the most threatening military, on Earth.

The 1973 agreement arguably had been delayed for years by the
United States, which prolonged the conflict in order to save its pride and
reputation, both domestically and abroad.  As this reality became known
not just to Congresspersons, other politicians and anti-war activists, but
also to soldiers and veterans, serious pressure mounted against the United
States government.  Ron Kovic in his autobiography, *Born on the Fourth
of July*, explains how he and other veterans, upon coming back from Vietnam, began to understand that American soldiers continued to die for what
many considered a lie.  The U.S. government had cited communism as
the major factor that led to the U.S. involvement.  United States troops,
as well as the general public, were trained to see a serious threat posed by
the possible expansion—or domino theory—of communist regimes.  To
save America, to protect freedom and democracy, the United States had no
choice but to attempt to save all of Vietnam from falling into communist
hands (or so the line goes).

Many soldiers, after witnessing the atrocities committed against
innocent Vietnamese civilians, seeing the lies being told to the American
public by the U.S. government, and realizing that the communist threat

wasn't so serious, came back to the United States and joined anti-war organizations such as Vietnam Veterans Against the War. For these former fighters to take such a critical stance against the war, even after taking in the U.S. government's rigorous, anti-communism propaganda campaigns, was a monumental and powerful addition to the anti-war struggle. These individuals were able to tell Americans firsthand what U.S. soldiers were dying for some 13,000 miles away.

The student movement on campuses is also not to be forgotten due to its perseverance and impact. There may not have been another time throughout the history of the United States when university and college campuses across the country erupted in protests and dissent to such a degree. Authors, including Zaroulis and Sullivan, argue that students became involved in such high numbers, at least in part, after becoming aware that they too might be called on to go to Vietnam. With thousands of U.S. casualties reported per week for quite some time, students were well aware they too could, at any time, be drafted and forced to risk their lives.

Yet, Howard Zinn disagrees and writes in *You Can't Be Neutral On A Moving Train*:

> We often read in the press—or heard from some young people—that the opposition to the war came from young people wanting to save their own lives. That was so clearly untrue; millions of people protested the war not because their own lives were at stake, but because they truly cared about other people's lives, the lives of Vietnamese, of fellow Americans (1994, p. 122).

In attempting to apply the student activity of the 1960s and early 1970s to the War Against Terrorism and Iraq currently conducted by the United States, it is crucial to understand just how so many people of the younger generation felt compelled to take part in protests and other actions. It is important to also ponder how groups such as SDS could actually have had a membership of over 100,000 students nationwide. Part of the answer did indeed lie with the reality of the draft, as previously mentioned. But there had to be—and there were—other factors. Education, largely taking on the form of teach-ins, also played an extremely important part. Also, just the purposeful creation of student organizations, such as SDS, on campuses gave students the opportunity to be exposed to information as well as get involved in activities against the war. It sounds quite a bit easier than it actually was, but at the time, at least a small national student anti-war movement could be formed just by a few experienced organizers traveling the country, educating local areas and setting up organizations. The maintenance, sustainability and growth of any new movement nowadays would be a far more complex battle to tackle.

Although the sheer multitude of participants in the anti-Vietnam War movement was incredible, the implemented strategies were not enough to force the U.S. government into stopping its Vietnam conflict. As a result of the struggle being single-issue, reformist minded and not focused on combating the U.S. government itself, the anti-war movement could not have effectively challenged U.S. militaristic policies in Vietnam or elsewhere.

# CHAPTER FOUR

# *The Algerian Revolution: A look at the FLN organization*

When the subjects of revolutions and social movements are examined, there are commonly a wealth of resources available arguing the historical success of absolutist, nonviolent practices. Whether it be Gandhi's work in South Africa and later India, Martin Luther King, Jr.'s activities in the U.S. civil rights movement, or Suffragettes in the United States struggling for the vote (just to name a few), there are volumes of literature promoting the belief that nonviolence as a revolutionary tool or catalyst for societal change is the only tactic historically successful and morally acceptable. In Western countries such as the United States, this category of educational resources is used in schooling, popular media (books, magazines, movies, television, newspapers, radio, etc.) and in other learning situations to suggest a morally-proper methodology for solving societal grievances.

Conversely, the investigation into political violence as a revolutionary strategy is met with difficulty due to a comparable void in available supporting documentation. While case histories involving political violence are readily available, there is a specific void concerning the ethics, morality, and strategies behind the tactic. Is this simply a result of revolutionary nonviolence having a greater success record historically? Has political violence simply not achieved the same feats globally as the practice of nonviolence? Looking into the matter, even slightly, it becomes evident that political violence has indeed played a major role historically in social movements and in political and societal revolutions. Why then, in the westernized countries such as the United States, is there not a greater array of supporting documentation as to the legitimacy of politically-motivated violence?

A simple answer is that in the perfect world, true global peace would be a reality. To promote this reality, many who share a Gandhian point of view would argue that we need to adhere to a strict policy of nonviolence—acting in the way we wish to live in our perfect utopia. In most, if not all, post-industrialized countries, the standard of living for many contains a comfort that allows for a certain level of luxury and privilege. Resulting from this privilege is the security and freedom of not facing life-and-death situations on a daily basis. The promotion of nonviolence and the availability of materials on the subject may very well exude from this privilege. The lack of acceptance in these same countries of the legitimacy of political violence (unless of course it originates from governments and their militaries), and the resulting absence of easily-available supporting literature, suggests a clear bias based on that same societal privilege.

Does this very basic analysis suffice, or are there further issues to be explored in this disparity between nonviolence and political violence information sources? Perhaps the most crucial questions of each of the strategies are *Do they work? Is there a legitimacy to them? Are they morally acceptable?* To understand if a strategy can be successful, an examination must be made of its use historically. Historical documentation and case studies allow for a more realistic and informed opinion to be formed regarding the legitimacy of political violence, in terms both of political and social movements seeking mere reform and of those advocating for complete revolution.

In this spirit, my attention became drawn to the Algerian Revolution, arguably one of the best-known examples of effective political violence. My interest primarily lies within the most famous and successful revolutionary organization at the time, the FLN or *Front of National Liberation*. From 1954 to 1962, in the French-colonized Algeria, the FLN waged a fierce campaign using a variety of tactics—predominantly terrorism—to gain independence for Algerians.

This particular chapter consists of an examination of the FLN and its use of political violence to achieve its desired results. Yet, in order to begin, some background information must be provided as to the social and political climate, as well as the history of the French in occupying Algerian territory. I tend to look at history as a giant puzzle, with each incident, each story, providing a crucial piece. As more and more pieces are provided for the puzzle, advanced insight can be gained regarding how to answer problems facing us all on a global basis today. This chapter on the FLN and the Algerian Revolution serves, at least to me, as one more piece of knowledge allowing a better understanding of the role of political violence in political and societal change.

*

When French troops first arrived in Algeria in 1830, they found that an estimated 3 million people inhabited the country. Approximately 2.5 million of these people were Arabs. As the troops continued on inland, they ran into indigenous resistance, largely centered in western Algeria. This main resistance to the colonization was headed by Emir Abdel Kader, who had previously built a sizeable empire off raiding neighboring tribes, especially from 1832 to 1839. When the French formally attacked this power in 1840, Kader called for a national campaign of resistance to the French, rallying tribes and villages all across Algeria. Kader's forces were defeated in two battles in 1843 and 1844, and Kader himself surrendered in 1847. This surrender of Kader signaled the beginning of the end of the French military conquest of Algeria.

Joseph Kraft, in his 1961 book, *The Struggle for Algeria*, discusses the immediate implications that the military invasion had on the Algerians. He writes, "Though hardly glorious, there did prevail a civilization with a delicate inner balance. This balance the French occupiers destroyed" (p. 16).

By 1870, over 200,000 Europeans had settled in Algeria. For the next fifty years thereafter, the Moslem population grew from almost 3 million to close to 5 million. Kraft states that "accompanying the demographic burst was a striking decline in the traditional base of subsistence. At least 2.5 million acres of tribal and village domain passed into the hands of the Europeans, either by sale or expropriation" (1961, p. 18). Resultantly, Moslems for the first time came to live directly next to Europeans in increasing numbers. They migrated to the larger cities, then under European economic control, seeking work and support for their families. Living in this close proximity, Moslems could, then more than ever, observe firsthand the effects of French colonization. This would be a major factor leading to Algerian pre-revolutionary conditions.

Additionally, the Moslem population was increasingly forced to rely upon the cash economy popularized with the French and European invasion. Kraft notes that "in 1870 not many thousand Moslems were city dwellers or paid farm workers. By 1920 at least a million Moslems depended on wages or buying and selling for a livelihood" (1961, p. 19).

In 1871, the last indigenous resistance fell, and the French ended their military colonization process by turning over the country to civilian rule. In *Revolutionary Terrorism: The FLN in Algeria, 1954-1962*, Martha Hutchinson argues that the French colonization left Algerians in a position ripe and ready for revolution. She writes:

> After 1871 Algeria was governed not in the interest of France or of the Muslim majority, but for the benefit of the European minority. The disastrous impact of the military conquest and of colonial rule on the social, cultural, linguistic, religious, and economic structures of Algeria was completely disregarded. The traditional life of Algeria was literally destroyed and replaced with an alien system from which Algerians were excluded. Lands, especially the most fertile coastal plains, were seized for European cultivation, leaving the Algerian peasants with sparse plots from which only a bare subsistence could be won. Partial famines were followed by serious epidemics of disease among the local populations in 1893, 1897, and 1920 (1978, p. 2).

In response to the quite noticeable disparities in everyday life brought about by the displacement of Moslems, protest movements began to form. The *North African Star* was formed in 1923 by Algerian Moslems working in France. The group was created as a splinter of the French Communist Party and was led by factory worker and World War I veteran Messali Hadj, who had learned principles of organizing from the Communist Party. Kraft writes, "the North African Star sought an independent, urbanized, socialist Algeria and chose as means subversive action by the proletariat" (1961, pp. 24-25). The group further intended to protect the moral, social, and material interests of North African Moslems.

Just two years prior to the founding of the *North African Star*, another protest organization was created called *Young Algeria*. Established by Ferhat Abbas, a pharmacist from Setif, *Young Algeria* was a middle-class movement that supported economic and political freedom but opposed nationalism. The group wanted its freedoms within the French Algeria, rather than expressing a desire for a truly independent country.

A third organization was formed in 1935 known as the *Association of Vlemas* (Arabic teachers). Created by Sheik Abdel-hamid ben Badis, Vlemas was a religious group that sought "regeneration and independence through a return to the pure practices of Islam" (Kraft, 1961, p. 25).

From 1923 to 1936, Hadj's *North African Star* was banned twice, and Hadj himself was arrested on multiple occasions. In 1936, Hadj became the leader of a new organization, the *National Union of North African Moslems*. With this group, Hadj toured the country energizing crowds and attracting as many as 11,000 people at meetings. Just one year later this new organization dissolved, and Hadj started the *Algerian People's Party* (PPA). On July 14, 1937, Hadj organized a massive parade in Algiers and for the first time since the French colonization, an Algerian flag was displayed publicly. The PPA became Algeria's first major party and claimed to have some 10,000 followers in Algeria and another 4,000 in France by the time World War II began.

An additional, important event occurred in 1936 that further frustrated Algerians. That year, legislation referred to as the Blum-Viollette bill was introduced into the National Assembly proposing that "certain categories of Muslims be allowed to become French citizens without exceptional encumbrances" (Hutchinson, 1978, p. 3). Hutchinson states that, "this would have been a step toward genuine assimilation, but the opposition of the colons, represented by their mayors, the traditional leaders of European protest, was vehement enough to cause the abandonment of any idea of reform" (p. 3). As a result, this failure created bitterness, anger, and disillusionment even among moderate Algerians toward the possibility of reform. This response translated into more support for the radical groups, the PPA and Vlamas.

Both the PPA and Vlamas then called a Muslim congress to attempt to organize and unite all the pro-Algerian groups. As the organizations realistically had differing goals and ideas on how to achieve them, the unity was very brief. For the next fifteen years, Kraft states that "the classic dilemma of reform versus direct action bedeviled the nationalist groups" (1961, p. 61). While the field organizers in Hadj's party pushed for violent strikes, the other two organizations advocated for more moderate action.

In 1943, World War II veteran and politician Ferhat Abbas led an effort to create a true unity between the groups. The Algerian Manifesto was written on February 10, 1943, a document meant to serve as a notice to the French government of Moslem expectations. Served as an appeal by Algerian politicians, the manifesto called for the creation of a constitution that would guarantee basic rights and political freedoms to Algerian Moslems. Under General De Gaulle, the French government rejected this proposal for a constitution, instead deciding to meagerly increase the Moslem electoral college in 1944.

Algerian opposition parties rejected these token reforms and instead vowed to work for an autonomous Algerian republic. Disagreements continued to be a reality though, in this case over whether or not this Algerian republic would be in any way federated with France. As an additional response to the rejection of the Algerian constitution, Moslem groups formed a joint organization called the Friends of the Algerian Manifesto (AMA). Within just one year, the AMA counted over 500,000 Moslem supporters.

But for the PPA, in particular, these reforms had only proved that armed revolt was necessary. Throughout 1944, the PPA—then led by Dr. Lamine-Debaghine—recruited new groups who were armed and ready for action. All through the country a tense atmosphere of potential unrest lurked about. A letter written by a settler group in 1944 to the French government describes the scene:

> Everywhere insecurity is increasing. There have been reports of attacks on property, of willful damage to water mains, of undisguised threats on the lives of isolated French inhabitants. In the cities, despite the official ban

on processions, the streets are full of demonstrators openly proclaiming that Algeria belongs to the Arabs. Local organizations - combat groups and groups formed to replace the French administration - have burgeoned in front of our eyes (Kraft, 1961, p. 62).

At the end of World War II, an event occurred on May 8, 1945 that would have a permanent impact on Algeria. Local Moslems in Setif had received permission to hold a "nonpolitical victory parade" under the PPA organization. While the parade was en route, Moslem marchers pulled out a green Algerian flag and displayed banners with PPA slogans. "LONG LIVE INDEPENDENT ALGERIA; DOWN WITH COLONIALISM" and "FREE MESSALI (Hadj)," the banners stated. When a police officer ordered the Moslems to put away the banners, they refused, and police began to struggle with the protesters. A first shot was fired by the police, and in return, Kraft writes "one band of PPA militants opened fire on the police, then poured through the streets of Setif, knifing and clubbing such settlers as they could find" (1961, p. 63). By the middle of the day, news of the revolt had spread through the territory and Moslems in other areas began rioting. Nearly 100 people died that first day.

The French declared martial law, responding with severe military force. They bombed Algerian villages, killing an estimated 40,000 Moslems. Kraft states:

> Planes, tanks, and in one case a cruiser bombarded Moslem villages. After the bombing came infantry detachments burning villages, searching huts, shooting suspects. Thousands of Moslems were bundled into barbed-wire camps (1961, p. 63).

Additionally, settlers immediately formed armed militias and set about seizing and burning homes and directly shooting Moslems. Nearly 5,000 Moslem political leaders were also arrested in connection with the May 8 revolt.

This extreme brutality by the French contributed to a further increase in Moslem hostility against the French and European settlers. It also gave rise to a heightened nationalism amongst Moslems. Perhaps most importantly though, the French response served as a reality check, and afterward Moslems ended all attempts at reform.

One year later, in 1946, Ferhat Abbas formed the *Union Democratique du Manifeste Algerien* (UMDA), which was set up specifically to campaign for the Algerian Manifesto. During the same time period, Messali Hadj returned from exile and converted the PPA into an above-ground party called the *Mouvement pour le Triomphe des Libertes Democratiques* (MTLD). Both of these two new parties concentrated their efforts on elections to various assemblies.

In 1948, out of sheer frustration with the election process, the MTLD set up an underground wing, the *Organisation Speciale* (O.S.). The main purpose of the O.S. was "extending and deepening the Messalist organization while at the same time striking blows of terror and sabotage against French rule" (Kraft, 1961, p. 65). Under the direction of Mohammed Khider, the O.S. focused much of its energy on organizational needs such as the creation of cells both in the back country and in Moslem quarters of Algiers. Additionally, it engaged in the storage of arms and "settled scores" with Moslems who demonstrated a loyalty to the French.

Nearly all of the actions of the O.S. involved the use of terror and violence. In early 1949, the O.S. even attempted to assassinate Governor General Naegelen at Mostaganem. Following a few more minor actions, a heavy French response of repression annihilated the O.S. organization.

All of this set the stage for the beginnings of the Moslem rebellion. After close to five years of organizational disputes, mostly over what sort of actions to take, Algerian Moslems could not wait any longer. Hutchinson writes:

> The Algerian masses, now numbering about nine million, had no hope of attaining equality of freedom within the French political system as long as the European population maintained its dominant position. No political reforms were in sight, nor were there plans to develop Algeria, to relieve the poverty and ignorance of its peasants, or to promote social, cultural, economic, or educational advancement. The Algerian population was doomed to permanent inferiority. Although they were discontented and frustrated, the existing Algerian political parties dissipated their energies in internal quarrels that prevented the emergence of a unified opposition. The creation of a new nationalist organization determined to use violence was opportune (1978, p. 6).

Thus, on November 1, 1954 the revolution began. Kraft documents:

> That night armed bands struck in fifty different actions all across Algeria. Biskra was rocked by bomb explosions. In the Batna the French army barracks was attacked and two sentries killed. Two bombs exploded in downtown Algiers. Arris was besieged. At Boufarik the European-owned agricultural cooperative was destroyed. In the Tighanimine Gorge armed bands stopped a bus, hauled out a caid and two Europeans, and shot them on the spot. In the Kabylia two policemen were killed and a storage depot was burned to the ground. Near Oran two settler farms were burned, a motorist killed, a power plant attacked. From Cairo, the "Voice of the Arabs" announced the establishment of a Front of National Liberation (F.L.N.) (1961, p. 69).

Nearly all of the revolutionaries at this time were men who had previously been involved in politics before 1954 and had witnessed the absolute failure of attempting to work within the system. Many of the men also had military training acquired while working in the French army. Hutchinson suggests that the war experience assisted in highlighting the disparities existing between the settlers and Moslems in Algeria. She asserts:

> The most important aspect of the wartime experience, however, had been its contribution to a sense of self-respect arising from having successfully competed with the Frenchmen and having been fairly treated in the process (1978, p. 7).

Coming back home, the Algerians easily recognized the major differences in the lives of Europeans and Moslems. Furthermore, Algerians also began to view France as not so powerful in light of the French defeat in World War II and Indochina. The French were then seen as vulnerable.

In 1954, various Algerian revolutionaries formed the *Comite Revolutionnaire d'Unite et d'Action* (CRUA). This organization directed the very beginnings of the Algerian revolution. The initial CRUA president at the time was Mohammed Boudiaf, who worked primarily with five others: Mourad Didouche, Larbi Ben M'ttid, Mustapha Ben Boulaid, Rabah Bitat, and Belkkacem Krim. The CRUA also formed an exterior delegation in Cairo that included Ahmed Ben Bella, Hocine Ait Ahmed, and Mohammed Khider. From the exterior of Algeria, this delegation focused on building support for the Algerian revolutionaries.

When the revolution began, the *Army of National Liberation* (ALN) was created as the military branch of the FLN. At the start, the ALN had only a mere 300 men who were armed with rifles and a few bombs. Lacking arms, ammunition, logistics, communications, safe bases, and regular systems of command, the ALN focused first on meeting these needs. As a strategy, the ALN engaged in what it referred to as the "grease spot strategy." This involved placing a few people outside of the French population. Their task was to mix in with the local populations, from which they drew recruits, sentries, hiding places, and food.

Meanwhile, the CRUA divided Algeria up into five different zones called 'Wilayas,' in addition to the Sahara. Ben Boulaid was in charge of the Aures, Didouche the North Constantine, Krim the Kabylia, Bitat the Algerois, and Ben M'Hidi the Oranie. These five men would be in charge of commanding the differing struggles in each zone.

The revolutionary bands, first and foremost, aimed at deliberately creating disorder. Through assassinations, bombings, strikes, boycotts, economic sabotage, and attacks on security forces, the main focus of the campaign was to disrupt French peace. Kraft suggests that "by the end of 1956 the rebels had achieved striking success" (1961, p. 70). One of the main rebel leaders wrote during that time period:

> The small groups of the Army of National Liberation, badly armed and isolated from each other, have not only held in check the formidable forces of French colonialism, but have spread the grease spot to... the whole national territory (Kraft, 1961, p. 70).

Late in 1954, Ben Boulaid pulled back his forces into a group of tiny villages on the western slopes of the Aures Chelia region. In December, he then headed south and organized a southern supply line that went from Egypt through Lybia, to the south of Tunisia and then up through the Aures. Just two months later, in February 1955, Boulaid was captured by the French while on a mission in Tunisia.

In his place stepped Bahir Chihani, who had organized some 2,000 square miles of rebel territory in the Aures by March. One of these newly-formed bands ambushed a convoy of three military trucks on April 13, 1955, seizing rifles and a machine gun. Three days later, a different group intercepted a military jeep, burning the vehicle and slaughtering its two occupants—a French army major and a chaplain. On April 24, the actions continued. Another band halted two trucks and a jeep, killing four French soldiers and the French Administrator from the local area. With these actions in particular, Kraft points out that "this band won over thirty Moslems in the French army" (1961, p. 71).

On May 1, 1955, a band of rebels stole rifles and over 800 rounds of ammunition from a forestry station at Jemmapes. Using these weapons, the rebels wounded two policemen by gunfire the next day. Seven days later, on May 8, a forest guard at Collo was murdered. The town of El Milia was completely blocked off on May 10 by rebels who cut down all the telephone poles and obstructed the roadways by cutting trees. Two policemen attempting to reach this town were killed the next day.

In August, 1955, a coordinated strike demonstrated the power that lay within the rebels' brand of terrorism. Kraft refers to this effort as "the most spectacular armed coup achieved by the rebels in the whole course of the war" (1961, pp. 72-73). The action consisted of organized strikes taking place in at least thirty different areas during the same time period. Kraft writes:

> At Constantine in the south, bombs were exploded in a police station, a barracks, and a movie house, while political personalities working with the French, one of them a nephew of Ferhat Abbas, were assassinated. At Oved-Zenati crowds of screaming Moslem women, pushed on by the rebels, stormed the city hall. At Ain-Abid, St. Charles, and El Arrouch European pedestrians were shot in the street. At the zinc mines of El-Hallia, outside Philippeville on the coast, the European community was massacred (1961, p. 73).

During these actions, an estimated 123 people were killed, at least 71 of them European. In response, the French counterattacked and chased all of the rebel forces away from the areas.

Desiring to re-organize the resistance, the revolutionaries planned a Congress for August 1956. At the Congress, held in the Soummam Valley, the attendees established two groups, the *Comite de Coordination et d'Execution* (CCE) and the *Conseil National de la Revolution Algerienne* (CNRA). The CNRA would act as an oversight committee for the revolution. It was allocated the highest power of the resistance and was the only group chosen to be allowed to call a cease fire.

Two additional decisions were made at the Congress: that the interior of the resistance would take precedence over the exterior, and that political interests were deemed more crucial than military ones in the progress of the revolution. The interior taking precedence simply meant that efforts would focus less on obtaining foreign support (from groups in such places as Cairo) and more on matters within Algeria itself. Political interests were considered more important than military ones for the revolution, as the rebels realized that they were far outnumbered, both in troop strength and weapon resources. Their aim was not to fight in a conventional military style, nor was it to attempt on any level to annihilate the French army. Rather, the rebels used political terrorism to simply cause an ongoing atmosphere of unrest and uncontrollability for the French government and European settlers.

One main goal of the ALN, discussed in length at the Soummam Valley Congress, was simply survival. They felt that the best use of the ALN was to try to weaken the French army, not allowing it to claim a military victory. One of the leading resistance fighters, Belkacem Krim, stated, "If the French mass, we disperse. If they guard the cities, we ambush the mountain roads. If they chase us in the mountains, we hole up in the city. We don't want to waste our forces" (Kraft, 1961, p. 78).

A prime example of this type of terrorism stemmed from another decision made at the Soummam Valley Congress. After the Congress in 1956, a group called the *Zone Autonome d'Alger* (ZAA) began a bombing campaign, inflicting massive casualties on European civilians, in addition to assassinations of those supporting the French empire, both Algerian and European. The ZAA referred to the zone region of Algiers set up by the rebels and controlled by the CCE. This "zone" of Algeria was divided up into three main regions and then into smaller sectors, subsectors, quarters, groups, and cells. Organized hierarchically, this underground was expansive enough to include nearly every Moslem home and business within the city. Different groups had varying duties, including fundraising, supply, intelligence, communications, and direct action. Additionally, the organization had secret presses, a bomb-making laboratory, and large numbers of

154

women volunteers.

One of the main focuses of the ZAA was to leave bombs in public places. In Algiers alone, an estimated several hundred bombs were set off between the fall of 1956 and the summer of 1957. ZAA fighters had received shipments of plastic from Morocco for bomb construction by November 1956. In one of the more famous actions by the rebels inside the ZAA (also dramatized in the legendary film, *The Battle of Algiers*), a bomb was detonated at the Milk Bar on September 30, 1956. At this popular downtown cafe, thirty Europeans were severely wounded. On June 9, 1957 another bomb was set at the Casino de la Corniche, killing eleven Europeans and wounding many more.

In January, 1957, the *Algerian Trade Union* (UGTA) was instrumental in organizing a week-long general strike, specifically timed to coincide with a United Nations discussion about the fate of Algeria. For eight days, the FLN called on Algerian Moslems to not engage in any economic or military activity, as a demonstration of strength to the U.N. This was not an easy task as by 1957, some 400,000 French troops were committed to Algeria.

Just prior to the strike, the French had called in the 10th Paratroop Division, headed by General Jacques Massau. Under Massau, the 10th Division was given the responsibility of restoring and maintaining order in Algeria. During the eight-day strike, the paratroopers actively attempted to break up the Moslem effort. Massau's Division soon was faced with growing criticisms, even from moderates and liberals in France, for using controversial tactics, including the outright torturing of suspects in an attempt to break up the FLN network. At the end of the eighth day, Massau had failed to stop the strike, and the FLN resumed its active campaign for independence.

As the bombings, assassinations, and other assorted tactics continued through 1957, a new organization formed to target the French in their homeland. Resulting from yet another decision made at the 1956 Soummam Valley Congress, the FLN expanded its activities to France. The *Federation de France du FLN* (FFFLN) was set up with the task of raising funds abroad for the Algerian revolution.

On September 19, 1958, the CCE was replaced by the *Gouvernement Provisoire de la Republique Algerienne* (GPRA). This new political organization was set up with the specific strategy in mind of attempting to force negotiations on Paris. The group felt this could be accomplished through a growing dissatisfaction with continued unrest inside Algeria and from pressure mounting in the international arena for decolonization.

Throughout 1958, 1959, 1960 and early into 1961, sabotage, assassinations, and other violence steadily continued. Kraft documents that "at no time did the rate of killing fall below ten a day" (1961, p. 87). The response from both Massau's 10th Division and of newly-organized European militia groups was increasing violent repression on the entire Moslem community.

The first negotiations between the French and the FLN occurred in June 1960. This first meeting appeared to be nothing more than a symbolic gesture on the part of DeGaulle who offered the FLN little in the way of a true freedom. Hutchinson writes:

> DeGaulle's intractability apparently caused their failure (1960 negotiations), but he later adopted a more conciliatory position and resorted to the characteristic tactic of a referendum on a proposed policy of self determination for Algeria (1978, p. 16).

In January 1961, a referendum vote in France was finally favorable. All that remained to be decided was the governing relations between the Algerian state-to-be and France. But as the talks went on in 1961, disagreements continued to delay any successful outcome for the FLN. Hutchinson states:

> DeGaulle's victory over the military rebels reinforced the authority of his regime, and negotiations with the GPRA followed at Evian in May and at Lugrin in July. The talks again floundered, however, as the military faction within the FLN rejected concessions on issues such as control over Saharan oil and the status of the future European minority... The stalemate in negotiations was accompanied by random and indiscriminate violence by the OAS both in Algerian and France. The metropolitan population —weary of the war, disturbed by the brutal image of the French army in Algeria, and irritated by the OAS plasticages—was eager to see an end to the struggle (1978, p. 16).

A long-awaited agreement was finally reached at Evian in March

1962. The agreement, known as The Evian Accords, "granted the FLN the complete independence and sovereignty it had originally demanded in November 1954" (Hutchinson, 1978, p. 17). Through the use of a variety of tactics, predominately political terrorism, the FLN was able to accomplish its goal, not through defeating the French militarily, but by causing a relentless atmosphere of unrest and fear.

Hutchinson proclaims that after the eight years of violent revolution, Algeria, amazingly enough, transformed itself into a fairly stable country. She writes:

> By the time of the July 1 referendum approving independence, most of the Europeans had left Algeria, although the OAS and the FLN had declared a private cease-fire in June. Some violence and extortion were practiced by irregular Algerian groups that were not under the control of the FLN, but internal order was restored fairly rapidly. After a period of internal maneuvering and bargaining, Ben Bella emerged as president of Algeria, although he was destined to be overthrown by Boumedienne in a bloodless coup in 1965. Since that time, the Algerian state has been remarkably stable; few traces of the violent process by which independence was attained are now visible (1978, p. 17).

In today's global society, there are not many people who would speak of terrorism in a favorable light or promote it as a positive reformist or revolutionary tactic. Especially with the events on September 11, 2001 in the United States, the fear, sense of loss, mourning, and hatred that often accompanies terrorist acts were brought home to U.S. citizens in a way that is unparalleled by few, if any, events in U.S. history. But for the FLN, terrorism, glorious or not, was a primary means by which the Algerian independence was indeed achieved.

As stated earlier in the chapter, and as documented by Kraft, Hutchinson, and Fanon, the revolutionaries involved in the FLN previously had been politicians. They had attempted, with no success, to achieve their desired results through the more socially-accepted, French-approved, political process. These attempts at reform, to grant basic rights to Moslem Algerians, were repeatedly denied. As a result of the frustration with achieving no positive advancements through the peaceful political process,

Moslem Algerians felt they were forced into violent activity. Hutchinson states that "in Algeria revolutionary conditions existed because the incumbent regime had denied peaceful means of political protest" (1978, p. 23). From a standpoint of basic intelligence, it simply does not make sense to even expect that a regime that colonized a country by military force would willingly grant liberties to the colonized population simply because that population asked nicely.

The FLN organization engaged in both rural and urban terrorism. Its rural strategies consisted primarily of attempting to recruit additional support in the way of direct fighters, as well as safe houses and the destruction of the roadways and other means of accessibility between villages. Additionally, the FLN used terrorism to specifically draw intense repression from the French in particular locations, with the expectation that this would lead to more hostility toward the French and support for the FLN. Hutchinson asserts:

> During the first ten days of July 1955, the ALN soldiers were to enlist the aid of local peasants in destroying roads and bridges, cutting telephone lines, ruining European crops, and liquidating "traitors." During the next ten days, ALN units were to attack towns, villages, or local markets, where they were to "settle accounts" with recalcitrants. Those who had disobeyed orders not to smoke or drink were to be mutilated by having their noses or lips cut off. From the twentieth to the thirtieth of the month, the ALN was to mount ambushes against French troops. It was then to disappear for a week, leaving the population to face certain french retaliation (1978, p. 44).

Political terrorism applied by the FLN consisted of a variety of types and targets. 'Compliance terrorism' is simply acts of terror conducted to achieve compliance either from the direct opposition (the French government or military), the indirect opposition (the European population in Algeria), the colonized population (Moslem Algerians not already involved in the revolution), and/or the members of the revolutionary organizations. By far, the FLN's compliance terrorism was most successful in forcing the compliance of the Moslem Algerians and members of its own organization or affiliates. Through tactics such as the assassination of those expressing any loyalty to the French government, mutilation or assassination of those found to be violating FLN laws (such as the ban on smoking or drinking) the FLN successfully enforced a strict compliance within the country.

'Endorsement terrorism' was another category utilized by the FLN. This type of terrorism is designed to be more shocking and terrifying than compliance terrorism. The FLN primarily used three types of endorsement terrorism. A first sort aimed to create respect and support within the "resonant mass." Moslem Algerians not already in support of the revolutionary cause and the FLN were targeted in order to gain this backing.

Secondly, endorsement terrorism was used to purposely provoke repression from the French. The FLN felt that the more repression that came from the French government, the more the Moslem Algerian population would be forced into a revolutionary atmosphere. As the repression became increasingly intense, the FLN thought that would equate to more direct support from Algerians. Hutchinson suggests that:

> Spontaneous and indiscriminate violence by french civilians and military against Algerians alienated the masses from the regime, enhanced Algerian solidarity, and increased support for the FLN. It thus served the goals of isolating the French and of gaining popular support (1978, p. 49).

Endorsement terrorism also served as "a method of satisfying Algerian demands for vengeance against those whom they considered their persecutors" (Hutchinson, 1978, p. 49). After French actions of repression, there consistently were cries from the Moslem Algerian population for retaliation. With the FLN stepping in and creating retaliatory situations, the organization answered the population's calls. There is sound evidence indicating that the FLN knew exactly what it was doing by ordering units to disappear after they had performed terrorist acts. FLN leaders understood that in doing so, the local populations would be left to face the repression from the French. As a result, local populations would become hostile to the French and increasingly loyal and supportive of the FLN.

Another strategy used by the FLN was 'destructive' or 'antiregime terrorism.' This can be broken into two main categories. The first aims to isolate the entire European community from the Algerian population. This included the regime, the military, and civilian colonists.

Secondly, destructive or anti-regime terrorism attempted to weaken the French administration and society in Algeria through the creation of an insecure atmosphere. Destructive/anti-regime terrorism was used quite successfully by the FLN and played a major role in gaining the same independence demands in 1962 as originally asked in 1954.

'Isolation terrorism' was also used by the FLN to attempt to cut off sources of French intelligence among the Algerian population. The tactic also aimed to enforce a complete non-cooperation with the French and to discourage European contact with Moslem Algerians. How this category of terrorism differs from compliance or destructive terrorism in terms of tactics is slight; however, the primary division lies within the intent. While it is difficult, if not impossible, to know and fully comprehend the minds and true motives of the FLN with each particular action, some assumptions can be made based on outcomes, FLN behaviors, and the limited writings by rebels during that time period.

One of the most interesting aspects of the Algerian revolution was that various rebel groups, mainly the FLN but also precursory organizations, did not come into an already-existing revolutionary atmosphere inside Algeria. Instead these organizations actually seem to have *created* the atmosphere of revolt. While to a certain degree these groups were aided by a colonization process that left Moslem Algerians in a state of discontent, that state on its own was not enough to start and sustain a successful revolution. Hutchinson asserts that:

> By 1954, many Algerian nationalists had decided that political progress was impossible under French rule, but the ideology of nationalism had not yet stimulated the traditional, politically apathetic, and poverty-stricken Algerian population to action. Mass revolution was a future possibility, not a present reality. All the necessary pre-evolutionary conditions existed; what was needed was a catalyst, and the efforts of the FLN provided it. Terrorism became one means of mobilizing the Algerian people and forcing them to participate in political decisions by choosing one side or the other in the war for independence (1978, p. 131).

At the beginning of the uprising in November 1954, the FLN had little in the way of weapons, fighters, support, and other resources. The organization logically chose terrorism to further its political agenda, as it knew it had no other recourse. "Terrorism," writes Hutchinson, "a low cost and easily implemented strategy, was the only feasible alternative for the new nationalist organization because the FLN lacked both the necessary material resources (money, arms, soldiers) and active popular support" (1987, p. 135). Sticking to a focused goal of creating an insecure French Algerian state through terrorism, the FLN was the primary factor in forcing the French to grant independence in 1962.

Does the notion that the FLN *created* the revolutionary atmosphere have any important bearing today in justice struggles? Certainly. As a political activist living in the United States, I have repeatedly heard arguments (usually from the liberal sector) that on various levels in varying situations, violent or not, an increase in tactical severity is not needed. On many occasions, I have witnessed individuals pursuing legal means of protest object, on the above basis, to any suggestion that illegal, non-violent civil disobedience be implemented in their campaign. Similarly, I have heard the same opposition when others have argued for the ideological support of property destruction in the environmental movement, for example. *There isn't the public support for those kinds of actions. The public will be against us and our cause.* Ironically, many political activists within the United States, while strongly opposing even the mere idea of an escalation in tactics within their homeland and issue, will simultaneously offer ideological support to violent resistance and revolutions occurring in foreign lands. Perhaps the most recognizable recent example of this phenomenon is the support raised for the Zapatistas in Chiapas.

Assuming critics of controversial tactical escalation in the United States are correct—that the atmosphere within this country is far from ready for a revolution, far from accepting illegal activity including violence—could that atmosphere be provoked? Could that atmosphere be created by a revolutionary movement, as the FLN did in Algeria? Certainly, the political factors dividing the two cases are abundant, but are there any similarities? While privileged, white political activists (such as me) experience a certain degree of comfort, safety, and health in this country, is this the case for the majority of Americans? What level of discontent is there actually within the United States, once you get beyond the mind-numbing societal vices such as television, corporate media, drugs, alcohol, etc.? What level of discontent does there need to be to provoke a revolutionary atmosphere? How close *does* it need to resemble the case in Algeria? For those within the United States who advocate a political revolution, these questions are crucial.

Was the FLN justified in using violence, primarily terrorism, to advance Algerian independence? To Moslem Algerians involved in the struggle, they had lost all hope that nonviolent political activities were going to lead to a successful outcome, or to any progress for that matter. They had tried. Repeated attempts were made to confront the French on nonviolent terms, and they failed. The FLN felt it had no choice but to resort to violence if it truly wanted to see independence for Algeria. As a justification, the FLN looked upon the wealth of violence and injustice committed against the Algerian people by the French colonists. Hutchinson suggests that:

> References to the wrongs done to Algerians by the colonial regime served as emotional justification for violence against the enemy, especially civilians. Evoking an image of Algerian suffering under colon domination undoubtedly assuaged feelings of guilt and released inhibitions... Blaming the French for the neglect, cruelty, and illegitimacy of years of colonial rule and appealing for independence from this oppression took on a dual role as both motivation and rationalization (1978, p. 135).

In their own minds, the FLN members felt that what they were doing was right for themselves, for Moslem Algerians, and for the nation of Algeria.

Rather than wait for an indefinite length of time to see if nonviolent approaches would ever stand any chance of advancing Algeria toward independence, the FLN chose to act in the present, to target the French government using the only weapons and strategy they felt would work—revolutionary terrorism. On an individual level, this activity served to free the mind of the colonized. Fanon further describes this phenomenon: "at the level of individuals, violence is a cleansing force. It frees the native from his inferiority complex and from his despair and inaction; it makes him fearless and restores his self-respect" (1963, p. 94). Hutchinson argues that terrorism has the ability to provoke action from the previously inactive, forcing them to make choices. She writes:

> The Algerian case supports the proposition that populations do not act solely from ideological preference. Terrorism can influence attitudes as well as behavior,

however. It can polarize opinion: confronted with terrorism, a threatened person can no longer remain neutral or uninvolved in a conflict (1978, p. 31).

Mouloud Feraoun, himself part of the struggle, stated:

It is fair however to say that the very violence of terrorism has made no small number among us leave our ease and our laziness in order to reflect. Each one has been obliged to consider the problem, to examine his conscience, to tremble for his skin because the skin of the Kabyle is not worth much in the eyes of the terrorist (Hutchinson, 1978, p. 31).

Additionally, former FLN leader Amar Ouzegane proclaimed that "terrorism is a safety valve... It served as a means of psychological liberation from French rule, or individual self-control, and of organizational discipline by relieving militant impatience and tension" (Hutchinson, 1978, p. 33).

The case of the FLN in Algeria illustrates a situation where violent tactics seemed unavoidable and where the implementation of those tactics proved successful. While each and every situation has some differences in terms of circumstances, this particular example demonstrates how a successful violent revolution may not always fit into the circle of violence theory. It additionally demonstrates a successful example of a reliance on strategies outside those sanctioned by the given society or state. The Algerian revolution actually led to a state of calm in Algeria in the post-colonized time—at least for a while.

# CHAPTER FIVE

# North Vietnamese Strategies During the Vietnam War

The Vietnam War could easily be considered one of the darkest times in U.S. history. With all the manpower and military might contained within this global superpower, one could have easily expected, as it seemed most U.S. government officials did, that the United States and the Allied forces would win a quick and decisive victory over the North Vietnamese communists. Backing the Diem puppet government, which the U.S. government help put in power (in clear violation of the 1954 Geneva Convention on Indochina), Allied forces refused to learn a lesson taught previously to the French by the North Vietnamese—Vietnamese nationalists, the people of Vietnam, could not be overpowered by conventional military force. Even with superior weaponry and mobilization ability, the

United States and its Allied friends could not defeat the North Vietnamese militarily or politically. When the Paris Agreement was officially signed on January 27, 1973, the United States was forced to evacuate the South and retreat without any semblance of victory.

To proclaim that the United States completely lost the Vietnam War would perhaps be misleading. Even though the U.S. government failed to keep the Diem regime alive and to stop the spread of communism throughout Vietnam, economically it can be easily argued that the U.S. did indeed achieve at least one of its aims—opening up a consumer market for western goods in Indochina. By this rationale, it could be suggested that the United States, while not winning the battle in Vietnam, did not altogether lose the conflict either. For certain, the real losers of the Vietnam War were the more than one million men, women, and children killed on all sides of the conflict.

That said, the communist forces operating first in North Vietnam, and eventually spreading throughout the South, were able to withstand an amazing degree of force supplied against them by the U.S. and Allied militaries. By combining intelligent political and military strategies, the North was able to prolong the conflict to the point where, politically, the United States was forced to back out. How the Northern and Southern communist forces were able to effectively oppose U.S. aggression has certainly been a topic of interest globally since the Vietnam War.

In this chapter, a brief look will be taken at the political and military strategies that were used by the communist forces to drive the United States out of Indochina. By understanding these strategies, insight can be gained to assist in struggles for independence, liberty, and justice within the United States.

*

I will begin this study with a look at the North Vietnamese victory against the French at Dien Bien Phu in 1953. During this particular battle, General Vo Nguyen Giap—the highly respected general of North Vietnam's army—and his colleagues came up with a simple strategy. The French were allowed to concentrate their forces at Dien Bien Phu, a main junction of roadways between China, Laos and Northern Vietnam. After the French forces were gathered en mass, they were then to be surrounded and isolated from any reinforcements. Simultaneously, Viet Minh forces were to create attacks on the other French bases in the area to keep them occupied. This strategy worked, and after much bloodshed, the North Vietnamese were victorious.

At the Geneva Conference on Indochina in 1954, all nations involved agreed to "respect the independence, sovereignty, unity, and territorial integrity of Vietnam, Cambodia, and Laos" (MHIV, 2002, p. 3). Additionally, all foreign troops were required to withdraw from Indochina. A free general election was also to be held within two years from when the conference ended to unify Vietnam. After the conference ended on July 21, 1954, the cease-fire agreement during the next two years provided that the 17th parallel would become a temporary military boundary line in Vietnam. In the North, the People's Army of Vietnam (PAVN) controlled the territory, and in the South, the French Allied army still occupied most of the area. On May 13, 1955, the last foreign soldiers withdrew from North Vietnam.

As the United States had been providing support to the French military in the conflict, they too were a participant at the 1954 Geneva Convention. Even so, President Eisenhower announced that the United States "is not bound by the terms of this agreement" (MHIV, 2002, pp. 3-4). In June 1954, the U.S. brought Ngo Dinh Diem in from the United States to establish a puppet government in South Vietnam. Immediately the U.S. National Security Council approved an emergency program of economic and military assistance to Diem in South Vietnam. Furthermore, the U.S. replaced French advisors with American advisors to Diem. A Southeast Asia Military Alliance (SEATO) was then created, consisting of U.S. Allied and Satellite nations. In September 1954, SEATO placed South Vietnam, Laos, and Cambodia under what it called its "umbrella of protection." Just two months prior, in mid July, Ho Chi Minh, in a direct response to SEATO, publicly declared, "the U.S. is not only the enemy of the people of the world, it has now become the principle, direct enemy of the people of Vietnam, Laos, and Cambodia" (MHIV, 2002, p. 4).

In November 1954, Eisenhower sent General Collins to Saigon to draw up a plan for the American role in South Vietnam. Named the Collins plan, the proposal called for direct U.S. support for the Diem regime. It supported the creation of an army for Diem that would be formed with U.S.-supplied equipment and training. The army would also be operating under the command of the United States military. Lastly, the Collins plan declared the need to enact social and economic programs such as the resettlement of the population, land reform, changing tax laws, etc. to maintain control and increase the income coming into the U.S.-backed

Diem regime. Perhaps most importantly, the plan would pave the way for U.S. economic interests to invade South Vietnam. The Military History Institute in Vietnam, in its 2002 book *Victory in Vietnam: The official history of the People's Army of Vietnam 1954-1975*, describes perhaps one of the main objectives of the Collins plan:

> These programs would benefit the capitalist and landlord classes and would allow U.S. capitalists to invest in South Vietnam. This was to be implemented through a puppet regime and puppet army and was an extremely dangerous form of disguised, covert colonialism on the part of the imperialists (p. 15).

By June 1955, the French expeditionary army completed its withdrawal from South Vietnam, in accordance with an agreement reached between France and the United States. The U.S. government then re-organized the local army, previously under French control, into a puppet army subservient to the Diem regime and ultimately the United States.

In March 1956, the Diem puppet government held elections attempting to legitimize the regime. This came after refusing to follow the Geneva Accords and meet with the Government of the Democratic Republic of Vietnam to discuss holding free elections to unify the nation. The Military History Institute in Vietnam describes the plan of the Diem regime:

> The U.S.-Diem clique made "denouncing communists and eliminating communists" their national policy and they savagely terrorized Party members, patriots who had participated in the resistance against the French, people sympathetic toward the revolution, and anyone who did not agree with their policy of selling out the nation, serving as lackeys of the American imperialists, and dividing the nation and the Vietnamese race (2002, p. 20).

Ho Chi Minh was well aware of the impending threat posed to North Vietnam by the United States. He stated in April 1956 during his closing speech to the 9th Plenum of the Party Central Committee:

> When assessing the prospects for achieving unification

of Vietnam through peaceful means, we must always remember that the enemies of our people, the American imperialists and their lackeys, still occupy one-half of our country, and that they are now preparing for war. Therefore, we must always raise high the flag of peace, but we must at the same time also raise high our defenses and our vigilance (MHIV, 2002, p. 18).

As a result of this perceived threat, the Party Central Committee, during the 12th Plenary Session in March 1957, approved a five-year plan to build the army and consolidate national defense in North Vietnam. From 1955 to 1959, the North Vietnamese government would attempt to increase its combat strength and readiness before any large-scale war broke out. It used this time as a serious preparation for what was considered to be a "large-scale war of national salvation against the Americans" (MHIV, 2002, p. 22).

Meanwhile in South Vietnam, the United States and Diem, within two years, had built up an armed force with 150,000 regular soldiers and 100,000 Regional Force militia, and police troops. The South Vietnamese people faced daily terror as anyone judged as opposing the Diem regime became targeted for severe repression. Debates waged between South Vietnamese nationalists at the time over whether or not to even attempt armed struggle against Diem and the Americans. It was obvious that Diem, backed by the Americans, had superior strength and firepower.

In August 1956, Le Duan, a member of the Politburo of the Central Committee, who had been ordered by Ho Chi Minh and the Politburo to lead the revolutionary movement in South Vietnam, wrote *The Tenets of the Revolution* for the South. In his proclamation, Duan affirmed that the road to advance the revolution in South Vietnam "was the road of revolutionary violence" (MHIV, 2002, p. 43). Yet, during a December 1956 conference held by the Cochin China Party Committee, a resolution was passed which sought to delay the use of armed struggle in the South. The resolution stated:

At the present time, when the entire South is conducting a political struggle, it is not yet time to launch guerrilla warfare. Instead our policy should be to conduct armed propaganda operations. Armed propaganda units are armed operation units. Propaganda team members and cadre will reveal the true face of the enemy to the people. They will encourage hatred, develop revolutionary organizations among the masses, suppress enemy thugs and intelligence agents, win the support of enemy troops, proselytize puppet troops and government personnel to support our mass struggle movements, and limit any combat with the enemy that might reveal our forces... (MHIV, 2002, pp 43-44).

In 1957, the Diem regime, with the assistance of the United States, mobilized a large percentage of their regular troops, local armed forces, and local government officials to increase acts of repression and terror against the South Vietnamese people. They began concentrating the population and formed "new farming land" areas and "population concentration" areas. A primary goal of this societal re-organization was to separate the people from the revolutionaries. Additionally, the Diem government established a new prison system for every local area, where they tortured and murdered Party members and people sympathetic to the revolution. Diem also made a strong effort to suppress all demonstrations and strikes by the workers and laboring classes in the cities. Those involved in the protests who were caught were subject to, at minimum, severe torture.

By 1959, the revolutionary forces in South Vietnam totaled 139 platoons in the Cochin China area, 34 platoons in the mountainous regions of the Interzone 5 area, and hundreds of covert, self-defense units at the village level. With the sharp increase in both political and military revolutionary forces and activity in South Vietnam, the Diem regime in March 1959 declared a state of war in South Vietnam. In May, Diem implemented law Number 10/59, which stated that anyone guilty of an act of "opposition to the regime" could be executed on the spot without a trial. Naturally, after the implementation of such laws and the general, ongoing repression by the Diem government against the people in the South, hatred against the regime was growing.

In January 1959, feeling confident of the growth of revolutionary forces in the South, the Party Central Committee held its 15th Plenary Session in Hanoi. At this meeting the committee decided to:

liberate South Vietnam from the yoke of oppression imposed by the imperialists and the feudalists; to secure national independence and grant land to the farmers; to complete the people's national democratic revolution in South Vietnam, and to build a peaceful, unified, indepen-dent, democratic, and prosperous Vietnam nation (MHIV, 2002, p. 50).

As far as the strategies to liberate the South, the Central Committee stated:

> The revolutionary methods to be used to accomplish these goals were to utilize the strength of the masses, relying primarily on the political forces of the masses (operat-ing in conjunction with large or small armed forces, depending on the situation) to overthrow the imperialist and feudalist rulers and establish a revolutionary regime belonging to the people. In order to achieve this goal, we must make vigorous preparations aimed at launching a popular uprising to overthrow the U.S.-Diem regime (MHIV, 2002, p. 50).

The Party Central Committee felt that the 15th Plenum Resolution demon-strated offensive revolutionary thinking and confirmed that for them, the liberation of South Vietnam would rely upon revolutionary violence.

As a result of the Resolution of the 15th Plenum of the Party Central Committee, the general Military Party Committee intensified its efforts to construct a modern, regular army. This was also based on what were considered successful results of the first military five-year plan (1955-1959), which built up the military forces. Preparations were then made to send the army to South Vietnam to join the resistance.

In May 1959, a staff agency under the General Military Party Committee was created to study the establishment of a supply route from North to South Vietnam. A regiment known as the Military Transportation Group 559 was created on May 19, 1959 to fulfill this task. By late sum-mer the group had built the supply road, and on August 20, 1959 the first shipment of supplies made its way South on what would be known as the Ho Chi Minh Trail.

In early 1959, uprisings in the South arose from the repressive tactics implemented by the Diem regime. In the mountainous regions of Interzone 5, many armed uprisings broke out, conducted largely by Viet-namese ethnic minorities who opposed Diem's attempts to place them into concentration camps. On February 7, 1959, in the Binh Thuan province, the Ra Giai tribal people rose up and destroyed the Diem regime concentration areas at Brau and Dong Day in the Bac Ai district. In April, they destroyed the Tam Ngan concentration area. Also in 1959, the Cham and Hre ethnic minorities in Tho Lo, Phu Yen province, and the Ede, Gia Rai, Xe Dang, etc., in Ta Booc and Mang Khenh, Kontum province, conducted a series of uprisings. In the process they killed many of Diem's forces and abandoned their old villages to return to the jungles, where they established new living quarters (an illegal move, according to a recent Diem regime law).

On August 28, 1959, while Diem troops were conducting searches on all the villages to force people to go out and vote in the election for Diem's national assembly, the people of Tra Quan, Tra Khe, Tra Nham, Tra Phong, and Tra Lanh villages launched simultaneous uprisings. The next day, Diem forces occupying outposts at Da Lip, Ta Lat, Tam Rung, and Nuoc Vot, fled their posts in terror. The Military History Institute of Vietnam documents even more occurrences at the end of August:

> The revolutionary masses, led by the soldiers of Unit 339, attacked the two remaining large enemy outposts in Tra Bong, located at Eo Chim and Eo Reo. After a two-day siege and after crippling an enemy company from the district capital that tried to come to their rescue, on 31 August the outposts at Eo Chim and Eo Reo were both taken (2002, p. 56).

In December 1959, the Region 8 Party Committee in central Cochin China held an expanded meeting to prepare for mass uprisings. Upon the completion of the meeting, the Party Committee decided to "mobilize the masses to rise up to break the enemy's grip and seize control of the rural areas" (MHIV, 2002, p. 60). The regional committee decided to begin the massive uprisings on January 17, 1960.

On that day, the people of Dinh Thuy village, along with an assault unit, rose up, surrounded, and destroyed a group of ten in Diem's forces. During the next two days, on the 18th and 19th, the people in the Phuoc Hiep and Binh Khanh areas also rose up and seized control. From January 17 to 24, the people in forty-seven villages in the districts of Mo Cay, Giong Trom, Chau Thanh, Ba Tri, and Thank Phu rose up in a massive simultaneous insurrection. According to the Military History Institute of Vietnam, the period, named the "week of uprisings by the entire population," was deemed quite successful, as "in 22 villages tyrants were eliminated, outposts were destroyed, the enemy's governing apparatus was crushed, and the entire village and its hamlets were completely liberated" (2002, p. 62).

In response to this insurrectionist activity, the Diem government sent an estimated 10,000 troops to encircle and clear the villages of Dinh Thuy, Phuoc Hiep, and Binh Khanh. The force, which included marines, paratroopers, Rangers, 70 military vehicles, 17 naval vessels and the entire Regional Force of the province, "viciously shot and killed people, burned and looted, and committed many extremely barbarous crimes. They buried 36 youths alive and murdered 80 others" (MHIV, 2002, p. 63).

The next day, North Vietnamese troops ambushed Diem's forces at Phuoc Hiep village, killing fifty troops and capturing a large number of weapons. The battle continued to other nearby villages and lasted for ten days before the communist forces declared a victory. The Military History Institute of Vietnam describes the unilateral effort by the entire province against the Diem troops:

> They fought the enemy for ten straight days, inflicting over 300 casualties on the enemy force. The people of the villages enthusiastically fed and housed our troops and guerrillas and cared for our wounded. Mothers and sisters tried to win over enemy troops or to detain or deceive them, thereby enabling our troops to move forward and attack the enemy (2002, p. 63).

This particular uprising was considered so victorious by the North Vietnamese military and government that it was used to educate soldiers for future battles.

> The victorious uprising of the people of Ben Tre provided a model for uprisings in the lowlands and for the tactic of conducting uprisings to seize government authority at the grass-roots level by using mass political forces as our primary weapon with an armed self-defense force element to provide support and serve as the assault spearhead of the uprising. This tactic created a composite power of revolutionary violence made up of two forces: political forces

and armed forces (MHIV, 2002, pp. 63-64).

The last sentence in the above statement has incredibly important connotations for the North Vietnamese efforts. Through this two-pronged sword of political and armed strategies, they would ultimately win the conflict against the United States global superpower.

In the United States, President Lyndon Johnson officially decided to send ground troops into Vietnam in 1965, no doubt due to the growing conflict there, in which the U.S. had already played a major part. This decision came just months after he had ordered a military strike in response to the alleged Gulf of Tonkin incident. In February 1965, in response to two attacks on "military advisors" at Pleiku and Quy Nhon, Johnson retaliated with Operation Rolling Thunder—a bombing campaign of North Vietnam. Additionally, Johnson was able to quickly get the Tonkin Gulf Resolution passed by Congress which was "a de facto declaration of war" (Taylor, 1999, p. 62). This resolution gave him unlimited power to respond to the alleged aggression from the North.

Sandra Taylor, in her 1999 book *Vietnamese Women at War: Fighting for Ho Chi Minh and the Revolution*, states:

> When the limited bombing did not succeed in bringing Hanoi to heel, Johnson decided to send American ground forces to Vietnam. Their first orders were to patrol the perimeters of the large air base constructed at Da Nang, protecting it from guerrilla attack so the ARVN could engage the enemy in the field. But when their presence had little effect, he sent American forces to engage in combat (p. 62).

So began the full U.S. involvement which would last until the Paris Accords were signed in 1973.

\*

In 1945, when Ho Chi Minh achieved power, he planned his political strategy on three assumptions. William Warbey documents these in his book, *Ho Chi Minh and the Struggle for an Independent Vietnam*:

First, that the liberation of Vietnam would be part of

a general liberation movement throughout the peasant countries of Southeast Asia; second, that in each country (except probably Thailand), the weak native bourgeoisie (mainly comprador merchants and managers of foreign capitalist enterprises and plantations) would cooperate readily with the peasants, who vastly outnumbered them, in the creation of a new, non-capitalist society; and third, that the advanced agrarian economy of Vietnam, with its exportable surplus of rice, fruits, vegetables, tea, rubber, minerals, and craft goods, would, once the consequences of war neglect and foreign plundering had been overcome, provide sufficient sustenance for the whole population during a prolonged and enforced transition to a socialist society (1972, pp. 114-115).

Ho Chi Minh's three assumptions were understood by the resistance movement and played a crucial part in the creation of the political and military strategies.

The proper combining of political and military strategies was called *Dau tranh* (which translates, roughly, into *The Struggle*). In Dau tranh strategy, it was believed that through the marriage of violence and politics, victory could be achieved. According to one PAVN (People's Army of Vietnam) soldier, "Dau tranh is all important to a revolutionary. It shapes his thinking, fixes his attitudes, dictates his behavior. His life, his revolutionary work, his whole world is Dau tranh" (Pike, 1986, p. 217).

Inside Dau tranh strategy lay an important social myth involving *khoi nghia* (general uprising) and the "General Strike." This myth consisted of the notion that "some day all the workers of the world will simultaneously launch a general strike, bringing all industry, transportation, society itself to a standstill; then the workers will simply pick up the controls of power" (Pike, 1986, p. 218).

The strategy of Dau tranh, or the proper combination of political and military tactics, was, at least in theory, applicable to a short war in which victory might be had within a few months. However, the real strength of dau tranh seemed to be in its ability to succeed in deliberately drawn-out conflicts. Ho Chi Minh wrote:

Time is the condition to be won to defeat the enemy. In military affairs time is of prime importance. Time ranks

first among the three factors necessary for victory, coming
before terrain and support of the people. Only with time
can we defeat the enemy (Pike, 1986, p. 218).

Ho Chi Minh and other Vietnamese strategists saw several advantages to a protracted conflict. For one, it could allow a heightened
degree of strength for the Vietnamese against the United States, which
had far greater size and power. By allowing the conflict to appear endless,
the larger force might be worn down. Not only could this have an effect
militarily with ongoing casualties, but also—and perhaps even more importantly—the psychological effect could greatly lower troop morale. It
was thought that if the enemy's troops could not see any end in sight, only
an ongoing battle, they would be less motivated in their mission and even
less firmly attached to their particular side.

The Vietnamese felt that protracted conflict dissolves the ability
for the external world to actually understand what is occurring. They saw
this as creating a situation of easy manipulation of external perception.
Pike writes:

> Aggression is not seen as aggression but as liberation.
> Incumbent government measures become not normal
> self-protection but offensive and somehow illegitimate
> actions, and the incumbent is held solely responsible for
> contributing to the protraction of the conflict (1986, p.
> 219).

But, once again, one of the most important points in Dau tranh strategy
was the ability to convince the opposing side that you could fight a protracted war of indefinite length, even if in reality you could not.

Organization was another key factor in the success of Dau tranh.
Pikes writes, "In fact, organization is the great god of Dau tranh strategy
and counts for more than ideology or military tactics" (1986, pp. 220-
221). The Vietnamese felt that the organization of the struggle must reach
and encompass all of the people. "Since the goal is a totally new social
order, this levies on the participant the demand of total involvement, total
immersion. It touches all persons of the society at all points of their existence" (p. 221). Communication abilities were the primary benefit of organization, and through proper organization and communication, effective
mobilization became possible. With mobilization, the Dau tranh strategy

insisted, comes motivation. "In the end, victory goes to the side that gets the best organized, and can most successfully disorganize the other" (p. 221).

This extensive organization and mobilization reached far beyond the typical military men and into all members of Vietnamese society. Taylor writes, "the conflict that engulfed Vietnam from 1945-1975 was a family affair, not only a war for independence from foreign control, but a struggle that frequently included all family members" (1999, p. 93). Women played a major role in various aspects of the struggle and were encouraged "to use revolutionary violence to kill Americans" whenever possible (p. 69). To aid in this task, a large percentage of women were armed with Russian weapons and taught how to use them.

Men and women weren't the only ones involved, as children also took part in the struggle. Older children played an active role in the actual fighting and defense, and children of varying ages were often given the tasks of planting mines, digging traps, carving stakes, and other useful jobs. Taylor asserts, "Boys also participated in sports programs that prepared them to join the guerrilla forces. Girls helped prepare medicines and bandages, and they mended clothing" (1999, p. 96). It truly was a struggle that left no one untouched or without involvement.

Dau tranh strategy, as previously stated, can be studied in two separate categories: armed and political. In armed Dau tranh, the tactics included regular military actions, but also such unconventional forms as institutionalized assassination, kidnapping, and other guerrilla-like operations. Armed Dau tranh was never thought of in purely military terms, but always in the political context, which was considered the highest importance. The day-to-day armed Dau tranh activities included such actions as guerrilla raids; tank assaults; ambushes; harassing fire; sniper assaults; destruction of roads, canals, and harbor facilities; assassinations; kidnapping and selective terror.

The strategy of armed Dau tranh, especially early in the war, was primarily based on the Chinese Three Stage Guerrilla War concept. While this concept was never fully implemented in Vietnam, it provided a primary backdrop from which Vietnamese strategies emerged. The three stages relate to categories of development. They include static-dynamic, military-political, and offensive-defensive terms.

In Stage One, the guerrilla's primary task is the hit, run, and hide scenario. Constant activity is stressed, involving infrequent offensive raids, in which a great degree of mobility is required. The main goal in

Stage One is to "decimate the enemy army piecemeal, weaken then eliminate the government's administrative control of the countryside, and block counter-efforts such as the various pacification programs" (Pike, 1986, p. 224). These efforts must be accomplished while keeping the guerrilla units intact. Therefore, the guerrilla chooses the targets wisely, is never caught in a direct battle, and strikes and retreats into invisibility.

Often referred to as the equilibrium level, Stage Two moves toward equalization as equilibrium can be seen between the two sides. While in Stage One, the main rule was conserving strength at all costs, in this scenario, *van dong chien* (war of movement) is practiced to strike the enemy even harder. As the stage progresses, the enemy is forced on the defensive and in a retreat mode. Pike writes:

> As the stage progresses the incumbent increasingly becomes defensive. He ceases active opposition in favor of consolidating what he has left and retreats to urban enclaves on the coast. The smell of defeat hangs over those enclaves. Guerrilla spirit soars. Government abandonment of the countryside enables the guerrilla to rapidly build his strength in men and material. The war escalates. Battles are larger and more frequent. Regiments and even divisions appear; the war becomes less guerrilla-like and resembles a conventional small-scale war (1986, p. 224).

The final stage in the Chinese Three Stage Guerrilla War concept was never fully implemented in Vietnam. However, certain parts were included into the overall strategy. These elements largely involved deception and trickery on various levels.

When the American and other Allied ground troops arrived in Vietnam in 1965, General Giap and his High Command needed to restructure the armed Dau tranh strategy. Giap realized that a new plan was needed to contend with the advantage held by the Allied forces in soldiers, weapons, and mobility. His answer was to develop two armed Dau tranh strategies, or what he referred to as "fighting methods." The first was the occasional military assault that Giap labeled the "coordinated fighting method" (*cach danh hop dong*). This consisted of a medium-sized attack against a relatively important target, such as an enemy battalion headquarters. Pike asserts, "The target is destroyed with surgical precision, and the impact on the enemy is not military so much as psychological" (1986, p.

226).

The second fighting method tactic Giap called the "independent fighting method." In this tactic, dozens of smaller actions are taken daily. The goal is not for any one of the small actions to have a large impact, but to have an overall, cumulative effect. Giap thought this would have a devastating effect on the enemy, raising anxiety levels and diminishing self-confidence. This tactic also allowed for small losses to be taken as long as the overall effect of destroying the enemy's initiative was accomplished.

These two techniques are then combined into one campaign in which military activity escalates to the point of a "comprehensive offensive." At the peak of the campaign, a massive psychological blow is delivered by destroying a politically or psychologically important target. When captured, this target destroys the enemies' will to continue fighting.

For three years, General Giap pursued this armed Dau trah strategy until it reached perhaps its purest form in the 1967-68 Winter-Spring Campaign, the main portion of which was the 1968 Tet Offensive. For Giap, this campaign was a military disaster, as he learned that his idea of Dau tranh was too costly to sustain against the Allied Forces. Giap became convinced that armed Dau trah strategy again needed to be re-worked.

After a few months, a new form of Dau tranh emerged called Neo Revolutionary Warfare, or the "Super-Guerrilla" concept. This new strategy was created by reforming the original Chinese three-stage methodology. The key difference in the new idea was the assertion that victory could be achieved at Stage Two of the guerrilla war without advancing to Stage Three. Achieving victory at Stage Two would ideally eliminate the concentration of forces where the enemy would then have the advantage of massive firepower. This assertion that victory could be won at Stage Two was a drastic change from the past thinking of Chairman Mao Tse-tung and Lin Piao, who felt the three stages were necessary for victory.

From 1968 to 1972, this new form of warfare was practiced extensively in Vietnam. "The purpose," Pike writes, "was not to decimate the enemy's military force but to occupy it, wear it out, limit its initiative" (1986, p. 228). Additionally, though, the other older types of armed Dau tranh continued to be practiced simultaneously with the new. This largely occurred as a result of divisions in thought within the PAVN High Command.

As mentioned previously, armed Dau tranh strategy was never isolated and used apart from the political struggle. In fact, throughout the war, in terms of the amount of activity, political Dau tranh actually was of greater importance and was used with a far greater frequency. It was this marriage of armed and political Dau tranh—a bit heavier on the political side—that made the Vietnam War fairly unique.

Political Dau tranh is divided into three main *van* ("action among") programs. The first is called *dich van* ("action among the enemy"). In this program, dich van simply referred to "action among the people who are controlled by the enemy." In the Vietnam War dich van consisted of the nonmilitary activity directed primarily at the pro-government South Vietnamese, as well as the Americans and others abroad.

One portion of this program involved a heavy mass media campaign. Pike suggests that this consisted of such activities as:

> during the weekend surreptitiously placing leaflets in students' desks in a provincial school; stopping cars along a main highway and taking passengers to a nearby woods to be lectured by an agit-prop cadre; floating a raft containing the effigies of President Lyndon Johnson and Madame Nho Dinh Nhu in obscene postures down a river, past a teeming marketplace; interpreting the war and world events for Radio Liberation broadcasts; creating systematic rumor campaigns; armed propaganda teams visiting villages to stage dramas that were part entertainment and part propaganda (1986, p. 236).

Aside from the mass media campaigns, the main essence of the dich van program was using the social movement as a means of communication. The primary tool in this strategy was the *struggle movement*, a village-level method of gaining support and enlisting troops. The struggle movement was itself divided into two categories: the face-to-face struggle meeting (which was specifically for propaganda in depth) and the "coacting" struggle meeting (to spread agitation). The coacting struggle meeting also had the primary task of raising the revolutionary consciousness at the village level.

Followers and practitioners of the dich van program were asked never to deviate from two basic principles. The first was that any and all struggles required complete advance planning and control during the execution. Opposing the idea that the struggle was simply a group of people spontaneously protesting a specific act or condition, the Vietnamese military strategists rather felt that nothing should be left up to chance; everything in the struggle should be performed according to the advanced plans. The second basic principle was that the Vietnamese should avoid struggles that they did not organize and could not control. Since without control one cannot be certain of any outcome, the only struggles to be involved with were those that could be planned for and controlled.

Specifically among the Americans, the dich van program operated on two levels:

> strategic, to shape perception by the Americans so as to convince them victory in Vietnam was impossible, and, therefore, undermine the war at home and American diplomacy worldwide; and tactical, that is, power nullification, to limit American response in Vietnam by inhibiting full use of American military capability there (Pike, 1986, p. 239).

Dich van techniques were used to specifically target American air power. During the 1965-68 air war period and again during the Christmas bombing of 1972, "a major dich van campaign was launched to force cessation of the air attacks" (p. 141).

The second of the three van programs was *binh van* ("action among the military"). Its primary goal was to weaken the governmental structure and GVN armed forces by non-military methods. This was to be accomplished through encouraging defection and attempting to lower the morale of individual enemy soldiers. Organized into special teams, the binh van program used simple communication on a small scale to influence the enemy and lower their enthusiasm to fight.

Lastly, the third and final van section of the van programs was referred to as *dan van* ("action among the people"). This directly applied to the people under the control of the National Liberation Front - People's Revolutionary Government (NLF-PRG). Consisting of administrative and motivational activity, the dan van program sought to organize the areas already under Communist control.

There were three main objectives of the dan van program: organization, recruitment, and financial. The main goal of the organization objective was to create an organization that the local villager could fit into and want to be a part of. The recruitment objective was simply the next step—to recruit the civilian population into organizations and naturally into the military. With the financial objective, the main motives were obvious—to raise funds by way of taxes, the "Viet Cong War Bonds," or by direct collection.

In addition to the organization of all areas under Communist control, the dan van program played a major role in local village administration, food production, medical care, and making sure the whole administrative system was functioning properly. By being involved with these tasks, the dan van program had two purposes. One was the actual functionality of providing a system for people to live under and take part in. Secondly, the program gave off (or at least attempted to) an external appearance of "a peaceful, tranquil place with an advanced egalitarian social order where not only hostility but even animosity had vanished" (Pike, 1986, p. 246).

Using Dau tranh strategy, the Vietnamese were able to sustain a prolonged conflict with the United States which, to reiterate, had much stronger military capabilities. Pike writes:

> The Allied forces in Vietnam had clear advantage in warfare's traditional criteria, mass and movement - they had more men, more firepower, greater logistical resources. But this proved of only limited advantage. It was difficult to bring the massive available power to bear against a force that was everywhere and nowhere, with no fixed command center, with no territory it was obliged to defend, or if such territory existed it was off limits (1986, p. 250).

That said, the North Vietnamese were never actually able to militarily defeat the United States. At the end of the battle, the South Vietnamese military force was left basically intact. The real victory came for the North Vietnamese through their political Dau tranh campaign that, as Pike suggests, was never fully understood and defeated by the Americans.

By far, the most important and successful trait of the Dau tranh strategy was its ability to last indefinitely in a prolonged conflict. Very few, if any, militaries, on a global basis, are prepared to and can effectively fight a lengthy battle where an end is never in sight. Pike writes, "the advocate of dau tranh strategy is proven correct in his basic calculation: that no democratic society—no society perhaps—can fight a fifty-year war" (1986, p. 252).

The People's Army of Vietnam (PAVN) also built and utilized an elaborate underground tunnel system as part of its guerrilla war. Sometimes consisting of four levels below the ground, the tunnels provided the out-gunned people's army with needed refuge and supplies. Hospitals, meeting rooms, weapons storage, sleeping chambers and kitchens all were commonly housed in the tunnels. In one of the only known tunnel manuals ever issued by the Communists, an unknown author writes:

> If the tunnels are dug so as to exploit their effectiveness fully, the villages and hamlets will become extremely strong fortresses. The enemy may be several times superior to us in strength and modern weapons, but he will not chase us from the battlefield, because we will launch surprise attacks from within the underground tunnels... we can see that underground tunnels are very favorable for armed forces as limited as ours, in strength and weaponry (Mangold & Penycate, 1985, pp. 69-70).

These tunnels played an instrumental part in the success of the Vietnamese, especially early on in the war. Later, when the U.S. B-52's began heavy bombing campaigns, they did destroy much of the tunnel systems, yet the tunnels by that time had already served an important purpose.

In addition to the tunnels, regular campsites for the PAVN soldiers had to meet three main criteria. First, they were to be built under dense foliage to be hidden from aerial view. Secondly, the distance between the campsites had to be close enough for soldiers to reach each within a single night's march. Lastly, the campsites had to be located in areas that would provide defensive capabilities.

Another important inclusion in the Vietnamese strategy was the use of revolutionary terrorism. According to Lanning and Cragg in their book *Inside the VC and the NVA: The Real Story of North Vietnam's Armed Forces*, the terrorism as practiced by the PAVN had three primary goals: "intimidation of the people, elimination of enemies, and propaganda" (1992, p. 174). The intimidation of the people amounted to assassinations, abductions, and harassment of the South Vietnamese population to force its cooperation. Additionally, this was used to gain laborers and porters for tax collection, food, supplies, and "to prevent the local inhabitants from giving intelligence to the Allied Forces" (pp. 186-187). The elimination of enemies specifically referred to those among the South Vietnamese who were deemed as disloyal or traitors. Terrorism, in the form of propaganda, also provided a demonstration of strength and presence of the people's army. Attacks gave inspiration to the people's army soldiers as well as publicity to their struggle.

Giap was frequently quoted defining guerrilla warfare as "the means by which the people of a weak, badly equipped country can stand up against an aggressive army possessing better equipment and techniques" (Pike, 1966, p. 34). Surely, this definition described, at least in part, what the Americans were up against during the Vietnam conflict. In a speech before a joint session of the U.S. House of Representatives and Senate on May 25, 1961, President John F. Kennedy described the threat of guerrilla warfare as practiced by the North Vietnamese communists. He stated:

> Yet their aggression is more often concealed than open. They have fired no missiles; and their troops are seldom seen. They send arms, agitators, aid, technicians and propaganda to every troubled area. But where fighting is required, it is usually done by others, by guerrillas striking at night, by assassins striking alone, assassins who have taken the lives of 4,000 civil officers in the last 12 months in Vietnam, by subversives and saboteurs and insurrectionists, who in some cases control whole areas inside of independent nations (p. 33).

While the armed guerrilla tactics surely frustrated the Americans and other Allied forces in Vietnam by allowing the war to continue on for an unknown period, the true strength of the Vietnamese communists appeared to be their political strategies. They were extremely effective at gaining the support of and mobilizing the population into action, demonizing the enemy, and creating a highly successful means of propaganda organization. In this sense, their tactics appear quite similar to the Zapatistas in Chiapas, Mexico. While they too openly carried arms, their main weapon up to this point had been a direct type of political strategy—communication and propaganda. Of course the Zapatista means of propaganda distribution has been heavily modernized with the use of the internet, but the key idea remains the same: Effective communication and propaganda are the key to winning most conflicts.

Could the North Vietnamese communists have defeated the Diem regime, the United States and unified all of Vietnam without the use of armed force and violence?  As I suggested earlier in this chapter, the non-violent, non-military tactics used by the North Vietnamese forces were one of the primary keys to their success.  However, those tactics could not have been separated from armed action.  In fact, nearly all of the nonviolent tactics were used specifically with the knowledge in mind that they would assist the overall, multi-tactic struggle for unification.  While the struggle's backbone may have been the non-military strategies and actions, the real teeth of the struggle lay in the ongoing ability for armed military action.  The two strategies complemented each other, required each another and could not have been effectively separated.

The case of the Indian Independence Movement, of which Gandhi was a major part, had a similar (even if not admitted to) multi-tactic struggle that ultimately proved useful in forcing the English to pull out of India.  While Gandhi would never admit that coercion could ever play a positive role in a campaign, he was involved in a movement, a nationalist struggle, which had a very violent contingency.  Was this violence effective?  Although it did not militarily even attempt to defeat the English forces, the violence (mostly unorganized, random, and reactionary) served the successful purpose of allowing the British to acknowledge that if they did not work to resolve things in a civil manner, they would be left to deal with the violent elements.  Gandhi himself was released from prison on at least one occasion after specifically agreeing to attempt to assist the British in calming the more violent elements of Indian society.

The marriage of military and political strategies has been used widely in wars, struggles, and other conflicts on a global basis throughout history.  To suggest that an extreme power such as the United States, when it has repeatedly proven itself to be an irrational, unrelenting proponent of injustice answering only to itself, can be defeated purely by nonviolent means is ridiculous.  There simply is no precedent on which to base this faulty suggestion.  For certain, this is even further the case if and when the actual power structure of the United States—the government and its economy—is threatened.  The U.S. government was set on stopping the spread of communism in Indochina, while simultaneously opening up a market for U.S. consumer goods.  There is simply no foreseeable way that the North Vietnamese could have succeeded in bringing down the Diem regime without the addition of armed force, which complemented the more powerful political tactics they implemented.  While there is little doubt in my mind that nonviolence theorists can argue the 'what-if' scenarios for any given situation to eternity, in reality there simply has not been any sort of convincing evidence that the U.S. government has the ability to be threatened by anything but the barrel of a gun—particularly one it cannot see.

Did the revolutionary violence used by the Vietnamese, on its own, win the war against the United States? No, but it did play a necessary part in ensuring that the U.S. did not militarily become victorious. While the Vietnamese communists achieved part of their desires at the expense of hundreds of thousands of casualties, the United States also met at least one of its aims—a foot in the door of the Indochina economic marketplace, which would eventually benefit U.S. corporations and thus its economy.

# CHAPTER SIX

# *The Cuban Revolution*

Growing up in the United States, I was not taught a great deal about Cuba in my public education. What little I did know amounted to Cuba having something to do with communism, and therefore it was bad according to U.S. standards. Additionally, I knew that the U.S. had put some sort of restrictions on its citizens traveling to Cuba and was also refusing any economic aid. That was pretty much my primary knowledge of Cuba up until the last few years—embarrassing, but true.

While studying political violence, especially for this book, it was difficult to select which case studies to analyze on a global basis. On a personal level, I was not only interested in finding instances that demonstrated a successful use of violent tactics and strategies to further a social and/or political cause. Successful or not, my main goal was to review historical moments when revolutionary violence became legitimized in the hearts and minds of not only those directly involved, but in the masses of a particular area. With this in mind, in addition to having a personal interest in learning more about Castro and Guevara, I decided to focus this chapter on the Cuban Revolution.

Now, when I mention the Cuban Revolution there were many different components that comprised this whole. There were the political, military, economic, and social changes that, over a lengthy period, transformed the country into a place vastly different from its existence prior to 1959. My particular focus is on the actual insurrectionary rebels of the Cuban Revolution that forced the Batista regime to crumble, an effort led largely by Fidel Castro. It is important to contemplate and attempt to understand how a small number of dedicated and visionary individuals created a successful revolution. Reminiscent of other successful applications of guerrilla warfare throughout history—the Vietnamese example against France and the United States comes to mind—the strategies of the Cuban revolutionaries are important to examine for anyone contemplating the revolutionary process. Furthermore, the case of Cuba provides an important example of political and societal change only becoming possible once reformist measures were abandoned.

Many primary problems in Cuba can be traced back to 1493, when Christopher Columbus first brought sugarcane to Hispaniola (Haiti and the Dominican Republic). From there, Spanish conquerors took the sugarcane to Cuba where bananas, coffee, citrus fruits, rice, and beans were also later introduced. But sugar in particular brought slavery. Herbert Mathews in his 1975 book, *Revolution in Cuba*, writes:

> The Indians were worked and diseased to death in a half century by the Spanish... The sugar plantations brought enormous profits to the owners and made Cuba at the turn of the seventeenth century one of the richest - perhaps per capita, the richest - of countries in the world. But the owners were few, immensely wealthy, and politically powerful. They depended on slavery, which, in turn, depended on a continuation of the Spanish colonial status (p. 19).

In 1886 slavery was officially abolished in Cuba, but the lives of former slaves did not improve much. Severe poverty kept most of the former slaves on the plantations, where they faced wages usually below the subsistence level and could only work four or five months out of the year. While official slavery was outlawed, poverty continued the barbaric tradition.

The first major revolt in Cuba came in 1868, when Cubans rose up against Spain in what would become the beginning of the Ten Year War. This battle, which lasted from 1868 to 1878, is considered the first stage in the thirty-year struggle for independence from Spain. During the Ten Year

War, Cuban nationalists were not victorious, at least in part, because Spain had received arms and gunboats from the United States. After ten years of fighting, one of the primary results was the relocation of thousands of small farmers who had been driven off their lands into the cities. Here, Mathews writes, they "became a restless proletariat, at the same time the former slaves, now wage earners, turned into a rural proletariat" (1975, p. 21).

On April 21, 1898, another revolutionary war began in Cuba that would be successful in gaining Cuba's independence from Spain. One hundred fourteen days later, on July 16, 1898, Spanish forces surrendered in Santiago de Cuba. While Cuba had won its independence from Spain, it did so with the assistance of the United States. As the Cuban economic market was important for the United States, the U.S. government had decided that the only way to stop the unrest in Cuba and promote stability was to help get rid of the Spanish. Of course that meant that Cuba would largely then be under the control of the United States.

At the end of the war, without any Cubans present, the United States signed a peace agreement in Paris that gave the U.S. Congress the right to determine the "civil rights and political status of the island" (Mathews, 1975, p. 22). Immediately, Cuban nationalists charged the United States with the violation of Article IV of the Congressional Resolution of April 20, 1898, which stated:

> That the United States hereby disclaims any disposition or intention to exercise sovereignty, jurisdiction, or control over said island except for the pacification thereof, and asserts its determination, when that is accomplished, to leave the government and control of the island to its people (Mathews, 1975, p. 23).

The Platt Amendment to the Cuban Constitution led to the establishment of the U.S. Navel Base at Guantanamo Bay. This, of course, has repeatedly been in the international spotlight recently, as the U.S. is holding many of the suspected terrorists there. Cuban nationalists found Article III of the Platt Amendment particularly oppositional. It states:

> That the government of Cuba consents that the United States may exercise the right to intervene for the preservation of Cuban independence, the maintenance of a

government adequate for the protection of life, property
and individual liberty, and for discharging the obligations
with respect to Cuba imposed by the Treaty of Paris on
the United States, now to be assumed and undertaken by
the Government of Cuba (Mathews, 1975, p. 24).

The first president of the Cuban Republic was Tomas Estrada
Palma, who served from 1902 to 1906. Hand selected and placed in power
by the United States, Palma engaged in electoral fraud and was re-elected
to the presidency in 1906. This obvious corruption by Palma angered
Cubans who began to create an atmosphere of unrest in the Republic. As
Cuba became faced with a possible civil war, the United States intervened
and sent in Judge Charles Magoon of Nebraska to rule Cuba from 1906
to 1909. On his way out of office Magoon selected a new president, Jose
Miguel Gomez, who also became known for his corruption.

After Gomez, General Mario Garcia Menocal stepped up to the
presidency. Following in his predecessor's footsteps, Menocal extended
his own presidential term for another four years in 1917. Once again,
Cubans threatened to revolt and cried for the overthrow of Menocal.
President Woodrow Wilson in the United States supported Menocal and
publicly stated that the United States would not recognize any Cuban government brought in by revolutionary means. Corruption must have been
acceptable for Wilson, especially if it was part of a regime the U.S. could
control. A revolutionary overthrow of the regime would mean the U.S.
might stand to lose that control. *Corruption good, revolution bad.*

In response to the increasingly tense situation, the U.S. sent Marines from the Guantanamo Base into Cuba, where they stayed until January 1922. From 1921 to 1925, Cuba was essentially ruled by an American
commission led by General Enoch Crowder. In 1926, Crowder's commission left, and more corrupt Cuban rulers were put back into power.

General Gerardo Machado, who came into presidency in 1925,
also ended up extending his term illegally. This created a violent reaction,
particularly among the student movement. Uprisings further intensified
when the Hawley-Smoot Tariff Act was passed in the United States in
1930, which raised the tariff on Cuban sugar from 1.76 cents to 2 cents per
pound. This negatively affected many Cubans, and Machado, while having good relations with the United States, was considered a thief and corrupt person by Cubans. Cubans then engaged in strikes, riots, and forms
of terrorism in response.

In May 1933, U.S. President Roosevelt sent Summer Welles to Havana to act as an ambassador to help calm the increasingly tense situation. On August 3, 1933, Cubans engaged in a general strike which lasted for nine days. At the end, Machado had been effectively driven from power, but the chaos continued.

During the next five months of extremely unstable conditions in Cuba, Sergeant Fulgencio Batista rose to power and became dictator of Cuba. While he had not taken part in the overthrow of Machado himself, Batista seized the opportunity for power in the post-Machado chaos. On September 4, 1933, Batista and a small number of his followers took over Camp Columbia in Havana. He immediately appointed himself chief of staff and eventually colonel.

In 1944, Batista publicly boasted that he had held democratic elections in Cuba. Except Batista's candidate did not win as expected. Instead, Ramon Grau San Martin, who headed the Autenticos (Authentic Revolutionary Cuban Party), won. Yet, as the Autenticos did not win a majority in Congress, the Batista coalition remained in control. Cubans had been excited about Ramon Grau San Martin and felt he represented honesty and Cuban nationalism. Unfortunately for the Cuban people, he deceived them and was incredibly corrupt himself.

This helped spark a new reform movement in Cuba on May 15, 1947 that attempted to abolish corruption in government and business. Taking the shape of a new political party called *Partido del Pueblo Cubano* ("Cuban People's Party"), the movement was led by a man named Eddy Chibas. Fidel Castro had been one of the members of this new effort. Unfortunately, the movement was primarily bourgeois, and many early on knew it was doomed to failure. Chibas shot himself at the end of one of his radio commentaries on August 5, 1951, thus ending the effort.

Another presidential election was scheduled for June 1, 1952 in Cuba. In a December 1951 poll taken by the *Bohemia* newspaper, the nationalist candidate Roberto Agramonte was in the lead. He was followed in second position by Carlos Hevia, who was an engineer for the Autenticos. In the far third place was Batista, who, while he wanted so much to become president, knew he could not do it legally. So with the assistance of supporting lower rank officers in the army, Batista staged a coup. On March 10, 1952, Batista and his supporting army officers seized Camp Columbia in Havana ousting the existing president, Prio Socarras, who gave in without a fight.

On March 13, Socarras left Cuba for Mexico and then Florida,

191

where he used some of his wealth to buy arms for Cubans to overthrow and/or kill Batista. Mathews writes that "about $50,000 of his money went to Fidel Castro to buy the yacht *Granma*, in which the revolutionaries sailed to Cuba in 1956" (1975, p. 33). On March 27, the U.S. government officially recognized the new Batista government. So much for the United States' refusal to recognize governments that came to power by revolutionary means.

On March 16, 1952, Fidel Castro made one of his first public speeches at the end of an Ortodoxo party meeting. The Ortodoxo party was along the same reform and nationalist approach. In protest of the Batista coup, Castro vowed to "never halt in the struggle to see the nation free" (Mathews, 1975, p. 33). In 1950, Castro had earned a law degree and opened up his own office with two friends.

As an attorney, Castro attempted to take legal action against Batista by filing a brief with the Court of Constitutional Guaranties arguing that it should declare General Batista's seizure of power to be unconstitutional. Castro also entered a charge in the Urgency Court asking that Batista be tried as a criminal. Unfortunately, Castro's legal attempts were completely unsuccessful. Disillusioned with the legal process as a result, Castro immediately began contemplating the overthrow of the Batista regime through revolutionary means. He began planning a revolution.

Within a short time period, Castro came up with a plan to attack the Moncada Barracks and its arsenal, which was in the center of Santiago de Cuba. This was the second largest garrison in Cuba. Castro figured that controlling the Barracks would provide a base from which to dominate the capital of the Oriente Province. With this plan, he hoped to start an uprising against Batista with volunteers who could be armed with weapons from the munitions storage in the Barracks.

Castro realized that the attack would have to be a surprise, since he and his supporters were poorly armed and heavily outnumbered. He also wanted to block reinforcements coming in from the north, so a small attack was also planned against the garrison in Bayamo. Castro decided to plan the attacks for July 26, 1953, during the time of the annual carnival in Santiago de Cuba. For sixteen months the attack was planned and included hundreds of men. The movement itself was divided into cells, with most of them being in or around the Havana area. Castro led both the civilian and military committees, which comprised the national leadership of the movement. Within the planning phase, the movement was able to purchase arms using $17,000-$18,000, which they raised mostly from people selling their shops, donating their savings, pawning items and other personal contributions. Castro stated that with the money:

> [they] bought forty shotguns, thirty-five 22-caliber rifles, twenty-four rifles of other calibers, sixty pistols, three Winchesters from the time of Buffalo Bill and a machine gun that had to be repaired and was almost useless (Mathews, 1975, p. 54).

On July 24, the men left for Santiago de Cuba and Bayamo. When they reached Santiago de Cuba, they separated into various hotels and rooming houses that had been reserved for them by a man named Renato Guitart. He had also rented a rooming house for the twenty-nine men who were to attack the garrison in Bayamo.

At 2:00 a.m. on July 26, Castro gathered with the group of 129 men and 2 women who would be taking part in the uprising. The meeting was held at a farm ten miles outside of Santiago. Here the rebels were given weapons, and Castro informed them of their objective and the plan for the attack. Next, Castro reminded them that they were volunteers, and right then would be the proper time to back out if they were having any doubts about the plan. Nine to ten of the rebels backed out at that point.

Castro's plan was for himself and ninety men to storm through Post No. 3 of the Moncada Barracks. From there, they would seize the barracks and the rest of the buildings, taking soldiers prisoner and acquiring weapons in the process. A man by the name of Abel Santamaria, along with twenty-one men and two women, would take the Civil Hospital and care for any wounded. Another group of the rebels would occupy the Palace of Justice, where a key firing position could be obtained on the top floor.

So with the plan set, the vehicles left the farm at 4:45 a.m. and headed for Santiago. Once in town, the hospital, which was unguarded, was immediately taken. At the same time, the group responsible for the Palace of Justice disarmed the guards there and settled into firing positions on the top floor. As these two groups were getting into place, they heard gun shots coming from Post No. 3.

When the vehicles carrying Castro and the other men planning the main attack reached Post No. 3, they were caught off guard by a patrol car carrying two soldiers armed with machine guns. As a result, this alerted the entire Barracks, and Castro and his men were quickly outnumbered.

Shooting quickly began, and it became obvious that Castro and his men were greatly overpowered. The few men who had succeeded in getting into the Barracks fought their way out after they realized the attack had failed. One man was killed in the process. The problems facing the men were amplified when Castro's reinforcements failed to arrive at the Barracks. Being unfamiliar with the area, they had become lost in the streets of Santiago.

Castro and his men then quickly retreated and headed for El Caney, a small town near Santiago, where Castro felt they could take the small garrison there to obtain more arms. He thought that by using the arms that would be obtained at the El Caney garrison, they could head into the mountains and then begin a guerrilla struggle. For both of the simultaneous actions, the large attack on Post No. 3 and the smaller on the Bayamo garrison, Castro's forces lost eight, and eight more were wounded. They killed nineteen of the government forces and wounded another twenty-two.

At dawn on August 1, Castro and two friends were captured as they slept in the mountains. More of Castro's rebels were caught nearby soon thereafter. At the trial on October 16, Castro acted as his own attorney and was sentenced to fifteen years in prison. Most of those caught received similar sentences. Fortunately for the rebels, they all were released on May 15, 1955, resulting from the pardon that came out of a deal between General Batista and the Autentico Party. The Autentico Party, which filled seventeen seats in the Senate, demanded that Congress pass an amnesty freeing all political prisoners.

Within weeks of his release, Castro decided to carry out an invasion of Cuba from Mexico. He left Cuba shortly thereafter and headed to Mexico, leaving a man by the name of Francisco Isaac Pais Garcia in charge of organizing the movement in Cuba. Eventually, Garcia was to engage in an uprising to coincide with a landing from Castro and his supporters from Mexico.

Preparations for the Cuban invasion began upon Castro's arrival in Mexico. It was at this time that Castro first met Ernesto Guevara, who would later be known internationally as Che Guevara, or simply "Che." Guevara would eventually become a leading force in the Cuban revolution and a specialist in guerrilla warfare.

While in Mexico, the Castro supporters underwent guerrilla training under the direction of Colonel Alberto Bayo. He was an experienced man who had studied and applied the strategy previously in Spanish Morocco and later in the Spanish Civil War. Bayo and Castro apparently severed their relationship after Bayo disapproved of Castro publicly boasting that he was going to invade Cuba in the near future.

In the middle of November, a large supply of arms for the invasion was seized by the Mexican police, and Castro was then ordered to leave Mexico City. Forced out, Castro decided this was a fit time to make his move. Along with his supporters, Castro began the final preparations for the invasion of Cuba.

President Socarras, who had been tossed out of power by Batista, gave Castro money to purchase a small, worn yacht to sail to Cuba for the invasion. Named the *Granma*, the yacht was designed to hold a maximum of fourteen people. Seeming to answer to no one, not even the laws of the yacht capacity, Castro sailed with eighty-two aboard.

On November 24, 1956 Castro sailed with his crew from Tuxpan. The weather was so horrible that day that the Mexican Marine had suspended permission to sail in that region of the Gulf. As a result, the trip was a disaster, with everyone becoming seasick, the food spoiling, the yacht constantly taking on water, and the storm blowing them way off course. As a result of the storm and the obvious lack of preparations, the *Granma* was late arriving in Cuba. Unfortunately for the crew, that meant they missed their important rendezvous with Crescencio Perez, a peasant sent to meet them with arms and supplies. The crew also ended up missing the November 30 uprising in Santiago led by Frank Pais, which was supposed to coincide with their landing. Castro and his crew could only listen to news of the uprising on a broken radio aboard the *Granma*.

Finally, a few days later, the *Granma* ran aground in shallow water a hundred yards off the Cuban shore. As Castro and his followers waded ashore, he began thinking about traveling into the Sierra Maestra Mountains to begin the guerrilla struggle. Slowly, the group made its way inland, and on December 5 the crew reached Alegria de Pio, about seven miles away from where they landed. They were immediately met by government troops, who killed many of Castro's rebels and imprisoned others. Castro later found out that a civilian guide he had trusted was to blame for the soldiers' arrival.

A man by the name of Juan Almeida quickly gathered a group from the remaining men and led them into the forest. Other, smaller groups also formed and scattered into differing areas to escape the government soldiers. Castro was in a group that was led by a peasant into the Sierra Maestra Mountains. Crescencio Perez successfully brought the wandering groups back together for a meeting at his brother's farmhouse. By this time Castro's forces, which had been eighty-two, now consisted of a mere twelve. They formalized their plan to continue into the Sierra Maestra mountains to prepare for the guerrilla struggle.

Castro and his followers reached the upper part of the Pico Turquino Mountain inside the Sierra Maestra range on December 25. Just under a month later, on January 17, the rebels won their first victory in an attack on a small army garrison at the mouth of the La Plata River. Five days later, the rebels succeeded again with an attack on January 22, 1957 at Arroya del Inferno. Both of these actions occurred without any rebel losses.

Early on, Castro had strategically decided that in contrast to Batista's torture and execution of captured political prisoners, the rebels would chose to take prisoners, tend to the wounded among them, and release the others unharmed. This common strategy of guerrilla warfare is specifically intended to produce support from not only the masses of people, but also from the opposition soldiers themselves. In the case of Cuba, by the rebels acting more humanely toward prisoners, anger from the masses could easily be produced against Batista, who was using more ruthless standards. Furthermore, Batista's soldiers who were captured by the rebels could—at least according to the theory of the strategy—begin to see the barbaric nature of Batista. Defection could then occur.

From February 9 to the end of May 1957, the rebels experienced a relatively quiet time in the Sierra Maestra. On March 15, fifty new men arrived to join them, and the rebels began planning their next move. Castro and Guevara planned another uprising to occur on May 28, 1957 against the El Uvero garrison. The *barbudos*, as they were then called (by then, Castro and all the other men were wearing long beards), succeeded in seizing arms and taking control of the garrison. By July 1957, Castro had about 200 armed and trained fighters in the Sierra Maestra. Near the end of the year, he set up a permanent headquarters at La Plata, located on the southern slope of the Sierra Maestra.

The response from the Batista regime in 1957 was increasingly hostile and tense. Early in the year, Batista had committed at least 3,000 men to finding and liquidating the rebels. This number continued to increase over the course of the year as it became apparent to Batista that the rebels were a growing threat.

In addition to Castro's forces, other anti-Batista groups began to form throughout Cuba. On November 1, 1957, seven anti-Batista groups met in Miami and agreed on a "unity pact" with a fairly moderate, democratic program. Castro was not notified about the meeting, and when he was later informed and had reviewed the text of the pact, he sent back an angry letter of opposition. He called the Miami pact an "outrage" and "unauthorized" (Mathews, 1975, p. 98). Some of these seven groups that met in Miami were communist organizations that, according to Guevara, "did not understand with sufficient clarity the role of the guerrilla force, nor Fidel's personal role on our revolutionary struggle" (pp. 98-99).

An agreement was finally reached in a meeting of all of the opposition groups (except the communists, who weren't invited) at Caracas, Venezuela on July 19-20, 1958. In this agreement, Castro was recognized as commander in chief of the revolutionary forces. This change of heart, so to speak, of the other anti-Batista groups came as a result of their observing the increasing success of Castro's rebel forces.

In 1958, the rebel forces added new means of propaganda to their arsenal. A small newspaper was started called *El Cubano Libre*, and Guevara began a rebel broadcasting station in Castro's military headquarters in the Sierra Maestra. On February 24, 1958 *Radio Rebelde* officially went on the air.

Castro, also early in 1958, had sent a messenger named Pedro Miret to San Jose, Costa Rica, to seek assistance from President Jose M. Figueres. Figueres complied with the request for support and sent Castro a planeload of arms to help the rebels. The plane delivered the arms to a farm near the Sierra Maestra, and from there they were transported to the rebels.

During early 1958, small, but continuous, battles were fought between the rebels and the Batista forces. Consolidated in the Sierra Maestra region, Castro decided to move some forces out of the area on March 10, 1958. He sent his brother Raul with a column of about fifty men toward the Sierra de Cristal on the North Coast of the Oriente Province. The goal of the column was to "disrupt transportation of all kinds and establish a base of operations" (Mathews, 1975, p. 101). They were called "Column 6," to give the perception that there were at least five other columns active—which of course there were not.

In only twenty hours after leaving the Sierra Maestra, Raul and his column successfully crossed the province, arriving at Piloto El Medio, where they established the Second Front in the Northern Oriente zone. Within a few weeks, Raul successfully cleared the area of enemy outposts, capturing arms in the process. Mathews suggests that Raul was very hard at work during these first few weeks. He writes:

> He had maps made; organized a telephone network, and intelligence corps, public works for transport, an arms factory to make guns and bombs; and established a school, a provisional hospital, and even a Cuerpo Juridico through which he imposed a rudimentary code of law and collected taxes" (1975, p. 102).

Raul claimed to have more than 1,000 rebels with him during this time.

Meanwhile, Batista set in and planned to destroy the rebels in the Sierra Maestra. Mathews states, "he gathered between 10,000 and 12,000 well-armed troops, supported by American Sherman tanks, armored cars, and mountain artillery, all backed by his navy and air force" (1975, p. 104). Having a quality intelligence team, Castro was able to be well prepared for the attack.

At this time Castro had a mere 300 men with arms, but they did have some clear advantages. For one, they were more familiar with geographical layout of the area. This was important as they could use this knowledge to their advantage to out-maneuver Batista troops. Second, the rebels had a familiarity with the ruggedness of the territory in the Sierra Maestra. This also would be of benefit, as the government troops would likely be caught off guard and unprepared for the harsh conditions. The rebels also had a good fighting spirit and were under excellent leadership by Castro. All of these factors combined were going to need to prosper over the 10,000-12,000 Batista troops.

On May 24, 1958, Batista began his offensive against Castro's forces with an attack on a rebel outpost at Las Mercedes. Batista's forces immediately pushed the rebels back. But just as previously speculated, Batista's forces were not equipped or trained to fight in the rugged mountain conditions of the Sierra Maestra. As Batista's troops stopped to rest and regroup, they were surrounded by the guerrillas. Two of Batista's battalions were destroyed in a week-long battle, which ended on June 20. The rebels captured the Batista unit's shortwave radio equipment and code book. Castro claimed that by gaining this information, the rebels "intercepted every order and even used the captured transmitter to direct government air strikes on its own positions and to drop food where the rebels were" (Mathews, 1975, pp. 105-106).

The main battle of the Sierra Maestra was fought at El Jigue, near

Castro's headquarters at La Plata, from July 11-20. During this fight, Batista's troops, who had already fought in some fourteen small battles against the rebels, were short on provisions as they moved in on Castro's forces. Rebels quickly trapped a main battalion of Batista's forces. Castro's forces succeeded in stopping all reinforcements for this battalion, and on July 20, Major Jose Quevedo and his 163 soldiers surrendered to the rebels. In keeping with their previous strategy, the rebels fed the soldiers and tended the wounded. Their weapons were taken and handed over to trained rebel volunteers. In late July, 1958, Batista ordered a complete withdrawal of forces from the Sierra Maestra. Mathews writes, "One battalion after another of the seventeen sent into the Sierra Maestra was decimated or fled" (1975, p. 106).

After Batista's attempt to annihilate the rebels failed, Castro issued an order stating, "The guerrilla war has ceased to exist; it has become a war of positions and movements" (Mathews, 1975, p. 107). This statement related to spreading the war from the Oriente Province to the rest of the island. Castro's plan was for his column, along with his brother's, to take Santiago de Cuba. Simultaneously, another column of 148 men under Guevara would move West through Las Villas Province to Sierra de Escambray and then on to Havana. A fourth column under Camilo Cienfuegos was to move parallel to Guevara's column and travel to the western province of Pinar del Rio.

Even though Batista was losing power to the rebels he, with the assistance of the United States, held a presidential "election" on November 3, 1958. His chosen candidate, Andres Rivero Aguero, won in the fixed scheme. Aguero immediately saw many towns and areas fall into the hands of the rebels while Batista continued to fight. In fact, Batista was still purchasing arms, tanks, and planes—largely from the United States—at this time to use against the rebels. But by this time in Cuba most, including Batista's own chief of staff, General Francisco Tabernilla, realized it was over.

General Tabernilla ordered General Eulogio Cantillo in mid-December to meet with Castro. On December 24 the two met at the Oriente sugar mill, where Castro asked Cantillo to surrender the Santiago and Bayamo garrisons. After Cantillo flew back to Havana and discussed the matter, Batista agreed to the surrender. Meanwhile, the rebels continued to take other areas of Cuba through fighting.

Instead of moving directly into Santa Clara, Guevara captured all the surrounding areas thereby isolating the capital of the province. On December 28, he then led an attack on Santa Clara. Batista, in a final effort, sent an armored train into Santa Clara with tanks and 350 soldiers. Guevara, at this time, had less than 300 men from his own column combined with men from the Revolucionario and the 26th of July Movement—both underground anti-Batista groups. (Castro had started the 26th of July Movement, which he referred to as the primary revolutionary effort, to commemorate those lives lost in the attempted barracks seizure on that date.) On December 29, the armored train arrived in Santa Clara. With tractors, Guevara's men pulled up the railroad tracks in front of and behind the train and then derailed it with dynamite charges. Once derailed, the train was set on fire by the rebels. The trapped officers and soldiers surrendered, and on December 31, 1958, Santa Clara was officially taken by the rebels.

During that same evening, Batista was notified that Santiago de Cuba could not be held and was soon to be taken by rebel forces. This meant that the rebels would be in full control of the Oriente Province. Based on the defeat of Santa Clara and the news of the loss of Santiago, Batista decided to immediately flee.

Julio Garcia Luis describes the atmosphere at the end of 1959 in his 2001 book, *Cuban Revolutionary Reader*. He writes:

> The last few hours of the Batista dictatorship ran out on the night of December 31, 1958. The end of the war was imminent because of the Rebel Army's sudden offensive on all fronts. A revolutionary force of fewer than 3,000 armed men had pushed the 80,000 members of the repressive bodies of the terrorist regime that had taken power on March 10, 1952, to the brink of collapse (p. 12).

With Batista gone, Guevara formed a group of three to demand the surrender of the main garrison on January 1, 1959. As the three rebels entered the area under a white flag, the soldiers warmly greeted them. By this time the rebel forces included a large number of defectors from Batista's forces. To Castro's credit, his policy of demonstrating humanity toward any prisoners taken by the rebels surely contributed to the high defection rate among Batista's soldiers.

So on January 1, 1959, the insurrection and the fighting ended, and Castro's social revolution began. This revolution would mean an attempt to transform Cuban life and end the sixty-year domination of Cuba by the

United States. In 1959, Castro knew a social revolution was needed, but he was unsure at that point how or what to make it. He did know certain features must be included—the building of schools, the establishment of free healthcare for all, a policy of agricultural reform (which immediately meant land rents were cut in half), an end to government corruption, and the reality that this must be a revolution not for the bourgeois, but for the poor.

Castro with his forces then set out to change the whole of Cuban society. This was not done in a small number of years but arguably still is going on today as Castro remains in power. Since 1959, his government has faced great difficulties, not just with the overwhelming task of transforming Cuba, but also from the United States, which engaged in everything from the Bay of Pigs fiasco, to repeated assassination attempts on Castro, to severe sanctions against the country. All of this action taken by the United States was due to the fear of communism growing in Latin America and the fear of the disruption of U.S. business in Cuba. Of course for most—if not all—of Castro's insurrection, he was anti-communist and largely refused to work with communists in Cuba—even those opposed to the Batista regime. After the victory in 1959, aid began to come from Russia, and although Castro did develop a socialist ideology and plan for his country, he arguably never accepted the communist doctrine.

Perhaps one of the primary criticisms of Castro and his forces is that over the many years since 1959, they have lost touch with the people of Cuba. They perhaps have lost touch with the poor masses that the revolution originally set out to serve. Certainly, Castro kept many of his promises; government corruption was immediately reduced and eliminated (to a certain extent) after 1959, schools were built, literacy rates went up, healthcare improved, and workers were no longer exploited by U.S. corporations. However, early on in the insurrection, when Castro was fighting in the Sierra Maestra, he promised that when the rebels were victorious there would be free and open elections. This was not to be a reality, as Castro constantly feared losing the revolution for which so many Cubans had given their lives.

The most remarkable feature of Castro's success at coming into power was how a few people ended up being victorious against a dictator and his thousands of forces. Guevara, in his 1961 book, *Guerrilla Warfare*, wrote about his experiences with Castro in the Cuban revolution. He states that the Cuban Revolution:

contributed three fundamental lessons to the conduct of revolutionary movements in Latin America. They are,
1) Popular forces can win a war against the army.
2) It is not necessary to wait until all conditions for making a revolution exist; the insurrection can create them.
3) In underdeveloped America the countryside is the basic area for armed fighting (p. 7).

In his first lesson, *popular forces can win a war against the army*, Guevara simplifies an extremely complex phenomenon. Indeed popular forces—meaning those of and by the people or the masses—can win a war against an army as was the case with the examples of the Vietnamese fighting the French and the United States. But there are many factors that have enabled these people's struggles to even stand a chance, when they were outnumbered and were weaker militarily. It is easily arguable that as the military technology in countries such as the United States becomes increasingly advanced, the ability for a successful armed insurrection by the mass of people against such a force greatly decreases. Not that it is impossible, but it is increasingly difficult.

Guevara writes that the fundamental principle in guerrilla warfare is that "no battle, combat or skirmish is to be fought unless it will be won" (1961, p. 12). This is crucial, as most often the rebel forces will be greatly outnumbered, and to lose any people can mean certain failure. He continues:

> At the outset, the essential task of the guerrilla fighter is to keep himself from being destroyed. Next the guerrilla, having taken up inaccessible positions out of reach of the enemy, or having assembled forces that deter the enemy from attacking, ought to proceed to the gradual weakening of the enemy... the blows should be continuous. The enemy soldier in a zone of operations ought not to be allowed to sleep; his outposts ought to be attacked and liquidated systematically. At every moment the impression ought to be created that he is surrounded by a complete circle (1961, pp. 15-16).

Guerrilla warfare seems to work most effectively by dominating the opposition through psychological means rather that by military victory.

By playing with the enemy's mind, always deceiving the opponent, guerrilla strategy has the capability of lowering morale while simultaneously increasing recruits from the masses. This definitely seemed to be the case in Cuba, as Castro and Guevara repeatedly used psychological means to dominate Batista. Through tricks such as naming a grouping or column a high number in order to imply many active columns, to quickly striking at random and then disappearing, to even allowing captured Batista soldiers to go free, these factors most definitely played a major role in the rebel victory.

A second fundamental lesson Guevara suggests was learned from the Cuban experience is that *it is not necessary to wait until all conditions for making a revolution exist; the insurrection can create them*. I find this perhaps the most interesting phenomenon of the Cuban revolution. Indeed, it does appear as if it was the case with Castro. As an attorney, Castro first tried to legally take measures against the Batista regime. When that did not work, he felt his only recourse was to develop an army and start an armed revolution. Of course at that time he was Fidel Castro, largely alone with his analysis. He did not know what it would mean in particular to start and win a revolution, but he knew in his heart that it had to be done. So through many failed attempts, Castro continued to fight on, gathering support along the way until his partial vision became a reality in 1959. Once the insurrection was won, the real revolution was to begin, and Castro himself stated at that time, "This is only the beginning."

Ramon Eduardo Ruiz, in *Cuba: The making of a revolution*, disagrees in part, suggesting that the Cuban Revolution was made possible by already existing conditions. He states:

> the Revolution of 1959 was made possible by Cuba's own revolutionary tradition. Since the middle of the nineteenth century every generation of Cubans had experienced revolution. Political and social turmoil had engulfed the island approximately every twenty-five years; the Ten Years War of 1868 to 1878, the struggle for independence that began in 1895, and the revolution of 1933. Between 1902 and 1920 the island suffered at least two political revolutions which, though limited in objectives, disrupted peace and order. On the basis of Cuban history, the Cubans could rightly claim the right—indeed the obligation—to revolt in order to eliminate old griev-

ances (1968, pp. 168-169).

Were there revolutionary conditions existing in Cuba during the beginning of Castro's attempts, or did he and his forces make them? Perhaps a bit of both. Naturally there was unrest in Cuba and a great amount of disdain for the Batista dictatorship. While it is feasible that someone or some forces would have come along eventually and overthrown Batista, it is doubtful that a true revolution to change all of Cuban society would have been possible without the revolutionaries creating the suitable atmosphere for prosperity. Some of the most important questions that come out of this analysis are as follows: How are revolutionary conditions created? What constitutes revolutionary conditions? Are the same set of conditions possible under a democracy (or pseudo democracy) as with a dictatorship?

Guevara's third lesson learned from the Cuban Revolution is that in the underdeveloped areas of the Americas, rural fighting is beneficial to the rebels. This definitely seems to have been the case in Cuba, as the rebels in the Sierra Maestra used that terrain for their own benefit. They knew the area's layout and rugged terrain better, and therefore were better equipped to fight there. Batista's forces suffered as a result of poor training for that particular terrain. Another benefit of the rural areas, particularly in the less-developed lands, is that the masses of people—the peasant populations—commonly lived nearby. This is where a lot of the rebel recruits came from, similar to the recruits gathered for the Vietnamese forces. Guerrilla warfare seems to be much more difficult to conduct in urban areas, where rebels would be forced to be much more out in the open and would have fewer options for hiding and escape.

With regard to the moral justification of armed revolution in the Cuban example, Cubans should have had every right to rise up and change their society into a sovereign one that benefited the people, rather than just the bourgeois and foreign corporations. Certainly a lot of lives were lost, but in the end, the society that Castro helped to mold was arguably much better than that which existed prior to 1959. When people are exploited and forced to live without liberty under tyrannical conditions, it should be their right to rebel, by any means necessary, to gain their humanity.

# CHAPTER SEVEN

# *The 1916 Easter Uprising*

It would be difficult to find a credible argument opposing the fact that the 1916 Easter Uprising in Ireland was a complete tactical failure. While the history of British rule in Ireland for some 700 years prior to the 1916 insurgency understandably led to the revolt, it was only afterward when nationalist events began to pose a threat to the stability of English governing. Militarily a disappointment, the uprising did serve the purpose of being in the line of Irish revolts aimed at removing the British from the country. Additionally, this particular uprising appeared to have taught individuals, such as Michael Collins, that the Irish would have to alter their strategies if they were going to make any progress with the British.

The 1916 Easter Uprising, in particular, has been credited by many historians as being a primary precursor to the beginnings of the elusive and militant Irish Republic Army (IRA). Indeed, the IRA and other nationalist organizations and efforts, to an impressive extent, have made it extremely difficult for the British to rule in the northern section of the country for many years. Furthermore, with the assistance of the Sinn Fein political wing of the IRA, the organization has been effective, at least to some extent, at forcing the English to the bargaining table. Most importantly, the 1916 Uprising demonstrated a legitimacy to political violence—that if people face oppression they have the right to use any means necessary to acquire justice. For these reasons in particular, the 1916 Easter Uprising is an interesting study.

The history of the British occupation in Ireland dates back over 700 years to the reign of Henry II, Pope Adrian IV. Being the only Englishman to ever sit on the throne of St. Peter, he publicly insisted that the Irish were in a chaotic state and could not govern themselves. During the reign of Elizabeth the first, the Irish were nearly successful at removing English rule. However, when Hugh O'Neill, Earl of Tyrone, failed in his efforts to stop England, the ancient Gaelic language and lifestyle became threatened. This additionally led to the continued colonization by successive English governments which resulted in the creation of two Irelands— one for the English landowners and the other for the poor natives.

Serious organized rebellion in Ireland dates back to the seventeenth century, when the country witnessed two failed insurgencies. During the eighteenth century, there was another unsuccessful rebellion, pushing the Irish into even a more extreme and desperate state. During the next hundred years, the state of the Irish at the hands of the British continued to decline. Max Caulfield, in his 1963 book, *The Easter Rebellion*, writes, "By the eighteen-forties however, war, waste, conquest, and the stoutly resisted Act of Union with England and Scotland of 1801 had so operated upon the country that the Irish had become the poorest people in Europe" (p. 18). An almost cliché story of colonization, the British landowners continued to become richer at the direct expense of the Irish. Caulfield continues:

> This was the time of the Anglo-Irish rakes; rapacious landlords who, with the one hand built elegant Palladian mansions, planted innumerable avenues of glorious trees opening onto vistas of glittering fountains, and with the other gulped down such oceans of claret that they could only sprawl senseless in their own vomit... (p. 18).

For the Irish during this time period, wages and employment, for the most part, did not exist. Thus, their level of poverty continued to grow.

At the beginning of the twentieth century, the Irish, to a certain extent, felt some hope for their country. A Home Rule Bill was being considered by the English government and many in Ireland felt that this, at least, may have been granted. Caulfield states:

> A sixth of the House of Commons at Westminister were
> Irish members and Home Rule had become the great mor-
> al touchstone of English politics. At long last, it began to
> look as though the two countries were about to embark
> upon a new era of mutual respect and goodwill (1963, pp.
> 19-20).

This would have simply meant that Ireland would be able to govern itself
but would still have to answer to England. Certainly, there still would
have been a clause in the Bill allowing for the British to, at any time they
deemed fit, interfere with home rule for the "preservation of peace and
order." Appearing at least like a small step along the route to eventual
independence, Home Rule seemed to many Irish and English to be capable
of appeasing the majority of Irish national sentiment.

Only a couple of major factors stood in the way of this Home Rule
Bill progressing. For one, the English Conservative Party was against any
and all independence for Ireland. Secondly, there were a sizable number
of primarily young men in Ireland who opposed any kind of integration
with England and therefore strongly opposed Home Rule. Additionally,
Caulfield writes:

> The Protestant Orangemen, who had enjoyed a local
> majority in the four northeastern counties since the great
> plantation of 1603 (when Irish lands had been seized and
> given to English or Scottish settlers) believed that Home
> Rule meant Rome Rule—to which, of course, hell was
> preferable (1963, pp. 19-20).

The Orangemen were a group named after the well known Protestant,
William of Orange, who defeated James the Second at the Battle of the
Boyne in 1690. Because of these forces in opposition, Home Rule was
not granted.

In 1905, a journalist by the name of Arthur Griffith, published a
revolutionary proposal based on his observations of Hungary's independence gained from Austria. Just as Hungary had refused to send representatives to the Parliament in Vienna, Griffith felt the Irish should refuse to
send representatives to Westminister. Griffith proclaimed that members of
Parliament should withdraw from Westminister and set up their own Irish
Council. Next, Irish courts, banks, a civil service, and a stock exchange

could be created to rid the Irish of dependence on the English. Griffith felt that if this Irish system were put into place, the English structure would likely disappear from lack of use. He named this policy *Sinn Fein*, which means "We Ourselves" or "We Rely on Ourselves."

Two militant organizations took a profound interest in Griffith and his ideas. The first was the Irish Republican Brotherhood, a secret group formed in the United States in 1857. This organization was closely linked to the more public Irish-American group. Also taking an interest in Griffith was the Irish Transport and General Workers Union. Caulfield suggests that the unionists were ripe for supporting the evacuation of England. He writes, "Housed in the worst slums in Europe and paid farcical wages, the victims of police oppression and frequent brutality, these trade unionists, militant and tough, supported the idea of a separate Ireland" (1963, p. 21). Important events would ensure that this newfound energy for Irish independence transformed into action.

In 1911, the Liberal Party was back in power in England and needed the support of the Irish Party's eighty-four members to continue ruling Ireland. In exchange for his support, John Redmond, leader of the Irish Party, demanded that the government introduce another Home Rule Bill. He felt this time the Bill would certainly pass. The Tories responded with anger, hiring Sir Edward Carson, K.C. who, through various means, persuaded 80,000 people from Belfast to sign a Solemn League and Covenant against Home Rule. Many Irish who refused to sign were tortured and/or killed.

Once these 80,000 signatures had been gathered, Carson next organized the large group into the Ulster Volunteers, an armed force dedicated to resisting Home Rule by force. Caulfield writes, "If it were legal for Orangemen to take up arms and defy the Government, then surely it must be legal for Southern Catholics to take them up in its defense" (1963, p. 21). The South then decided to form its own armies.

Two more organizations also came about during this time period. The Dublin Trade Unionists formed the Irish Citizen Army, and in 1913, poets, professors, intellectuals, and professionals formed the Irish Volunteers. By the end of 1913, the membership in the Irish Volunteers had grown to over 10,000.

As the Home Rule Bill, despite the efforts of Carson, looked as though it might be finally successful, the beginning of the war set it on the back burner of English politics. A sizable portion of Ireland supported England during the war, feeling as if England would be likely to thank the

Irish for their support afterward by granting Home Rule. Two divisions of Irish troops even voluntarily agreed to travel to France on England's behalf.

But for many of those who refused to support England during the war, they saw the time as being an excellent opportunity to stage an insurrection. Additionally, attempts were made to contact the Germans to ask for support for the uprising. While officially England and therefore Ireland were considered the enemies of Germany, the Germans might be likely to listen to any additional efforts aimed against England.

At a meeting held on September 5, 1914, the Supreme Council of the Irish Republican Brotherhood decided to stage an insurrection and to accept whatever assistance Germany could offer. It was agreed that the uprising should definitely occur if the Germans were to invade Ireland, if the English attempted to force conscription on the country, or if it appeared like the war was coming to an end. Caulfield writes that:

> the insurrection would be accompanied by a declaration of war on Britain and a demand that the Provisional Government be represented as the envoys of a belligerent nation at the Peace Conference which must inevitably follow the end of hostilities (1963, p. 25).

Irish nationalists increasingly found it easier to recruit new members, as young Irishmen were reluctant to fight for England, with which they felt no loyalty. As the war continued to progress, increasing numbers —especially of young men—began to fill the ranks of the insurrectionists. The numbers continued to rise as England increasingly turned to Ireland as a source for army soldiers. Many men in England who were skilled workers became exempt from military service, and so England looked toward Ireland, where the British government considered there to be a large pool of technologically-unskilled labor.

So the massive insurrection was then planned for Easter Sunday and, at least for a while, looked like it was to be a threatening force against Britain. Caulfield states:

> Until Holy Thursday, April 20, the great insurrection promised to be a really serious and impressive affair. If every Irish Volunteer, in the event, had answered the call, ten thousand would have been in action. If, in addition,

once the fighting had started, Redmond's National Volunteers had joined in—as was hoped—there would have been more than one hundred thousand men under arms" (1963, p. 38).

Unfortunately for them, the Irish Volunteers went into action with two hundred citizen army men and less than a tenth of the Irish Volunteer membership.

Up until April 20, the organizers from the Irish Volunteers had expected a large shipment of arms and ammunition from Germany. By way of hand-delivered letter, the Volunteers had contacted the German forces, informed them of their planned insurrection and asked for assistance. While Germany refused to land troops in support, they did load up one ship, the *Aud*, and sent it to meet the insurrectionists in Ireland.

The original plan for the uprising rested on the Germans' delivery of arms in Southwest Ireland, and then German submarines would assist by closing down the Dublin and Kingstown ports. Once armed, the Volunteers would then develop a line based on the River Shannon and advance to the capital. Along the way, the insurrectionists would attack and annihilate military and police barracks. Once in Dublin, principal buildings were to be seized and fortresses established to blockade roads and railways that would be used to transport military reinforcements for England.

While the German *Aud* did succeed in making it to the coast of Ireland, it was never met, except by English authorities. The communication between the insurrectionists and Germany had been so poor that the rebels did not expect the German ship in for a few more days. The ship ended up being sunk, and the crew, comprised of three men (at least two of which were from the Irish resistance) either drowned or were later executed by the English. This of course did not bode well for the insurrection, which was desperately relying on the German shipment of arms.

The Irish Volunteers, now realizing that England was conscious of their planned rebellion, felt they either had to fight or were sure to be faced with extreme repression. Yet, not all within the leadership of the Volunteers felt that an insurrection would be a wise move. John MacNeill, Chief of Staff of the Irish Volunteers, actively campaigned to prevent the rebellion and went as far as to forbid the insurrection. He immediately issued an order on April 22, 1916 stating, "Volunteers completely deceived. All orders for special action are hereby canceled, and on no account will action be taken" (Caulfield, 1963, p. 55). Next, MacNeill traveled to meet an editor from a newspaper in Dublin, who agreed to publish an announcement the following day. The message read:

> Owing to the very critical position, all orders given to Irish Volunteers for tomorrow, Easter Sunday, are hereby rescinded and no parades, marches, or other movement of Irish Volunteers will take place. Each individual Volunteer will obey this order strictly in every particular (Caulfield, 1963, p. 55).

The next morning news of MacNeill's cancellation had reached volunteers all over Ireland. At a breakfast meeting of key Volunteer organizers, after debating whether or not to go ahead with the planned insurrection, it was agreed to postpone it to the following day at noon. So for the next twenty-four hours, Volunteer organizers busily prepared for the long-awaited revolt.

Early the next morning, on Monday, April 24, rebel leaders sent couriers around the Dublin area to round up the insurrectionists. Each carried a piece of paper signed by the organizers stating that "four city battalions will parade for inspection and route march at 10 a.m. today" (De Rosa, 1990, p. 241). A large number of rebels did not answer their doors, either being too drunk, since it was a holiday, or not home. Owing to the confusing and conflicting orders that had been given during the last few days, once the news broke on Sunday that the insurrection had been called off, many rebels had left Dublin. Most of the insurgents that did show up initially thought they were just preparing for usual maneuvers.

Edward Daly was put in charge of the first battalion of volunteers. His mission was to seize the enormous Royal Barracks, a military fortress that would have an estimated military force twenty times the size of his battalion. Daly had been counting on at least 350 men to take part, yet only 120 showed up Monday morning.

The second battalion also only consisted of 150 men armed with rifles, pickaxes, and sledgehammers. Led by Thomas MacDonagh, their goal was to seize the Jacob's Biscuit Company building, which contained two tall towers from which they could view the entire Dublin area. MacDonagh, like Daly, had counted on many more men taking part.

Eamon de Valera led the third battalion that aimed to defend the eastern approaches to Dublin. This would hopefully stop any British reinforcements coming in from the East. It was determined that de Valera needed at least 500 men to accomplish this feat but, like his two colleagues, he only received 130.

The fourth battalion was led by Eamonn Kent, who was assigned the task of taking over the South Dublin Union. This was a facility that housed poor and elderly people in a closed and guarded facility on fifty acres. The location of the Union was near the British military headquarters in the Royal Hospital and multiple other British military camps. Seizing this location, so the rebels thought, would be a strategic success in the heart of the British military positions. Of the 1,000 men expected for this mission, Kent only received 130. A fifth battalion was then also formed to operate outside of Dublin to the north.

All of the rest of the remaining rebels were asked to assemble in front of Liberty Hall beginning at 10:00 a.m. At the Hall, the Citizen's Army formed these volunteers into three groups. The first group left and marched to Stephen's Green. There the group planned to take the Shelbourne Hotel, which strategically would have meant controlling the immediate adjacent area. However, not enough men showed up for the action so those taking part were put to work digging trenches in the Green.

A second group, led by James Connolly, was preparing to march from Liberty Hall to the Castle. The group had been instructed not to attempt to take the Castle since it was a Red Cross Hospital. Rather, the group's goal was to merely seal off its entrances to prevent any troops from entering or leaving the premises. The third group of about seventy volunteers gathered in front of the Hall and became the Headquarters Battalion.

So at 12:04 p.m. on Easter Monday, April 24, 1916, the rebellion began. Many of the organizers knew the insurrection was doomed from the start. Not only had they failed to acquire the arms shipment or any aid from Germany, but only a fraction of their recruits actually showed up for the rebellion. Earlier that morning, Connolly spoke to his friend William O'Brien, "Bill, we're going out to be slaughtered" (Caulfield, 1963, p. 8).

On the way to the Castle, Connolly's battalion decided to take the Post Office. Peter De Rosa writes, "For the sheer hell of it, Connolly yelled, 'Charge', and his troops with pikes, rifles, and bayonets held high, galloped through the columns into the Post Office" (1990, p. 254). Everyone was quickly evacuated from the Post Office. and the two British military officers who happened to be inside were taken prisoner.

Moments later, Connolly's detachment, wearing dark green uniforms and hats with their red hand union badge, marched on the Castle. Pushing past a priest who tried to block them and killing a policeman, the rebels moved in on the guard post. The six men on duty were busy cooking food at the time and were naturally startled by the rebels. They became easily overpowered after the insurrectionists threw a homemade bomb through their window, stunning them long enough for a group of the rebels to enter. Once inside, the rebels seized the guard post and took the guards prisoner.

Once the guard post was seized, the rebels did not attempt to move further into the Castle, fearing there were great numbers of military forces inside. They had no idea that the Castle was largely empty, except for a few civil servants and could have been easily taken. But this was also not part of their intended mission, as they were instructed only to stop the access to and from the Castle.

Instead of penetrating further into the Castle, Volunteer organizer Connolly divided his troops, sending one group to capture the Henry and James outfitters at the corner of Parliament Street. This location was adjacent to the Castle gate, and controlling it meant controlling access to the Castle. A second unit was sent to the *Mail and Express* newspaper officers on the opposite corner, where the staff members were removed by bayonet. The third unit, led by Connolly, retreated into City Hall, gaining access by a specially-impressed key.

As rebels continued to slowly make their way around Dublin taking more small businesses for strategic defense purposes, Patrick Pearse, a key Volunteer organizer emerged at 12:45 from the General Post Office (G.P.O.). He read aloud the Proclamation of the Republic which stated in part:

> In the name of God and of the dead generations... Ireland, through us, summons her children to her flag and strikes for her freedom... We hereby proclaim the Irish Republic as a sovereign state... The Republic guarantees religious and civil liberty, equal rights and opportunities to all its citizens... cherishing all the children of the nation equally (De Rosa, 1990, p. 268).

A small crowd of observers cheered after Pearse completed his reading.

Meanwhile, British troops began to mobilize and make immediate plans to take back the Post Office and the Castle. Heavy exchanges of gunfire occurred between the rebels and British military in the early Dublin afternoon. While British soldiers for hours were falling at the hands of the well-positioned insurrectionists, rebel forces began to suffer casualties later in the day.

In many of the Dublin streets, the rebels set up barricades made up of trams, bicycles, motorcycles and sidecars all wired together. Other barricades consisted of pieced-together furniture from nearby houses. Most of these walls proved highly ineffective, as either they were quickly raided by looters, or the British soldiers merely went around them. The looting was not limited only to the structures erected by the rebels, as many Irish citizens broke store windows and took whatever they could carry in their arms.

Next, the rebels set in on taking over the College of Surgeons, a three-story building on the west side of the Green. After being shot at by the caretaker, they strong-armed their way in and took up sniper positions on the roof. For the rest of the day, the insurgents worked to fortify the college and stock it with supplies.

Pearse, meanwhile, began receiving intelligence from women in a group called *Cumann na mBan*, who bicycled around the city. According to this intelligence, all four of the rebel battalions were in position covering the British Barracks. Along the way these four had also taken some, but not all, of the railway stations in the area. Some of the key stations, Amiens Street and Kingsbridge, still lay in British domain.

Unfortunately for the rebel forces, a great portion of Dublin citizens seemed opposed to the uprising. Pearse had received reports of women in the streets throwing bricks at the insurgents. Other citizens were purely angry at the reality that the rebels had interrupted their holiday. People on their way to various churches cursed the rebels for their sinful ways, and many elderly people were angry at the rebels because the British were giving them pensions every Friday morning. This opposition, from the public whom the rebels were supposedly representing, only added to the downfall of the insurrection.

Adding to the public's anger and opposition to the insurgency was the execution of countless Dublin citizens for physically opposing or simply getting in the way of the rebels. One man who tried to get back his cart, which had been taken and used as part of a barricade, was shot in the head after he refused the rebel orders. The public began to hate the rebels.

That first night the British declared a cease fire until the morning, still unsure of the strength of the rebels. They also were unsure if the rebels had backing from the Germans, and so they had spent the day mobilizing their forces and carefully setting out on fact-finding missions. In their various buildings-turned-bunkers, the rebels set in for at least a short night's sleep.

Early Tuesday morning, the British troops again mobilized and set out to take back City Hall. Through underground corridors, windows, and roofs of other adjacent buildings, the British soldiers stormed the building. They were surprised to find that the entire City Hall was being held by a mere nine rebels. Instantly, the rebel group in the building surrendered.

Later that morning, the British sent for 18-pounder firing guns, which were to be shipped from Althone via roadway. The guns, dreaded by the rebels, destroyed virtually everything in their path along the route to Dublin. Later that afternoon, the guns arrived in the Dublin area.

Late in the day, just before 5:50 p.m., the rebels succeeded in setting up a transmitter powerful enough to be received outside of Ireland. Connolly created a message "telling the outside world that an Irish Republic had been declared in Dublin and that a Republican army, authorized by a Republican government was controlling the capital" (De Rosa, 1990, p. 310). The American press received this message in time for the next day's newspapers.

As the day ended, sixty rebels retreated to the G.P.O., forced from the suburbs of Dublin. After they ate, Pearse divided them and sent them off to local positions. Just as the men attempted to settle in for the night at the G.P.O., an intelligence report came in stating that the British were mobilizing for a bayonet charge. The rebels once again took up all their positions at the G.P.O., where they stayed for the duration of the night.

Early Wednesday morning, the British military set out to take Liberty Hall. The plan was to fire a large gun from the *Helga*, a small armed fisheries patrol boat, at the Hall. Once the Hall was hit, the troops would then charge and storm into the building. The *Helga* fired two shots with the second striking a major blow to the Hall's roof. A third shot forced the main door of the facility to explode outward. For over an hour, the British continually fired shots from the large gun held on the *Helga*. After such time, the roof was destroyed, as was the complete interior structure of the building.

During midday, 2,000 more British troops landed in Ireland and marched to Dublin. De Valera, who was one of those in charge of securing the roads and rail lines against troop reinforcements, was faced with attempting to stop this British force. De Valera only had thirteen men left.

The rebels were able to hold their ground on Wednesday at the Mount Street Bridge, the one bridge they still skillfully occupied. A large battalion of British soldiers was reduced to next to nothing, as snipers fired upon them from many directions. Failing to correctly identify the locations of all the snipers, the British continued to fall, as the battle went on for hours. Only a small handful of snipers, strategically placed, comprised this rebel hold.

Pearse, back at the G.P.O., was still under the false assumption that German forces might land to assist in the battle against the British. He felt that capitalist governments would only use heavy artillery against their cities if they were in real trouble. So when the 18-pound guns arrived and began tearing buildings to pieces, Pearse took that as a sign that the Germans might be on their way.

Intense fighting went on throughout the rest of the day in the inner city area. Other than the brief success the rebels had at holding the British back at the bridge, they were slowly, but surely, losing their ground. As the day ended, many of the rebel troops had been killed, and those alive were short on food and nearly out of ammunition.

At dawn on Thursday, the G.P.O. was attacked by gunfire from all sides. Throughout the rest of the day, British artillery shells struck buildings all over the downtown Dublin area killing, many rebels and forcing others to retreat back to the G.P.O. While the G.P.O. had been hit extensively, it still housed a sizable portion of insurgents. As all the rebel guard posts had to be abandoned on the building, Pearse and his soldiers felt increasingly trapped. They decided to attempt to get out of the building the next day. With a large portion of Dublin in flames, the rebels once again set in for the night.

At daylight on Friday morning, the 18-pound guns again took aim at the G.P.O. It became further clear to the rebels inside that they could not hold out much longer. A key concern was that fires that were ablaze on the roof would spread to the basement, where all of the explosives were being stored. As machine guns and massive artillery continuously hit the roof of the building large fires began to run out of control. The rebels quickly gave up trying to fight the fire from above and retreated to secure the lower floors.

At 6:30 p.m., it was clear to all inside the G.P.O. that the building was a loss. They either had to wave the white flag and surrender or find a way to break out and find a safe destination. They located a soap and sweet factory called "Williams and Wood" on a nearby street that was built like a fortress. The only problem is that they would have to break through a British barricade to get there.

The men began preparing to leave, stuffing as much of the food rations as possible into their bags. For certain, all were aware of their impending fate—either they would escape or die in the process. A man by the name of O'Rahilly, who had originally been opposed to the entire uprising but then later reconsidered once it began, volunteered to lead a group of thirty rebels out of the G.P.O. After Pearse gave O'Rahilly a last handshake, the men stormed out of the building and headed for the Williams and Wood building.

After passing one of their own posts, they broke into two divisions and headed for the British blockade. Coming under intense fire, twenty-one of the men were quickly hit. O'Rahilly was struck by a bullet in his stomach, and, after dropping to the ground in pain, got up again to lead another charge at the British. He was instantly hit many more times.

At 8:30 p.m., another group led by Michael Collins prepared to leave the G.P.O. for the Williams and Wood building. They hoped that the first group under O'Rahilly had been successful, but they had no real way of knowing. As they ran out, they also came under heavy fire from the British. Again, most of these rebels were hit, and those who survived ran into alleys and houses to hide. Shortly thereafter, another group left the G.P.O. and faced the same fate.

The fourth and final party left the G.P.O. after another short while. This group included both Pearse and Connolly, who was wounded and had to be carried on a stretcher. Hit with severe fire power from the British, this group also attempted to duck into barns, houses, or any shelter. Pearse then ordered the remaining men to try to burrow from house to house toward Williams and Wood. All night long men worked underground, building tunnels to try to provide a safer escape than the alternative—getting shot out in the open by the British.

Early Saturday morning, after eating a makeshift breakfast, the remaining leaders and men crawled through the newly-built tunnels to a new headquarters inside Hanlon's fish market. During a meeting held at this new location, it was decided that their only hope was to attempt to get west and link up with the rebel contingent at Four Courts. To do this, though, they definitely needed some sort of diversion. As the remaining leaders concentrated on a plan, Pearse gave the order to various houses that there would be no more firing until further notice.

While a portion of the remaining leaders wanted to fight until the death, Pearse was fully conscious of the fact that their insurrection was causing ongoing massive civilian deaths. After pausing for a long moment, Pearse stated, "For the sake of our fellow citizens and our comrades across this city who are likely to be shot or burned to death, I propose... we surrender" (De Rosa, 1990, p. 375). Instantly, a handkerchief was tied to a stick and waved outside. It was met with gunshots from the British soldiers. After the flag was again waved outside the fish market, there was silence. All of the rebels feared though that they would be shot anyway, just as many others who had attempted to surrender under the white flag had been shot.

Elizabeth O' Farrel was given the task of walking out into the open with the white flag. Part of the rebel forces and supporters, Farrel had been working in the insurrection as a medic and Red Cross Volunteer. She approached the British with a message: "The Commandant-General of the Irish Republican Army wishes to treat with the Commander of the British Forces in Ireland" (De Rosa, 1990, p. 376). After first being laughed at and dismissed, she was then taken seriously. General Lowe of the British military apologized to Farrel for the rudeness of his men, and asked her to repeat her message. After she did, Lowe ordered a cease fire in the area and sent a signed reply to Pearse in writing. The message stated:

> A woman has come in and tells me you wish to negotiate with me. I am prepared to receive you in Great Britain Street at the North End of Moore Street provided you surrender unconditionally.
>
> You will proceed up Moore Street accompanied by the woman who brings you this note, under a white flag.
>
> W.N.C. Lowe, Brigadier-General (p. 378).

After Farrel returned to Pearse and the remaining other leaders, Pearse read Lowe's message aloud, and they once again held a meeting. Pearse then drafted a reply to Lowe's message, and asked Farrel to take it back as their response. Lowe, furious at Pearse's letter, wrote a final ultimatum, which instructed Pearse to surrender unconditionally before anything was discussed.

Once Farrel delivered this note back to Pearse, he looked around at the faces in the room and then agreed to go. At 3:30 p.m. the two opposing commanders met at the top of Moore Street. Pearse symbolically handed Lowe his sword feeling, like they were at least victorious in creating the most effective Irish uprising to occur in a couple hundred years. He then stepped into a car and was driven to a meeting with British General Maxwell.

At the meeting, Maxwell instructed Pearse to write a message to be sent to all of his remaining men to lay down their arms. After the messages were typed, they were then distributed to the remaining rebel outposts in Dublin. Many of the rebels were at first furious at this surrender, arguing that they could have fought on. But insurrectionist leaders continually told the rebels that they were surrendering to protect the Irish citizens from further bloodshed. Unfortunately, the message did not get out to all the rebel posts before nightfall.

Once the surrender message had been delivered, some of the remaining rebels were taken into custody and herded into an open area, where they spent the night without food, water, or toilet facilities. The few women who had been with the rebels and the Red Cross were treated like the men and forced to relieve themselves where they slept. Pearse was sent off to the Arbour Hill Detention Barracks.

Early Sunday morning, Farrel was instructed to once again take the surrender message to the few remaining rebels. These last rebels, skeptic of the surrender note, refused to lay down their arms without directly talking to General Lowe. At noon, Lowe met the remaining rebel leader, MacDonagh, and convinced him that the surrender note signed by Pearse was legitimate and not written under force. By 3:00 p.m., the surrender had taken effect, and the remaining men were laying down their arms.

Days later in his trial, Pearse offered the following explanation for his actions:

> From my earliest youth I have regarded the connection between Ireland and Great Britain as the curse of the Irish nation, and felt convinced that while it lasted, this country could never be free or happy.
>
> When I was a child of ten I went down on my bare knees by my bedside one night and promised God that I should devote my life to an effort to free my country. I have kept that promise.
>
> We seem to have lost. We have not lost. To re-

fuse to fight would have been to lose; to fight is to win. We have kept faith with the past, and handed on a tradition to the future.

I repudiate the assertion that I sought to aid and abet England's enemy. Germany is no more to me than England is. My aim was to win Irish freedom; we struck the first blow ourselves but we should have been glad of an ally's aid.

I assume that I am speaking to Englishmen who value their freedom and who profess to be fighting for the freedom of Belgium and Serbia.

Believe that we, too, love freedom and desire it. To us it is more desirable than anything else in the world. If you strike us down now, we shall rise again and renew the fight.

You cannot conquer Ireland. You cannot extinguish the Irish passion for freedom. If our deed has not been sufficient to win freedom, then our children will win it by a better deed (De Rosa, 1990, pp. 416-417).

Pearse, along with other leaders, was found guilty and shot on May 3, 1916. The rest of the rebel volunteers were either shot or sent to prison.

While for all practical purposes, the Easter Uprising was a failure in the sense of not obtaining Irish freedom and independence from England, the Volunteer leaders were proud of the attempt they had made. They strongly believed that their insurrection was needed, and even though it may have been doomed from the start, it would provide a spark to ignite a future fire of revolt in Ireland. Little did they know that this egotistical ideal of themselves and their effort would hold somewhat true. When Michael Collins and a few of the imprisoned volunteers were released a few years later, a more successful force was then created.

Largely to the credit of the direction and effort of Collins, this new force would prove to be powerful enough to drive the British to the bargaining table and grant home rule to at least half of Ireland. Of course this meant that Ireland would be divided, and this decision brought problems and opposition of its own. Some Republicans, angered partly at the fame and power Collins had achieved and refusing to agree to any cooperation with the British, began to fight against Collins and his supporters. Unfortunately, this led to what could be considered a civil war in Ireland. For better or worse, that is where Ireland has stayed for the bulk of modern history—half under British military occupation and half under home rule, but both sides always ultimately answering to England.

Strategically, the 1916 Uprising was horribly planned and executed. Not only was there no feasible way the rebels could have been victorious over the larger and more powerful British military, but they could not have even sustained their effort at provoking continuous unrest. While it is true they may have been more successful and lasted longer against the British forces if they had more rebel fighters, weapons, and even backing from Germany, none of this became a reality. When news reached the rebel leaders that the German arms ship had been captured, the rebels had to decide whether or not to continue with their plans. Their choice lay between calling it off (and facing the inevitable wrath of repression that would come from the British, who then knew of the plan for insurrection) and going ahead with the uprising with less arms and backing. To make matters further complicated for the rebel leaders, that confusing message went out on Easter Sunday publicly declaring that the uprising was called off. Unfortunately for the insurrectionists, many rebel men read this and were either not around or not sober enough to hear the calls to action the next day.

To the rebel leaders, though, for their country—their pride and heritage—they knew they had to fight. As Pearse stated in his trial, "To refuse to fight would have been to lose; to fight is to win. We have kept faith with the past, and handed on a tradition to the future" (De Rosa, 1990, p.417). In this sense, the uprising using political violence had legitimacy—to act against injustice is a legitimate right.

# PART TWO

# Nonviolence and Political Violence Used in Pursuit of Political and Social Change

# CHAPTER EIGHT

# *Theories of Nonviolence*

I will begin this chapter by looking at the Gandhian principle and theory of nonviolence. Gandhi was not the first or the last individual to engage in or have theories about nonviolence, but because of his fame and thorough development of the practice, I find him a suitable base to begin.

Owing to his strongly religious base, being Hindu himself and yet extracting various qualities contained within many religions, Gandhi felt that the pursuit of truth is perhaps the noblest cause in life. He defined the highest truth as *anything and everything that has the greatest good for the most.*

In past workshops I have given, I recall attempting to explain this definition by looking at a specific example. For instance, suppose that I did not know, and had never heard, anything about the effort to stop the cutting of old growth trees in Northern California. Then one day, I decided to define the highest truth to myself as it applied to this situation. I would need to carefully review all arguments on both sides of the debate. Next, I would ask questions such as *who stands to benefit in any way from the old growth trees being cut down?* My answer would be *the loggers, the lumber companies, distributors, retail establishments, perhaps governments by way of taxation, all the way down to the consumer who purchases and uses the wood product.* So a lot of people benefit. My next question would then be *who would be hurt by the logging of those trees?* My answer would be *people (who may own homes near potential mudslides, who may rely on nearby water for their drinking supply, everyone suffering from a dramatic decrease in global air quality, etc.), and nonhuman animals (those who rely on the area in question for habitat, those who rely on the particular ecosystem in question for survival, etc.).* My conclusion would then be that because the logging of old growth trees potentially hurts more life than it benefits, I would support efforts to stop the logging. My highest truth—again, anything and everything that holds the greatest good for the most—would be to let those trees stand. This personal example is one I always used to rationalize my belief in Gandhi's definition of truth.

*Satyagraha* was the term, coined by Gandhi, labeling this nonviolent pursuit of truth. According to Gandhi, no one is capable of knowing the absolute truth, and therefore, Satyagraha excludes the use of violence. This idea is based on the assumption that one who uses violence claims to know the absolute truth. Satyagraha relies on the notion that the moral appeal to the conscience and heart is more effective than an appeal based on threats and violence. "For the Satyagrahi (practitioner of satyagraha), this wider truth cannot be achieved through violence (which violates human needs and destroys life), because violence is itself is a form of injustice" (Burrowes, 1996, p. 108).

Gandhi felt that there must be no separation between means and ends and was bold enough to assert that if the means are correct (referring to the correct application of nonviolence), then the desired end will come naturally. He thoroughly rejected the eye-for-an-eye strategy, which he felt would just lead to a universally blind world. Instead, Gandhi sought to reverse the cycle of violence by engaging in Satyagraha, or *soul force* as he sometimes referred to it (Fischer, 1954, p. 35).

Rather than answering an opponent's violence with violence, Gandhi felt it crucial to demonstrate love, respect, and a certain degree of self suffering. In his book, *Non-violent Resistance*, Gandhi wrote, "In the application of Satyagraha I discovered in the earliest stages that pursuit of truth did not admit of violence being inflicted on one's opponent but that he must be weaned from error by patience and sympathy" (1961, p. 6). He further explains the doctrine of Satyagraha as meaning "vindication of truth not by infliction of suffering on the opponent but on one's self" (1961, p. 6).

The notion of self suffering is difficult to grasp at first, and a more in depth analysis leads to further complexities. The basic theory entails a belief that the individual holds the power (or as Gandhi would say the *soul force*) to allow the opponent to see the evils in his or her own actions and voluntarily change. Having sound faith in the decency of humanity and the strength of conscience, Gandhi felt that the opponent could see his or her own evils through a reaction to the Satyagrahi's self suffering.

One of the classic examples that has been used to illustrate this process occurred with the raid on the Dharsana Salt Works by Satyagrahis in India during 1930. The British Government (then colonial ruler of India) had declared it illegal for Indians to produce their own salt. Instead, the natives had to not only purchase salt from British owned companies, but they had to pay taxes on the salt as well. After a remarkable civil disobedience action led by Gandhi, in which he and several thousand others marched 241 miles to the sea to illegally make salt, Gandhi had next planned to raid a British-owned salt manufacturer. As Gandhi was arrested at the end of the Salt March, a poet named Mrs. Sarojini led the raid with 2500 volunteers. The following is an account of an eyewitness newsman, Webb Miller, who first reported the information in dispatches and then in his book, *I Found No Peace*:

> In complete silence the Gandhi men drew up and halted a hundred yards from the stockade. A picked column advanced from the crowd, waded the ditches, and approached the barbed-wire stockade. Suddenly, at a word of command, scores of native policemen rushed upon the advancing marchers and rained blows on their heads with their steel-shod lathis (staves). Not one of the marchers even raised an arm to fend off the blows. They went down like ten-pins. From where I stood I heard the sickening wack of the clubs on unprotected skulls. The waiting crowd of marchers groaned and sucked in their breath in sympathetic pain at every blow. Those struck down fell sprawling, unconscious or writhing with fractured skulls or broken shoulders... The survivors without breaking ranks, silently and doggedly marched on until struck down. Although everyone knew that within a few minutes he would be beaten down, perhaps killed, I could detect no sign of wavering or fear. They marched steadily, with heads up, without the encouragement of music or

cheering or any possibility that they might escape injury or death. The police methodically and mechanically beat down the second column. There was no fight, no struggle, the marchers simply walked forward until struck down (Fischer, 1954, p. 101).

Reportedly, the raids and beatings continued for many days.

This boldly defiant act of civil disobedience signaled the birth of moral freedom for India and would help lead to the eventual independence for the country. It allowed the British to further see India's resolve to rule itself and to sacrifice itself for its own freedom. Followers of the Gandhi-an ethic, such as Louis Fischer in his book *Gandhi: His Life and Message for the World*, states that this dramatic example of nonviolent disobedience "showed England was powerless and India invincible" (1954, p. 102).

A strategic perplexity immediately comes to mind when analyzing this or countless other examples of nonviolent civil disobedience. There can be no realistic denial of the reliance of the Satyagraha philosophy and of the practice of nonviolent civil disobedience on the working, healthy conscience of the opponent. The implicit assumption contained within the Satyagraha theory—that one must be weaned from error by patience and sympathy and that love and respect will win over the opponent—is based on the belief that the opponent's conscience has the ability to function according to the Satyagrahi's needs (or as Gandhi would assert, to provide for justice, humanity, and truth). While it is obvious that Gandhi and his followers throughout generations have held humankind in the highest regard and considered all capable of love and decency, this stems far from a realistic analysis of societal problems. In fact, it is a trivial approach to injustice, based on various historical religious doctrines.

What does it take to have a working and healthy conscience? I would suggest that directly implies the ability to decipher between good and evil, right and wrong, justice and injustice. The important question then needs to be asked: *Does an individual knowingly involved in an injustice have a working or healthy conscience?* Take, for instance, the example of the large tobacco companies, who for years have marketed products known to cause cancer and other health problems in humans. The problem is not that the executives of such companies are unaware of the health risks associated with tobacco, but that they are aware and proceed to market and sell their products to addicted consumers.

What signs, if any, are there that executives of the tobacco companies have working consciences? An honest look would reveal none. On the contrary, there have been clear indications for years that the consciences of these executives are far from healthy. A working conscience would have upheld the position that the human lives are more important than a company's profits. To assume that nonviolence would have worked in this scenario, to stop tobacco companies from selling products, is a far stretch from reality. Sure, progress could have been made perhaps with public boycotts, since these businesses are concerned with profit and loss margins. Yet the nonviolence ethic that states that *one must see the evil in his or her own actions and voluntarily change* would have been extremely ineffective. An individual who is unable (due to an unhealthy conscience) to knowingly decide whether or not to create (or continuing creating) a massive injustice must also be considered unable to voluntarily change his or her actions, based on decisions formed by his or her own conscience responding to outside opposing interests.

A more extreme example to illustrate my point can be found by referring to the case of the Nazi Holocaust. When asked if nonviolence, or Satyagraha, could be successful in stopping the Nazis, Gandhi replied that it could, but not without great casualties. While I agree the casualties would be, and were, tremendous, I take great exception to the assertion that nonviolence would have had any ability to succeed against Hitler and his forces. Why? The Nazis were operating on the mythical belief that the Aryan race is superior to all, and others (specifically Jews, homosexuals, and more) were fit only to be enslaved or executed. The extremity of these beliefs and severe nature of the repressive tactics used by Hitler would strongly suggest that a healthy, working conscience was not present. To imply that a small, or even massive, movement of nonviolent resisters could have successfully stopped the Holocaust serves to only lighten and trivialize the suffering and murder of Holocaust victims.

Gandhi also believed that conflict is largely the result of the denial of human needs through social structural problems (Burrowes, 1996, p. 112). He therefore identified, as a part of success, the creation of a superior social structure. This directly opposes the eye- for-an-eye strategy by making the argument that if the intention is a just world, unjust techniques and methodologies must not be utilized to accomplish that end. While there is an obvious amount of logic to this argument, logic also suggests this ideological vision of a utopian world through peaceful means is not a realistic approach for all.

Those preaching and adhering to a strict nonviolence policy in most westernized, post-industrial societies differ from those who may be engaged in armed self defense in less industrialized nations. The main difference lies within the idea of privilege. Those in post-industrial societies usually have more time, resources, and security to think about how best to get to utopia (and even what utopia may be) than those who are in an everyday battle to defend their lives, communities, and culture.

Gandhi also felt that in nonviolence, the Satyagrahi must be able to separate the individual from the individual's actions. "Hate the sin and not the sinner," he wrote in his book, *Gandhi: An Autobiography* (1968, p. 230). The importance of separating the individual from the action directly relates to the belief that all are capable of goodness. It is this outstanding faith in the human conscience that assumes even Hitler should be separated from his deeds, since he may have had the ability to change for the better. In idealistic terms this may be fairly plausible, but in reality it must be remembered that it is the very individual that is *taking* or *causing* the action in the first place.

Gandhi's effectual influences in creating his nonviolent adherence and strategies stemmed from a long history of religious beliefs to various forms of nonviolent applications. Tolstoy once wrote, in discussing the matter of civil disobedience and nonviolence, "You are told from the Gospel that one should not only refrain from killing his brothers, but should not do that which leads to murder: one should not be angry with one's brothers, nor hate one's enemies, but love them" (Tolstoy, 1967, p. 40). While Gandhi was not the first to understand the importance of nonviolent action, he did serve to influence others, who would follow in his footsteps studying the issue or becoming nonviolent Satyagrahis themselves.

There are various other theories and strategies regarding nonviolence and its potential applications. Now with a brief look at the Gandhian belief, other examples can be more clearly demonstrated.

One such theorist, Gene Sharp, has spent a great number of years analyzing nonviolent approaches to conflict and has developed his own in-depth study entitled *The Politics of Nonviolent Action*. This three-part series, published in 1973, is divided into *Power and Struggle, The Methods of Nonviolent Action*, and *The Dynamics of Nonviolent Action*. Appearing to be largely based upon the Gandhian approach to the issue, Sharp's study does deviate slightly, with attention to minor details.

Sharp writes in Volume 3, *The Dynamics of Nonviolent Action*, that nonviolent behavior is likely to contribute to a variety of positive accomplishments. "Four of these are 1) winning sympathy and support, 2) reducing casualties, 3) inducing mutiny of the opponent's troops, 4) attracting maximum participation in the nonviolent struggle" (p. 595). He cites the example of three young civil rights workers murdered in Mississippi in 1964 as demonstrating that casualties will occur. However, he writes, "But this does not refute this tendency on nonviolent behavior to limit the repression" (p. 596).

This limiting of repression appears to have been quite unsuccessful in the limited attempts at nonviolent resistance during the Holocaust. There are accounts of Norwegian and Danish nonviolent resistance, in addition to passive resistance used by the Jews. Yet, the outcome was perhaps as horrifying as one can imagine, and it is a far stretch to assume that these limited examples of nonviolence strategy did anything to reduce casualties. As I previously suggested, the passivity and lack of other more extreme action by various parties, both those inside and outside the concentration camps, directly enabled the systematic murder of a massive number of people and the near successful implementation of the Nazis' *Final Solution* to their perceived Jewish problem.

Sharp cites three ways that nonviolent action is successfully achieved. The first way is through *conversion*, in which the opponent becomes changed inwardly. The second is through *accommodation*, in which the opponent decides it is best to give in but still disagrees. The third way is through *nonviolent coercion*, in which the opponent "disagrees and wants to continue the conflict but is unable to do so" (p. 706).

The notion of nonviolent coercion is greatly controversial among scholars and practitioners of nonviolence. Gandhi felt that the person who uses coercion is guilty of purposeful violence (Burrowes, 1996, p. 119). He refused to acknowledge any coercion contained within Satyagraha. Yet, it is most certain that coercion is, in fact, a part of the nonviolent application. Even if the opponent admits to voluntarily changing his or her unjust ways, that change was prompted by the nonviolent action in theory. The opponent did not decide on his or her own to change but was affected by outside interests intent on having the change made. When the opponent changes but still disagrees and doesn't want to change, that is a clear indication of coercion. The nonviolent party, through his or her actions, in a way theoretically forces the opponent to change against his or her will. Remarkably, this is also the basis of more extreme forms of action, including armed revolution.

The same mythical phenomena seen in the Gandhian nonviolence theories are also present in Sharp's methodology. The absolute faith in the power of the nonviolent activist is demonstrated by Sharp in the following passage:

> If the nonviolent actionists remain fearless, keep their nonviolent discipline are willing to accept the sufferings inflicted for their defiance, and are determined to persist, then the opponent's attempt to force them to submit to his will is likely to be thwarted. He may be able to imprison them, to injure them, or even to execute them, but as long as they hold out, his will remains unfulfilled. Even if only a single person remains defiant, to that degree the opponent is defeated (1973, p. 636).

Ward Churchill, in his book *Pacifism as Pathology*, cites the example of Jews in the Holocaust period as a reminder of how unrealistic Sharp's idealistic theory can be.
He writes, in contrast:

> Eventually the SS could count upon the brundt of the nazi liquidation policy carried out by *Sonderkommandos*, which were largely composed of the Jews themselves. It was largely Jews who dragged the gassed bodies of their exterminated people to the crematoria in death camps such as Auschwitz/Birkenau, each motivated by the desire to prolong his own life. Even this became rationalized as 'resistance'; the very act of surviving was viewed as 'defeating' the nazi program. By 1945, Jewish passivity and nonviolence in the face of the *weltanschauung der untermenschen* had done nothing to prevent the loss of millions of lives" (1998, p.33).

With the systematic execution of more than five million Jews during the Holocaust, it remains to be seen how Sharp's notion of mere survival equaling resistance or revolution is indeed a plausible outcome of real-life, serious conflicts (Hilberg, pp. 1047-48).

Sabotage is another area widely condemned by most nonviolent theorists. Sharp sees sabotage as only seriously weakening a nonviolent movement. He goes as far as to list nine different reasons that sabotage will have this negative effect on nonviolence struggles. One reason is that the use of sabotage always involves the risk of injury or even death to opponents or innocent bystanders. While this may be true in many types of sabotage, it is fruitless to apply this idea unilaterally. For instance, if one decided to burn a piece of the opponent's property, then Sharp's concerns would be well founded. Obviously, the use of fire is dangerous and can result in injury or death to others, whether they are the opponent, innocent bystanders or fire fighters. But Sharp's rationale would not apply so directly to a billboard advertisement that is damaged or destroyed, for example. The risk of injury to the opponent or bystanders in this example is next to nothing.

Another reason Sharp opposes sabotage is the belief that it requires a willingness to use violence if the saboteurs are caught or their plan revealed. This directly depends on the parties involved in the sabotage and what strategies they have decided to implement. I have seen no evidence that would lead me to believe that this notion of a willingness to use violence if caught is adhered to by a majority, let alone all saboteurs.

He also takes notion with the supposed secrecy aspect of sabotage. While I will admit that the majority of sabotage actions do involve a high level of secrecy (largely due to their illegality and the reality of charges, such as conspiracy), secrecy is not a necessary aspect. A recent example of a successful sabotage action occurred in the French countryside, when numerous individuals announced publicly they were going to trespass on private land and destroy multiple acres of genetically-engineered crops (owned in part by the U.S.-based Monsanto). There was little, if any, secrecy involved with this action, and the group succeeded with its goal of destroying all of the modified crops.

Sharp feels that only a few people are needed to commit sabotage, and that greatly reduces the numbers of "effective resisters" (Sharp, 1973, p. 610). In his own perception of nonviolence as cited above, Sharp places heavy value on the power of one or just a few individuals. (*If a single person remains defiant, to that degree the opponent is defeated.*) Strategically speaking, it is logical to assume that in both nonviolent action and sabotage, a few can act on a particular methodology, but the more acting the better off the movement would be.

As the fifth reason that sabotage pollutes the pool of nonviolent resistance, Sharp cites that "confidence in the adequacy of nonviolent action is a great aid to its successful application" (1973 p. 610). While I would agree that confidence in nonviolence is helpful, it is likewise desired for any type of movement using any tactical means. The army using conventional warfare relies on the confidence of its troops to fulfill its destiny. The ability for saboteurs to successfully commit actions rests directly on their level of confidence.

Sharp next comes to a belief on a perceived problem of sabotage for nonviolence. He merely makes the distinction between nonviolent strategy as that which is based upon a challenge in "human terms" by humans to humans rather than sabotage being based on destruction of property (1973, p. 610). Going back to the argument over coercion, I think the underlying trait of each strategy is trying to force one's opponents to change their ways. Force does not have to be physical but can be psychological as well. Gandhi, who himself despised the idea of using coercion, named his nonviolent strategy Satyagraha, which he has translated into meaning, in short, *soul force*. This force of the soul, not unlike the force of property destruction, is placing a psychological pressure on the opponents to change their ways, often against their will.

Sharp's statement about the appeal in human terms to the opponent is another example of the utmost faith placed in humans and a failure to understand the nature and outcome of conflicts throughout history. It is an assumption that appears to rest upon the belief that the other tactics are inhuman or even subhuman, and are needless and harmful for the realization of humanity.

Another reason proposed by Sharp is that sabotage is likely to produce a greater amount of repression against the saboteurs or innocent bystanders. This belief is directly taken from the *Circle of Violence Theory*, which states that violence applied toward one's opponent will only result in a greater degree of violence applied back to oneself. Thus the spiral of violence is never ending until one party annihilates the other.

Yet, there is strong evidence suggesting that the opponent will respond accordingly to a perceived threat. In the example of revolutionary practices within a particular nation, that given government is going to respond with an increase in repression the more it feels its power is threatened. Nonviolent theorists, such as Sharp, will assert that nonviolence can lessen the degree of repression by not provoking the circle of violence. In reality, it is practical to assume that nonviolent tactics have on occasion been met with less repression directly because the tactics did not actually threaten the power of the state. It is arguable that instead, nonviolent tactics only have served to reinforce the power of certain states by succumbing to state-sanctioned forms of dissent, which, while making the participants feel better about themselves, have accomplished little if anything in practical terms of revolutionary change.

Sharp believes that where sabotage is concerned, if there is a loss of lives, it will reflect negatively on the nonviolent movement. The casualties will, in theory, diminish the opponent's respect for the nonviolent activists. This assertion rests entirely on the belief that the opponent is able to have an ounce of respect for the nonviolent activists in the first place. I discussed this matter earlier in the chapter.

The ninth and final reason Sharp gives as to why sabotage harms nonviolent movements is the belief that both tactics are based on different premises about how to "undermine the opponent" (1973, p. 610). It is interesting Sharp chose to use the term "undermine," which implies working secretly against a person. While it is obvious that there are some sharp differences in the two philosophies, the nature of secrecy and coercion can be contained within both.

In his book, *Exploring Nonviolent Alternatives*, Sharp explains nonviolent action as being a largely generic term, and he tells us that "it includes the large class of phenomena variously called nonviolent resistance, satyagraha, passive resistance, positive action, and nonviolent direct action" (1970, p.31). Gandhi, on the other hand, felt that true nonviolent action was void of passivity, and he sought to differentiate his tactics from some of those employed by the suffragettes in England around the turn of the century. He wrote, "Passive resistance has been conceived and is regarded as a weapon of the weak" (Gandhi, 1951, p. 1). Rather, he saw Satyagraha as a tool of strength and discipline to resist violence and temptation.

Sharp was also perhaps one of the first to use the term political *jiu-jitsu*. This has been described as the opponent's violence and repression acting against his or her own power position (Sharp, 1970, 56). The belief is that the more violent repression is used against a nonviolent movement, the more the opponent will look foolish and evil in the eyes of bystanders. My only question to this is: *What if the only bystanders are too politically weak to act or care about this repression?* How can that benefit the nonviolent movement? I am not certain it can, at least in all cases.

Another philosopher of the power of nonviolence, whose writings on the subject have influenced massive populations including Gandhi, was Henry David Thoreau. In his famous essay, *Civil Disobedience*, Thoreau theorized about the nature of nonviolent civil disobedience. Like Gandhi, Thoreau placed a high level of faith in the conscience of the individual and in humanity in general. He writes:

Can there not be a government in which majorities do
not virtually decide right and wrong, but conscience? - in
which majorities decide only those questions to which the
rule of expediency is applicable?  Must the citizen ever
for a moment, or in the least degree, resign his conscience
to the legislator?  Why has every man a conscience then?
(Thomas, 1966, p. 224).

He provides strong evidence of his belief in the importance of
means equaling ends when he writes, "What I have to do is to see, at any
rate, that I do not lend myself to the wrong which I condemn" (1966, p.
231).  This relates directly to the belief in conducting oneself at all times in
the manner one wishes to be treated and in the way one wishes the world to
change.  This concept, shared by Gandhi and other nonviolence theorists,
was perhaps picked up by Thoreau in his readings of the *Bhagavad-Gita*
and portions of the sacred Hindu *Upanishads* (Fischer, 1954, p. 38).

One of the most important influence Gandhi may have extracted
from Thoreau's writings was the notion of the duty of the self in listening
to the just conscience.  Thoreau writes in 1849, in protest of slavery and
the invasion of Mexico, "The only obligation I have the right to assume is
to do at any time what I think is right" (Thomas, 1966, p. 225).  This notion of the *right* may well have helped influence Gandhi's vision of truth
and its relation to the conscience.

Thoreau created his sought-after essay after spending the night in
jail for refusing to pay taxes.  His spiritual outlook on his brief time behind
bars can be definitely seen as downplaying the repressive nature of the
prison system.  "I saw that, if there was a wall of stone between me and my
townsmen, there was a still more difficult one to climb or break through,
before they could get to be as free as I was.  I did not for a moment feel
confined, and the walls seemed a great waste of stone and mortar" (1966,
p. 236).
While I understand Thoreau's idealistic approach to prison, I find his
analysis not well grounded, being chiefly based on his twenty-four hour
period of incarceration.  In theory, one who has spent years behind bars
most likely agrees with the ineffectiveness of the prison system.  Yet, it
would be far fetched to suggest that spending years in lock-up does not
restrict both a person's physical and mental freedom.

Influenced by Gandhi and Jesus, among others, Martin Luther
King, Jr. also lived devoted to preaching and acting on nonviolence.  King

was convinced that nonviolent struggle was the best methodology for the civil rights movement in the United States. He wrote, "Now the plain, inexorable fact is that any attempt of the American Negro to overthrow his oppressor with violence will not work" (King, 1967, p. 56).

Like Thoreau and Gandhi, King had a strong belief in the inherent goodness inside all of humanity. As Gandhi believed in the *soul force*, King pushed the idea of love as a revolutionary tool. He preached, "Only through our adherence to nonviolence—which also means love in its strong and commanding sense—will the fear in the white community be mitigated" (King, 1967, pp. 59-60). Especially in the cases of Gandhi and King, the idea of appealing to the opponent's good nature through compassion, love, and respect was universal.

Another recurring theme shared by both Gandhi and King is the belief in the circle of violence theory. Regarding the use of violence, King felt that "returning violence for violence multiplies violence, adding deeper darkness to a night already devoid of stars. Darkness cannot drive out darkness: only light can do that. Hate cannot drive out hate: only love can do that" (King, 1967, p. 63). He also believed that by resorting to the use of violent tactics, the Black Power and/or civil rights movements would be imitating white society's values, which were objectionable.

In his book, *Where Do We Go From Here: Chaos or Community?*, King outlines six aspects of a complete nonviolent struggle: (1) "somebodyness," (2) "group identity," (3) "full and constructive use of the freedom we already have," (4) "powerful action programs," (5) "a continuing job of organization," and (6) "giving society an new sense of values" (1967, pp. 122-132). King felt that nonviolent campaigns were just one aspect of an overall nonviolence struggle. This clearly demonstrates the concern King shared with others for the actual transformation of the values, ethics, and thought process of the society as a whole.

In the first aspect, *somebodyness*, King places emphasis on having a strong sense of self worth. The individual, who has been demoralized by the injustice, needs to overcome "a disastrous sense of his own worthlessness...a terrible feeling of being less than human" (1967, p. 122). While King was perhaps speaking of specifically the oppression and exploitation of blacks throughout the history of the United States, the message can be applied to various situations. Commonly, where an individual is faced with injustice, some form of dehumanization accompanies the process. In King's eyes, part of the methodology of liberation or justice is to demonstrate an extreme amount of self worth, shedding all clues that the dehumanizing was the least bit successful.

The second aspect, *group identity*, naturally follows placing worth in the self. Here King suggests that the next logical step after realizing one's own worth is the realization of the worth of one's group identity. Where injustice is applied to a vast population, whether based on religion, race, gender, sexual orientation, or nationality, dehumanization will have also occurred. This entire population then needs to realize its own worth to be strong and healthy. A good example of this theory is not only African Americans in the civil rights movement, but the extreme rise of gays and lesbians *coming out* during the last twenty to thirty years. King believed that the recognition of self worth would be a common bond joining people in the struggle to overcome discrimination. He spoke, "This form of group unity can do definitely more to liberate the Negro than any action of individuals. We have been oppressed as a group and we must overcome that oppression as a group" (1967, p. 125).

King's third aspect of a nonviolent struggle is *full and constructive use of the freedom we already have*. Just as Gandhi once volunteered to scrub the toilets while imprisoned, King believed that even during the struggle for justice, even with all the discrimination an individual or population may face, it is necessary at all times to demonstrate the highest level of humanity. He felt it necessary to simultaneously campaign vigorously against discrimination and demonstrate the true abilities of the African American individual. Indeed, these activities are one and the same to King, Gandhi, and perhaps even Thoreau.

Next, King's aspect of the *powerful action program* comes to play. Here he stresses the importance of nonviolent campaigns, which he felt have the ability to change not only the individual, but also entire structures. While demonstrating the humanity and self worth of the individual and population, King deemed it necessary to go further and take action to alleviate societal injustices. He wrote, "If the Negro does not add persistent pressure to his patient plea, he will end up empty handed...So every ethical appeal to the white man must be accomplished by nonviolent pressure" (1967, pp.128-129).

King's goal here with the use of nonviolent campaigns was definitely reform, rather than revolution. He felt that with the idea of reform, nonviolent strategies held the highest possibility of success. "The American racial revolution has been a revolution to 'get in' rather than to overthrow...This goal itself indicates that a social change in America must be nonviolent. If one is in search of a better job, it does not help to burn down the factory" (1967, p.130). *Unless of course, it is the very factory that is preventing one from acquiring the better job!*

King's fifth aspect of nonviolent struggle was *a continuing job of organization*. The extreme value and importance of organizing is high-lighted in this aspect. King not only felt that the oppressed population needs to be organized, but he was also concerned with how the organization would be accomplished. Looking at social divisions, King preached the need for middle-class African Americans to organize together with the lower-class or economically-deprived section of the population. The more a movement is successfully organized, the greater ability it has to create the changes it so desires.

This leads directly to King's sixth aspect for nonviolent struggle. King realized that in many cases, it is just not one particular population that is being oppressed on its own. Instead many populations may experience similar injustices due to the same societal policies. Acknowledging this, King felt that it is necessary "to be ever mindful of enlarging the whole society, and giving it a new sense of values as we seek to solve our particular problem" (1967, p. 132).

King's six aspects for a nonviolent struggle indicate a conscious concern for the state of the whole society. It is also a great demonstration of the value he shared with Gandhi in the means, rather than ends, of solving conflict. While I agree with the concept that society does need an incredible transformation, I am not convinced that can be successfully accomplished with insider reform and restructuring. Rather, we need to adopt a clear revolutionary approach that identifies the very social and political structure of many societies (but especially in the United States) as one of the main problems.

It is not just a mere coincidence that the majority of nonviolent theorists come predominantly from a background of privilege. It is easily arguable that the reason nonviolence is so popular in countries such as the United States is the high level of physical and economic security of its residents. Even in their own times, amongst their own populations, Gandhi and King were in positions of privilege. Gandhi, who began his career as an English-schooled attorney, had the majority of his expenses paid for throughout his nonviolent experimentation. King, likewise, was not among the poorest sectors of black society, but held—to a degree—a position of power and authority.

This notion, that nonviolence is primarily preached by those in privileged positions, is important to note. Rarely have there been occasions when individuals or mass populations, threatened with mere survival on a daily basis, have decided that nonviolence is the morally proper and strategically-sound methodology to follow. For many, this decision is not even an option, as all focus goes into protecting one's life, family, community or nation by any means necessary.

Unfortunately, the decision to follow a strategy of nonviolence in political and social justice pursuits comes from the above-identified position of privilege and also from overt or underlying religious beliefs. These factors constitute the chief reasoning behind the decision, which is made most often without considering the crucial question: *Does nonviolence strategy have the ability to produce the necessary change to allow for social and political justice?* I would argue that it does *not* have this ability, due to its failure to contain the potentiality to actually confront and overthrow particular, militaristic power structures, such as the U.S. government.

# CHAPTER NINE

# *On Political Violence*

The topic of methodologies of social change is virtually a timeless matter of international interest. The means by which progress can best be achieved has been debated for years and will no doubt continue to be discussed and argued over as long as the imperfection of societies is a reality. On one side of this argument sit proponents of nonviolence, ranging from those proclaiming a strict adherence to others who, at least on a minimal basis, understand and practice the principles. In this category, there are ample volumes of literature dedicated to explaining the rationale—the justification on a moral and philosophical level—for engaging in nonviolent social struggle.

However, on the other side of the fence, opponents argue against a strict adherence to nonviolence. While few scholars, theorists, and outright revolutionaries openly declare their love and desire for armed struggle on any level, many do promote the right to self defense, which can, and often does, include the use of political violence. On a sociological and psychological level, there is a wealth of resources attempting to understand the mindset of the group or individual who takes up arms and violence in pursuit of justice. Additionally, on a purely tactical basis, from guerrilla warfare to massive, armed insurrection involving full, conventional militaries, there is also a substantial amount of literature. Yet, to the direct counter of the nonviolent theorist who maintains the means-versus-ends argument, there is little in the way of explanation from a rational standpoint of why one takes up arms.

In this chapter I intend to discuss the strategy of political violence, particularly the tactical, moral, and philosophical justifications for the use of armed force in attempting to create a just world. It will most likely be helpful to first reiterate a couple of definitions. To begin, violence is often defined in varying terms. For the purpose of this work, it is defined as that which physically harms humans. Regardless of my personal beliefs—as well as the bulk of information supporting the notion that violence can also be both psychological and can be inflicted against any life form (other animals, the natural environment)—the above simplistic definition will suffice.

Political violence, therefore, can be defined as actions harming humans, taken for political purposes. This explanation may well include violence committed by nation states against other nation states (such as the United States against Afghanistan, Iraq and many others in recent history); violence taken by nation states against international, non-domestic populations (such as the U.S. military action against Al Qaida); action by nation states against their own population (such as the Mexican government against the Zapatistas or the United States against Natives and African Americans); domestic groups against nation states (such as the Weathermen against the U.S. government or the Angry Brigade against the English government) and domestic groups against one another (groups such as the Earth Liberation Front targeting industry and commerce in contemporary times) and, on the individual level, persons taking action against one another, populations, groups, and governments. Under this broad definition, political violence incorporates many varied opportunities, and there are numerous examples of each type throughout recent history. For this particular chapter, however, I would like to concentrate on political violence perpetrated at the individual and group level, by those who, for one reason or many, decide to use violence as a means for achieving justice and positive social change.

The reasoning for the use of violence can be divided into at least two separate schools of thought. The first revolves around the idea that violence in some way is a natural reaction to various situations, especially those that are life threatening. For instance, when an oppressive government comes down upon a specific sector of a population, perhaps targeting them for annihilation (as in the case of Nazi Germany), that population often times will react in a violent nature, as a matter of self defense. While the overwhelming majority of Jews targeted by the Nazis did not react violently, a minimal proportion did throughout the implementation of the Nazi's *Final Solution*.

Another example can be found by looking at the Algerian Revolution. Moslem Algerians took up arms to fight the French only after it was evident that their very existence was at stake. The most extreme example illustrating this point occurs when an individual, who is targeted for assassination by a government, fights back with violence just prior to the execution. In these situations the decision to use violence is not so much a well thought-out, conscious, and deliberate one, as it is a matter of necessity, of urgency, and last resort.

In his essay *Let My People Go*, printed in *When All Else Fails: Christian Arguments on Violent Revolution*, Duclos states:

> The violence of the poor is a violence that has been imposed on them, a violence that is necessary. He knows very well that the poor are the first and worst sufferers from violence, because the order of the powerful never hesitates to augment its violence when the "little ones" lift their heads. The violence of the poor is sacrificial. They spill their blood for a common liberation from injustice, for love of their fellows. It is a resistance of the spirit, an explosion of their dignity that has been left no other means for expressing itself. All ways of human expression have been closed to them, every dialogue refused, no attention has been paid to their painful and patient complaints. Nothing remains to them other than organized refusal, the deliberate will to die rather than continue living in slow motion (IDOC, 1970, p. 221).

In these particular cases, as Duclos explains, when a disgruntled sector of the population is attacked and left no other recourse, the violent reaction that results often stems from a last-ditch attempt to fight to the death to uphold the given principles.

This particular category also encompasses those who engage in political violence purely as a means of self defense. In these instances, there is often not the time, ability or luxury of debating what tactics are morally justifiable. Instead, the targeted individual, group, or population is in such a desperate struggle for survival that they, without contemplation, use whatever means they have available. A *by-any-means-necessary* approach, if you will. Examples of this can be seen within the few cases in Nazi-occupied Europe, when Jews on their way to the gas chambers would revolt and, in an effort to save their own lives, attack guards.

The second area of thought on individual and small group political violence focuses on those who actually plan, strategize, and engage in violence out of a belief in its necessity for change. For this grouping, the act of violence is far more premeditated than spontaneous. Additionally, whereas the former group of discussion largely takes on a reactionary role of self defense and rarely engages in proactive violence, this latter category does indeed not only use the tactic as a matter of defense, but also in offensive actions.

Resources pertaining to the first school of thought are fairly abundant, with many theorists attempting to prove or disprove the notion that violence is a natural reaction, and others attempting to explain why, in sociological or psychological terms, the violent reaction occurs. Yet, in the second category, that of organized and premeditated political violence, written material is somewhat scarce. While both schools of thought should be of interest to anyone concerned with the subject of political violence, my primary investigative leaning is toward the latter.

Political violence has, as a matter of documented fact, been with humanity throughout its history. Davies, in his 1971 book, *When Men Revolt and Why*, argues that:

> Violence among citizens, of which revolution is the most extreme sort, probably goes as far back (as)in the history of government... Indeed it may be argued that violence of citizen against citizen, government against citizen, and citizen against government has always come before orderly political processes (p. 3).

While this does not constitute a sound basis on its own for the continuance of political violence, there is an abundance of information to be gained by acknowledging and understanding its historic role. Some do, however, argue that humankind, with all its alleged intelligence and progress, should have found an alternative to violence by now, if there were a more viable alternative available. In his 1980 book, *The Riddle of Violence*, Kaunda states, "Man has suffered so greatly in wars throughout recorded time it must be assumed that if there were a more efficient way of achieving whatever end war serves, he would have found and applied it years ago" (p. 81).

Of the available material discussing possible motives and factors provoking a violent pursuit of political goals, a common belief among theorists is that a state of frustration, deprivation, repression, and oppression is often present. In an essay entitled *Social Change and Political Violence: Cross National Patterns* contained within *Anger, Violence and Politics: Theories and Research*, the authors argue that "our theoretical assumption linking change to violence begins with the notion that political turmoil is the consequence of social discontent" (Feierabend et al, 1972, p. 108). They continue on to suggest that frustration can be defined as:

> the thwarting at or interference with the attainment of goals, aspirations, or expectations. On the basis of frustration-aggression theory, it is postulated that frustration induced by the social system creates the social strain and discontent that in turn are the indispensable preconditions of violence (p. 108).

Some, such as Fanon and Duclos, go as far as to suggest that the act of violence in itself allows the applicant to regain his or her dignity and sense of worth. In one of his most renowned works, *The Wretched of the Earth*, Fanon states, "At the level of individuals, violence is a cleansing force. It frees the native from his inferiority complex and from his despair and inaction; it makes him fearless and restores his self-respect" (1963, p. 94). Duclos adds, "To die in refusal, in revolt, seems like the first gesture of the rebirth of oppressed man. For him it will be the assertion of his existence, of his consciousness of being human, a consciousness that refuses to let itself be alienated by other men" (1970, p. 221).

The above-stated hypotheses of causes of political violence are quite simplistic and, one might say, obvious. It seems like common knowledge that in the mind of someone committing political violence, that person feels he or she has been neglected or wronged in some way by the opposition. In many cases, this may be completely true. But why then do some choose to engage in political violence while others, perhaps under a similar set of circumstances, follow a less violent or even a nonviolent path?

The answer is not easily found. One realistic and grounded analysis differentiates between the various circumstances premeditating the outbreak of political violence. Like those Jews in the Holocaust who rebelled on the way to their execution, there is a higher likelihood of violence being used when the applicants perceive they are in a direct and immediate struggle for their lives. In other situations, when those who have a feeling of being wronged are not (or do not feel as though they are) in a desperate and immediate battle for their lives, there often is more time for contemplation, for analyzing and discussing the proper strategies by which to proceed. In some of these cases, the decision might then be made to engage in less violent, or nonviolent tactics. Arguably, whether those in this particular situation would admit it or not, the decision to follow a path less violent likely depends on the amount of personal safety, and even privilege, that is perceived at a given time.

The next logical question that should be contemplated is *why then do those who may not be in an immediate and desperate position of protecting themselves choose to resort to violence as a means of addressing their grievances?* This question is problematic for at least two reasons. First, the notion of an immediate and desperate position of protecting one's life is very relative. Any number of people may perceive the threats to their lives in varying degrees of seriousness. A man involved in the drug trade, for instance, who learns there is a contract out on his life, knows full well that he is in a desperate and immediate situation. But often the issue is much fuzzier. Members of the Earth Liberation Front have stated in their communiqués that protecting the environment is a matter of self defense. They feel that the threat to the natural world is so severe, desperate, and immediate that they engage in actions of sabotage to try to protect what they see as all life on the planet. Likewise, Dr. Ted Kazcinski, also referred to as "the Unabomber," conducted a multi-year campaign of violence against what he saw as a technological world threatening all life. As the above examples demonstrate, there often is a considerable discrepancy between what constitutes the notions of desperate and immediate.

A second problem with the question of why one chooses to resort to violence is that in many instances, the parties involved do not feel as though they are choosing. Instead, more often than not, the applicators of political violence feel as though they have no choice, that they were left no other option but to resort to some sort of armed struggle. Nelson Mandela, who led the armed wing of the African National Congress during South Africa's freedom fight, stated:

The time comes in the life of any nation when there remain only two choices: submit or fight. That time has now come to South Africa. We shall not submit and we have no choice but to hit back by all means within our power in defence of our people, our future and our freedom (Mandela, 1986, p. 122).

Mandela called for the addition of violent tactics to be used in the liberation struggle in 1961 after "a long and anxious assessment of the South Africa situation" (Mandela, 1986, p. 166). He goes on to better describe the decision:

This conclusion was not easily arrived at. It was only when all else had failed, when all channels of peaceful protest had been barred to us, that the decision was made to embark on violent forms of political struggle, and to form Umkhonto we Sizwe. We did so not because we desired such a course, but solely because the government had left us with no other choice (p. 166).

This lack-of-choice justification is perhaps the most common reason given by individuals and groups who use political violence to further their own agendas. On a basic level of progression the argument makes sense—if tactics A, B, and C do not work on their own you either give up and submit or take things to the next level. For many who have first attempted more nonviolent and state-sanctioned pursuits, they feel there is no other recourse left but to step up the pressure.

It can be said that the Black Power movement in the United States came about, at least in part, due to the observation by many African Americans that nonviolent tactics on their own were not succeeding in advancing civil rights. In a 1965 interview that appeared in the *Young Socialist*, Malcolm X stated:

I don't favor violence. If we could bring about recognition and respect of our people by peaceful means, well and good. Everybody would like to reach his objectives peacefully. But I am also a realist... I believe we should protect ourselves by any means necessary when we are attacked by racists (X, 1965, p.17).

A decade before Malcolm came into the heavy limelight, Robert Williams was arguing the need for blacks to arm themselves in self defense, to pick up where the law was lacking.  In the late 1950s, Williams was the president of the Monroe, North Carolina branch of the NAACP. There he proclaimed:

> Rather than submit to violence, Negroes must be willing to defend themselves, their women, their children and their homes.  Nowhere in the annals of history does the record show a people delivered from bondage by patience alone (Tyson, 1999, p. 215).

Williams also practiced what he preached.  He and a number of his followers used machine guns, dynamite, and Molotov cocktails to confront the Klu Klux Klan.

The formation of the Young Lords Party in the 1960s also revealed a frustration that came as a result of attempting various nonviolent tactics. A U.S.-based organization advocating for human rights, particularly for Puerto Ricans and Latinos, the Young Lords stated in its thirteen-point program:

> We are opposed to violence—the violence of hungry children, illiterate adults, diseased old people, and the violence of poverty and profit.  We have asked, petitioned, gone to courts, demonstrated peacefully, and voted for politicians full of empty promises.  But still we ain't free.  The time has come to defend the lives of our people against repression and for revolutionary war against the businessman, politician and police.  When a government oppresses our people, we have the right to abolish it and create a new one.

Again, the recurring theme is displayed here of those who argue they have attempted less severe and nonviolent tactics, but they simply did not work.

The above statement brings up two interesting points.  The argument that nonviolent tactics did not work can simply be met by questioning

248

the strategy of the implemented activities, as well as the timeline on which they occurred. Criticisms can easily be imagined from the nonviolence sector arguing that the violent offender did not give nonviolent tactics enough time to work. But in the minds of political violence proponents, it is commonly argued that their own personal time limit set for less severe tactics has expired.

The question, *how long is one supposed to wait to see if a particular tactic is going to be effective?*, is an important one but is also relative to each situation. For example, middle-class citizens of the United States, of the leftist or liberal persuasion, arguably have far more time to debate tactics and experiment with strategies on general progressive "issues" than say a member of the PLO, who rightfully believes that Palestinians are in a immediate and desperate struggle for their lives and sovereignty against Israel. Thus, to reiterate, the perception of the urgency and severity of the threat to one's life plays a definite role in deciding how able one is to argue for and take part in an adherence to nonviolent principles.

The second point that the above statement highlights is why nonviolence did not work, at least for those who argue for the necessity of political violence. There is a belief held by many proponents of political violence that nonviolence can only work when the opposition has the capability of decency, compassion, and a healthy and working conscience. Nonviolence philosophies, as preached by Gandhi and King, assume that an oppressive agent in any and every case has the ability to see the evils in his or her own actions and voluntarily change. Critics argue that not every opponent or agent of oppression has this capability.

T. Melville, in his essay *The Present State of the Church in Latin America*, writes:

> The revolution can only be peaceful when those who control the structures—the rich oligarchy—are willing to allow such a change to occur, recognizing the long-denied rights of the poor masses. To the degree that they oppose such a change, the masses will be forced to use ever more drastic measures, to take power into their own hands and thus effect change by themselves. It is the rich then, with those of allied interests, who have the real say as to whether the process will be peaceful or violent (IDOC, 1970, p. 217).

Rejecting even the slightest notion that nonviolence could actually play a part in revolution as they saw it, members of the Angry Brigade in England conducted a multi-year bombing and sabotage campaign. Advocating the overthrow of the capitalist system by the working class, the Angry Brigade was primarily active in the early 1970s. On February 19, 1971, their sixth communiqué was printed in *The Times*. It stated:

FELLOW REVOLUTIONARIES... We have sat quietly and suffered the violence of the system for too long. We are being attacked daily. Violence does not only exist in the army, the police and prisons. It exists in the shoddy alienating culture pushed out by TV, films and magazines, it exits in the ugly sterility of urban life. It exists in the daily exploitation of our Labour, which gives big Bosses the power to control our lives and run the system for their own ends. How many Rolls Royces... how many Northern Irelands... how many anti-Trade Union bills will it take to demonstrate that in a crisis of capitalism the ruling class can only react by attacking the people politically? But the system will never collapse or capitulate by itself. More and more workers now realise this and are transforming union consciousness into offensive political militancy. In one week, one million workers were on strike... Fords, Post Office, BEA, oil delivery workers... Our role is to deepen the political contradictions at every level. We will not achieve this by concentrating on 'issues' or by using watered down socialist platitudes. In Northern Ireland the British Army and its minions has found a practising range: the CS gas and bullets in Belfast will be in Derby and Dagenham tomorrow. OUR attack is violent... Our violence is organised.

The question is not whether the revolution will be violent. Organised militant struggle and organised terrorism go side by side. These are the tactics of the revolutionary class movement. Where two or three revolutionaries use organised violence to attack the class system... there is the Angry Brigade. Revolutionaries all over England are already using the name to publicise their attacks on the system. No Revolution was ever won without violence. Just as the structures and programmes of a new revolutionary society must be incorporated into every organised base at every point in the struggle, so must organised violence accompany every point of the struggle until, armed the revolutionary working class overthrows the capitalist system. COMMUNIQUÉ 6. THE ANGRY BRIGADE (Vague, 1997, p. 42).

This communiqué contains some of the classic factors common in the mindset of those conducting or advocating political violence. There is the reality of their frustration in being faced with years of violence and lower-class, poverty conditions. Also present is the vocal abandonment of any hope that nonviolent tactics could be successfully utilized.

Across the Atlantic, in the United States during roughly the same time period, the Weather Underground was calling for a massive armed revolutionary movement against U.S. imperialism. In its 1974 book, *Prairie Fire: The Politics of Revolutionary Anti-Imperialism*, the group also demonstrated its lack of faith in the nonviolent struggle, writing:

It is an illusion that imperialism will decay peacefully. Imperialism has meant constant war. Imperialists defend their control of the means of life with terrible force. There is no reason to believe they will become humane or relinquish power. As matters deteriorate for imperialism, there is every reason to believe they will tighten control, pass their contradictions on to the people, and struggle for every last bit of power. To not prepare the people for this struggle is to disarm them ideologically and physically and to perpetuate a cruel hoax (p. 3).

The question over whether or not certain opponents are able to have their own behaviors formulated by nonviolence is definitely crucial. There is some validity to the opinion that not everyone has this capability. For instance, it can be argued that a healthy, working conscience would not allow someone to be involved in overt, oppressive and even outright murderous practices. A person's own sense of goodness and decency, two components which should be present within any working conscience, would hypothetically prevent him or her from doing so. Therefore, in certain circumstances, one who is involved in such overt and obvious activities could be perceived as not having that conscience required for theories of nonviolence to succeed.

The executives whose factories pump extreme amounts of toxins into the environment must be aware of the pollutants and their adverse health effects on humans and other life forms. In some cases, the factories will knowingly continue to release this poison, simply because it is more cost efficient than not doing so. Likewise, it has been a matter of simple knowledge within the environmental advocacy community that automobile manufacturers continually give birth to larger gas-guzzling vehicles, even though more efficient and less polluting engine technology has been around for years. In many of these situations, the decision is purely financial.

In the above examples, it is debatable whether or not the parties guilty of the unjust acts would have the ability to respond to a campaign of nonviolence. Since they are already engaged in violent practices that directly affect the health of life forms globally, it can only be assumed they would not hesitate to use the same or even increased violence against a nonviolent opponent.

In *The Politics of Violence: Revolution in the Modern World*, Leiden and Schmitt argue that "the presence of violence in a community does not of itself mean that revolution becomes necessarily more likely, but it does suggest that revolution, if it does appear, will be accompanied by violence in generous quantities" (1968, p. 21). This statement makes a great deal of sense. In societies where there is little violence, especially of the state-sponsored variety, it could be suggested that the people and governments may be more receptive to nonviolent approaches for change. Unfortunately, in countries where there is a tremendous amount of state-sponsored violence, the possibilities of solving grievances in a strictly nonviolent fashion may be, at best, minimal.

Fanon adds:

> In fact, as always, the settler has shown him the way he should take if he is to become free. The argument the native chooses has been furnished by the settler, and by an ironic turning of the tables it is the native who now affirms that the colonialist understands nothing but force (1963, p. 84).

Robert Williams also felt that the strategy of nonviolence relied upon the willingness of the oppressor to concede to the requests of the peaceful. Tyson suggests that:

> The problem as Williams presented it, however, was that nonviolence depended on the conscience of the adversary; rattlesnakes, he observed, were immune to such appeals, as were many Southern white supremacists (1999, p. 214).

Williams himself stated, "Nonviolence is a very potent weapon when the opponent is civilized, but nonviolence is no repellent for a sadist" (p. 214). He further demonstrated his lack of expectations in the oppressive opposition when he wrote *Negroes with Guns*. In it Williams argues, "When an oppressed people show a willingness to defend themselves, the enemy, who is a moral weakling and coward is more willing to grant concessions and work for a respectable compromise" (Katope & Zolbrod, 1970, p. 396).

Mandela felt that nonviolence not only had not worked in the South African freedom struggle, but had actually provoked more violence from the government. He stated:

> The government has interpreted the peacefulness of the movement as weakness; the people's non-violent policies have been taken as a green light for government violence. Refusal to resort to force has been interpreted by the government to use armed force against the people without any fear of reprisals (1986, p. 123).

It is also seemingly ironic that those who preach about the adherence to nonviolent philosophies and tactics directly have often benefited from political violence. Here in the United States, the public schooling system teaches youth to have pride in this country's history. Simultaneously, the same nation will argue that only nonviolent, state-sanctioned tactics are deemed socially and politically tolerable. Yet, the foundations of this country are built upon political violence—the armed uprisings that led directly to the American Revolution. The educational system also teaches the heroic actions of the Boston Tea Party—interestingly enough, perhaps one of the earliest, best-known examples of politically-motivated property destruction. Not only was the United States formed through extreme political violence, both against European powers and indigenous nations, but more importantly the country has maintained its power only through political violence. Regardless of its perceived immorality, it is a fact. Still, advocates of social and political change within this country argue that strict adherence to nonviolence will indeed be able to achieve justice and true freedom for all.

Bakunin, who many identify as being one of the founders of anarchist theory, wrote about this mythological higher ethic that the oppressing parties are supposed to inherently possess:

> It is clear that the people, longing for emancipation, cannot expect it from the theoretical triumph of abstract right; they must win liberty by force, for which purpose they must organize their powers apart from and against the State (Maximoff, 1953, p. 376).

He goes even further to question the historical role nonviolence has played in class struggles, asking, "Was there ever, at any period, or in any country, a single example of a privileged and dominant class which granted concessions freely, spontaneously, and without being driven to it by force or fear?" (p. 377).

For many, the question of whether or not to consider employing political violence comes down to one of strategy. Is political violence capable of advancing social and political movements? Is it viable as a means of successful self defense? What is the historical success record of violent tactics? All of these questions are detrimental in contemplating this controversial subject.

Martin Luther King, Jr. once wrote that:

> violence exercised merely in self-defense, all societies, from the most primitive to the most cultured and civilized, is accepted as moral and legal. The principle of self-defense, even involving weapons and bloodshed, has never been condemned, even by Gandhi (Tyson, 1999, p. 215).

This is an amazingly powerful quote from King that partially debunks the myths held by nonviolent absolutists in their worshiping of Gandhi.

254

In an essay entitled *Political Violence in Analytical Perspective*, Apter admits the historical importance of political violence. He writes:

> It becomes difficult to ignore the heroic side of political violence. Reallocations of wealth, moral teleologies of human betterment, doctrines of how to realize it, these are also inseparable from political violence. It would be hard to envisage the evolution of democracy or for that matter the English, French, and American revolutions without such violence and indeed fears of its potentiality. The list of reforms which were successfully pushed and prodded by confrontational violence is a long one. Nor can violence be completely separated from institutional politics. The right to organize, and the actual organization of trade unions, or civil rights required a certain tandem connection between political violence and the ballot box, extra-institutional protest movements and political parties. It takes confrontation, outside the law to make the law itself. Few basic changes in the content and scope, logic and practices of liberty and equality occur peacefully, contained within the framework of institutional politics (Apter, 1997, p. 3).

Walter Laqueur, in his 1987 book, *The Age of Terrorism*, argues that terrorism—a form of political violence—can be effective on a short term basis. He writes:

> Where terrorism has been successful its aims have usually been limited and clearly defined. The daily wage of American iron workers (AFL) went up from $2.00 to $4.30 (for shorter hours) between 1905 and 1910 as the result of the bombing of some one hundred buildings and bridges. Spanish workers, using similar methods, improved their wages during the first world war (p. 75).

To followers of nonviolence practice and philosophy, perhaps the most important discussion is over the means-versus-ends argument. Nonviolent theorists hold as a foundation of their beliefs that the ends do not justify the means. Many suggest that it is unproductive to engage in strategies that do not fall within the ideal world one is seeking to create. Additionally, there is the circle of violence notion that implies that violence met with violence creates an endless spiral of destruction. Often times it is argued that only nonviolent tactics can break this vicious circle.

While in circumstances of immediate and desperate self defense, often one does not have the luxury of debating the means-versus-ends topic. The Jews who resorted to violence on the way to the gas chambers arguably did so not after a lengthy contemplation of means and ends, but because there was an immediate realization made that they were threatened with annihilation.

In times of urgent self defense *and* in calculated offensive action, Kaunda felt that it is often more important to stop the immediate evil at hand than to let it continue due to a reluctance of engaging in political violence. He writes:

> War is just like Bush clearing - the moment you stop, the jungle comes back even thicker, but for a little while you can plant and grow a crop in the ground you have won at such terrible cost (1980, p. 78).

As simplistic as it is, this statement by Kaunda is perhaps one of the more honest realities of struggle. For many, there simply is not the opportunity, as they perceive it, to limit their tactics to those only which they would like used on them in the utopian world.

Responding to the second biblical commandment, *I must love my neighbor as myself,* Kaunda asks, "Can I reconcile my love for my neighbor with watching him from a distance being brutalized and tormented and reduced to the level of an animal and do nothing about it?" (1980, p. 88). This is an extremely potent question. While the logic of Gandhian nonviolence, among others, holds that one must have and demonstrate love and compassion for the opponent and restrict any physical suffering to one's self, a conflict of interest arises when friends, family, neighbors, and nations greatly suffer from this lack of more direct rebellion. On a smaller scale, a rape situation is perhaps the most compelling in illustrating this problem. If one is a witness to a rape, and it is clear that nonviolent tactics (if there is time to consider them) will not work to stop the attack, is it not more violent to do nothing and allow the act to continue? Is it not more violent to refuse to engage in whatever tactics may be necessary to stop the rape? This same logic can be applied in larger confrontations in which matters of justice, liberty, and life are concerned.

Kaunda continues:

> You have no option but to be a pacifist if you believe that
> the worst thing you can do to a man is kill him. But you
> may think that there is something worse you can do to
> him—connive at the business of allowing him to become
> a real devil as he robs others of their humanity and de-
> faces the image of God in them. And to do that you need
> to do absolutely nothing - just fold your arms, shake your
> head in despair and watch him take himself and his victim
> to Hell (p. 89).

If your family, if your people, if your nation is being attacked, is it not a
greater evil to allow the horrific cruelties of warfare to take their toll on
those you identify with?

Former concentration camp inmate during the Nazi Holocaust,
Bruno Bettelheim, has harshly criticized Jews during this period who did
not fight back against the oppressive and murderous conditions. He asserts that nonviolence not only did not help the plight of the Jews, but actually assisted in their smooth and speedy liquidation. Speaking in reference
to the revolt of the twelfth Sonderkommando, Bettelheim states:

> They did only what we should expect all human beings to
> do; to use their death, if they could not save their lives, to
> weaken or hinder the enemy as much as possible; to use
> even their doomed selves for making extermination hard-
> er, or maybe impossible, not a smooth-running process...
> If they could do it, so could others. Why didn't they?
> Why did they throw their lives away instead of making
> things hard for the enemy? Why did they make a present
> of their very being to the SS instead of to their families,
> their friends, even to their fellow prisoners? (Churchill,
> 1998, pp. 35-36).

Should the Jews, particularly those who did revolt—such as the twelfth
Sonderkommando unit—have not engaged in such violent rebellion out of
some moral hierarchy of beliefs regarding means and ends? To most in the
current day, this notion constitutes one of the highest levels of absurdity.

To the twelfth Sonderkommando and others in similar circumstances, death was imminent and to not act, to not offer any direct form of confrontation meant, as Abbie Hoffman reiterated in 1969, to die like lambs to the slaughter.

To suggest that there is a legitimacy of political violence can be a controversial and even dangerous move in this day and age. This is particularly the case in the post-September 11, 2001 atmosphere of heightened anti-terrorism hysteria and political repression within the United States. However, there is a documented history, on a global basis, of the crucial role political violence has played in progressing struggles for justice.

This notion of legitimacy is intended to produce neither a moral condemnation nor support of political violence, but rather to advance the idea that it does exist as a viable option for political and social movements. One standard definition of legitimacy, as it exists in the 1933 Oxford Universal Dictionary, is *conformity to rule or principle, or to sound reasoning.* As discussed earlier in this essay, one may easily question whether or not *sound reasoning* would allow oppressed people to not engage in political violence when their life and the lives of their people are at stake. Ball-Rokeach, in an essay entitled *The Legitimization of Violence*, defines legitimacy as "a collective judgment that attributes the qualities of 'goodness' or 'morality' or 'righteousness' to behavior" (Short & Wolfgang, 1972, p. 101).

In defending the right to step beyond nonviolent tactics, Mandela wrote, "World history in general, and that of South Africa in particular, teaches that resort(ing) to violence may in certain cases be perfectly legitimate" (1986, p. 185). Apter states that some theorists declare, "applied to autocracies, political violence becomes self-legitimizing, an expression of the natural desire for freedom and liberty" (1997, p. 7).

Global history has demonstrated that a universal key to the progression of justice struggles is a combination of tactics and strategies. Rather than limiting a particular movement to one set of strategies, there is a conclusive amount of evidence which indicates every tool in the toolbox must be available for use. Apter suggests that:

> It is common for a given movement to combine extra-institutional protest with an underground wing using terrorism, aiming to create a revolutionary disjunction. Such combinations allow different strategies and modalities of action by different parts of the same organization (1997,

p. 10).

Churchill argues that the goal of political and social movements should not be to simply replace nonviolent tactics with those of political violence but rather:

> it is the realization that, in order to be effective and ul-
> timately successful, any revolutionary movement within
> advanced capitalist nations must develop the broadest
> possible range of thinking/action by which to confront
> the state (1998, p. 103).

In the history of the United States, many movements for justice and liberty have relied upon this mixture of strategies. In the abolitionist struggle, blacks did not progress merely as a result of asking the white power structure nicely. It came as a result of both legal and illegal actions, from the Underground Railroad to the scattered slave revolts. Likewise, the Suffragette movement relied upon not just the Susan B. Anthony main-stream efforts, but in addition, those with a more militant leaning, such as Alice Paul, who engaged in illegal activities. In labor issues, the organizing of the workplace, peaceful protests and boycotts, were perhaps just as crucial as the riots and revolts in obtaining more tolerable working conditions. The progress of the civil rights movement, itself founded upon the illegal civil disobedience campaigns against segregation and disenfranchisement, was aided in the emergence of the Black Power struggle, which made nonviolent campaigns much more attractive to the white racists.

Even outside of the United States, examples can be cited to demonstrate the legitimacy of political violence. The Indian Independence Movement, by far one of the most classic and often referred-to examples of successful nonviolent application, contained both legal and illegal, violent and nonviolent components. Churchill asserts that Gandhi's success relied upon not only his nonviolent Satyagraha principles and practices, but also such key factors as the "the decline in British power brought about by two world wars within a thirty-year period" (1998, p. 42). He continues:

> Prior to the decimation of British troop strength and the
> virtual bankruptcy of the Imperial treasury during World
> War II, Gandhi's movement showed little likelihood

of forcing England's abandonment of India. Without the global violence that destroyed the Empire's ability to forcibly control its colonial territories (and passive populations), India might have continued indefinitely in the pattern of minority rule marking the majority of South Africa's modern history, the first locale in which the Gandhian recipe for liberation struck the reef of reality. Hence, while the Mahatma and his followers were able to remain "pure," their victory was contingent upon others physically gutting their opponents for them (1998, p. 42).

Similar to the civil rights movement in the United States, Gandhi's nonviolent struggle was made much more appealing by the actual armed revolts and threat of further violence. It is easily argued that, deliberate or not, multiple forces—including violent and nonviolent action—worked together to force the British to give up India.

In reference to the legitimacy of political violence, often, in the minds of those arguing for and/or committing the acts themselves, there is a belief that the decision to resort to violence comes from *sound reasoning*. Additionally, political violence has a long documented history globally, as a practice which has and continues to play a role in political activity. For these reasons alone, it is safe to proclaim there is legitimacy to political violence.

Today, the threat to life on the planet is so severe that political violence must remain a viable option. To refuse this consideration constitutes a refusal to acknowledge the dire state of the world and the historical legitimacy of political violence in justice pursuits. The ability for justice to ever become a reality—especially in regards to the United States—directly depends on the willingness of individuals to do whatever it takes, to use any means necessary, to stop global murder, exploitation, and destruction of life.

No one in their right mind wants to use or resort to violence at any time during their lives. Instead, it is honestly more desirable to petition for peace and have the luxury and privilege to engage in the respectable means-versus-ends debate. That said, it is also a matter of realism to state that it is impossible to have peace without justice. In pursuing justice, when nonviolent means of social and political change have been exhausted, one is left with the choice either to advance tactics to a level of political violence or to do nothing. Of course, for multitudes of people in many circumstances, to do nothing means sheer suicide. It is a timeless dilemma, a debate that is often dominated by the nonviolence sector, coming from a position of privilege, regardless of historical facts. For me and for my own acknowledgment of my humanity, I can only hope that if I were one of the Jews on the way to the execution chamber, I too would have risen up in defiance, attempting to kill as many SS as possible, not only for myself, but for the sake of justice.

# *Applying Historical Lessons to Current and Future Pursuits for Justice in the United States*

In my own life, I have made a personal progression in strategies from a total adherence to nonviolent pursuits at all times, to where I am today: arguing for the legitimacy—and in the case of the United States, the necessity—of political violence. This was not a decision I came to easily, nor one out of a demented glorification of violence. Throughout my life I have always been opposed to violence and destruction, but I also have grown to learn that true peace can never come without justice. I do firmly believe, as the seven case studies help to demonstrate, that at certain points throughout world history and even that of the United States, the pursuit of justice has required a variety of strategies, including violence. Unfortunately, from all my experiences and my education, I have learned that political violence is also crucial to any current and future attempts at justice within the United States.

In my introduction I provided a list of the *Rules for the Game of Social and Political Change in the United States of America.* This contradictory set of guidelines has been heavily pushed by the status quo and ruling elite throughout the modern history of the country. *Why?* Do politicians, law enforcement, and even corporate interests really believe that an adherence to these rules will threaten their careers, their lives, and the entire manner in which the U.S. society functions? Of course not, and that is the point.

In one form or another, these rules have been taught throughout history in U.S. schooling systems and news and entertainment media. The rules have been promoted as a part of the incredible freedom that allegedly exists in this country. Our politicians have gone as far as to repeatedly use the public's access to the rules of political and social change as a demonstration of the democracy and freedom that exists. Of course, the only contradictory portion of this constant promotion of the rules is that they provide a far-from-accurate portrayal of how social change has occurred globally, and specifically in the United States.

The seven case studies presented in this book provide crucial lessons for those seeking justice, particularly in the United States. Those lessons specifically suggest that political and social change within the United States will not be possible without abandoning an adherence to the *Rules for the Game of Social and Political Change.* These state-sanctioned, society-approved methodologies cannot, by their own design, produce the necessary pressure on the U.S. government to stop its numerous unjust acts. Justice within the United States, and to an extent globally, depends on the very willingness of Americans to accept these and other historical lessons of political and social change.

The case of *The Jewish Resistance to Genocide in World War II Europe* horrifically demonstrates that nonviolence, and an adherence to "business-as-usual" policies and societal-approved rules cannot work against a morally incompetent opponent. Hitler is an extreme example, but multitudes of others can be found in current times among U.S. corporate executives and government officials. Those who knowingly, and even purposely, engage in extreme atrocities (often out of monetary interest) successfully demonstrate they have not only a severe immorality, but also a lack of any working, healthy conscience. Only by stepping out of the state-sanctioned, society-approved strategies can these individuals be defeated. It took the Allied military action to stop Hitler, and likewise, it will take radical, extreme activity to stop the U.S. government.

*The Civil Rights Movement in the United States* demonstrated that, due to its reformist nature, it could not, and did not, achieve an ultimate victory for African Americans. While acquiring desegregation and limited enfranchisement, the civil rights movement was unable, due to its focus, strategy, and intent, to actually threaten the very power structure that causes the injustice and discrimination. Because of the very design of the U.S. political system, revolution would be required to abolish the white power structure and enable a more honest equality.

Likewise, *The Vietnam Anti-War Movement in the United States* mirrored this reformist lesson. Even though hundreds of thousands, if not millions, of people took part in "The Movement," the efforts were not enough to stop the U.S. military action in Vietnam. Similar to the civil rights movement, the anti-war struggle was not successful due to its being a reformist pursuit, not meant to actually target the entire political system. By playing by the very rules for social and political change dictated by the status quo and U.S. government, the movement could *not* have succeeded without taking on a revolutionary strategy.

*The Algerian Revolution* provided an excellent example of the successful use of political violence. Members of the FLN organization had first attempted to obtain Algerian sovereignty from the French using societal-approved methods. Once it became clear these strategies were not working, the FLN was formed and used political violence—specifically terrorism—to accomplish its desire for presenting the French with an unstable Algeria.

Additionally, the FLN and the Algerian Revolution demonstrated that revolutionary conditions may actually be able to be created by the insurrectionists themselves. This lesson is extremely important in countering a common argument from the U.S. Left that implies a revolution can only be even considered when "certain" conditions are met.

*The North Vietnamese Strategies during the Vietnam War* provided another impressive example of a successful use of political violence. The Viet Cong were able to remarkably prevent any U.S. victory even though they were the clear underdog, having fewer resources, weaponry, and capabilities. While the casualties on all sides of the conflict were indeed enormous, the political violence utilized by the Viet Cong handed the United States its first, and still its worst, military embarrassment.

*The Cuban Revolution* then provided a lesson of the importance of using a by-any-means-necessary approach when it comes to social and political change. Castro had attempted to first play by the rules as an attorney legally fighting the Batista regime. When it became clear the rules were not working and *would not* work, he realized that only by stepping outside of the rules could social and political change become a reality. Castro's revolutionary action involving political violence enabled his forces to successfully overthrow the Batista regime and create a different society.

Finally, the case of *The 1916 Easter Uprising* in Ireland highlighted the notion that political violence has legitimacy. This specific failed insurrection was instrumental in the formation of the Irish Republican Army. While those involved in the 1916 Uprising knew, even before it began, they would not be victorious, the action still commenced out of a desire by the participants to do anything they could to pursue justice. In this sense, I conclude that the act of revolution involving political violence has legitimacy to those involved relating to the history of social and political change and possibilities for justice in the future.

In the case of the United States, reform has not produced the necessary fundamental pressure on the government needed for overall political and societal justice. By its own design, of accepting the underlying political system as working and healthy, reform can *never* pose a serious threat to the white upper class man's method of rule. The most it is capable of is very minor single-issue gains, while each individual concern is never fully resolved.

In the worst sense, reformism and its associated myths of progressiveness may actually be worse than no action whatsoever. Reformist propaganda teaches people that reform is working, that is has worked, and that it will work in the future. Thus, it becomes more difficult for justice seekers to understand the importance and necessity of a political and societal revolution in the United States. By failing to possess the ability to actually ever threaten the political structure of the country, reformism does indeed *allow* a greater degree of exploitation, murder, and injustice to continue.

The only viable means by which justice struggles in the United States can actually progress are revolution and the abandonment of any adherence to the state-sanctioned rules. As I have already stated, due to the history of the U.S. government, the formation of the country, and its day-to-day policies even currently, a revolution within this country *must* involve the use of political violence. There simply is no alternative, and there is an abundance of proof that the U.S. political system can never be threatened by nonviolence alone.

266

# CONCLUSION

With assistance from historical models, I have demonstrated in this book that 1) reformism has failed, and will continue to fail, to provide justice in the United States, 2) a political and societal revolution is necessary, and 3) that political violence is legitimate and must be included in any U.S.-based revolutionary movement. After digesting these three main points, the most important question is *what do we do now? Do we stop engaging in single issue reformist measures in pursuit of revolution?* Precisely. Those who truly seek justice—who want to actually put an end to the massive state-sponsored murder and destruction that occur on a daily basis, and who want to live in a society where life is categorically placed ahead of profits—must understand the logic and necessity of revolution.

Used in the sense of justice pursuits, of working to stop massive innocent bloodshed, political violence certainly is legitimate. Few argued with the Allied military action that was used to finally defeat the Nazis and close the concentration camps. To have refused this political violence and allowed Hitler to see the success of the *Final Solution* with total extermination of Jews would have allowed far greater atrocity. The same can be said in regards to struggles for justice in the United States. If we, as justice seekers, do not act by any means necessary to stop the ongoing domestic and international murder and destruction caused by the U.S. government, we are actually guilty of allowing extreme atrocities to continue. As the old anti-war slogan goes, *How many more lives must be taken before you decide to act?*

It is time for us all to stop being the *good citizens*. It is time to stop pretending that our own inactions are serving any purpose but to appease personal consciences. It is time to step out of the position of privilege into one of reality, taking responsibility for our obligation to stop the most diseased and violent political system in history. It is time for a revolution in the United States of America.

# *References*

Ainsztein, R. (1974) . *Jewish resistance in Nazi-occupied eastern Europe*. London: Harper and Row.

Anderson, T. (1995) . *The movement and the sixties: Protest in America from Greensboro to Wounded Knee*. New York: Oxford University Press.

Apter, D.E. [Ed.] . (1997) . *The legitimization of violence*. New York: New York University Press.

Arad, Y. (1987) . *Operation Rheinhard death camps: Belzec, Sobibor, Treblinka*. Bloomington: Indiana University Press.

Arad, Y. (1990) . *Vilna ghetto*. In Y. Gutman (Ed.), *Encyclopedia of the holocaust*. New York: MacMillan.

Ball-Rokeach, S.J. (1972) . *The legitimization of violence*. Printed in Short, J.F. & Wolfgang, M.E. [Ed.] . Collective violence. Chicago: Aldine-Atherton.

Bauer, Y. (1997) . *Jewish resistance to holocaust*. In R. S. Powers & W. B. Vogele (Ed.), *Protest, power, and change: An encyclopedia of nonviolent action from ACT-UP to wom ens suffrage*. New York: Garland Publishing.

Bender, S. & Prekerowa, T. (1990) . *Bialystok*. In Y. Gutman (Ed.), *Encyclopedia of the holocaust*. New York: Macmillan.

Birnbaum, J., & Taylor, C. (Ed.) . (2000) . *Civil rights since 1787: A reader on the black struggle*. New York: New York University.

Burrowes, R. J. (1996) . *The strategy of nonviolent defense: A Gandhian approach*. Albany: State University of New York Press.

Buszko, J. (1990) . *Resistance at Auschwitz*. In Y. Gutman (Ed.), *Encyclopedia of the holocaust*. New York: MacMillan.

Carson, C. (1981) . *In struggle: SNCC and the black awakening of the 1960s*. Cambridge: Harvard University Press.

Caulfield, M. (1963) . *The easter rebellion*. New York: Holt, Rinehart and Winston.

Cholawski, S. (1990) . *Resistance in Belorussia*. In Y. Gutman (Ed.), *Encyclopedia of the holocaust*. New York: MacMillan.

Churchill, W. (1998) . *Pacifism as pathology: Reflections on the role of armed struggle in North America*. Winnipeg: Arbeiter Ring.

Clark, S. (1986) . *Ready from within: Septima Clark and the civil rights movement*. Navarro, CA: Wild Trees Press.

Cohen (1990) . *France*. In Y. Gutman (Ed.), *Encycopedia of the holocaust*. New York: MacMillan.

Cooper, K. & Ludlow, J. (Producers) . (2002) . *Fidel* [Film] . Showtime.

Currey, C. B. (1997) . *Victory at any cost: The genius of Vietnam's Gen. Vo Nguyen Giap*. Dulles: Brassey's, Inc.

Davies, J.C. [Ed.] . (1971) . *When men revolt and why*. New York: The Free Press.

Davies, P. (1973) . *The truth about Kent State: A challenge to the American Conscience*. New York: Farrar Straus Giroux.

De Rosa, P. (1990) . *Rebels: The Irish rising of 1916*. New York: Fawcett Columbine.

Douglass, F. (1845) . *Narrative of the life of Frederick Douglass: An American slave*. Boston: The Anti-Slavery Office.

Duclos, B. (1970) . *Let my people go*. Printed in IDOC [Ed.] . *When all else fails: Christian arguments on violent revolution*. Philadelphia: Pilgrim Press.

Egerton, J. (1994) . *Speak now against the day: The generation before the civil rights movement in the south*. New York: Knopf.

Fanon, F. (1963) . *The wretched of the earth*. New York: Grove Press.

Fanon, F. (1965) . *A dying colonialism*. New York: Grove Press.

Feierabend, I.K. & Feierabend, R.L. [Ed.] . (1972) . *Anger, violence, and politics:*

# REFERENCES

*Theories and research*. Englewood Cliffs: Prentice-Hall, Inc.

Fischer, L. (1954) . *Gandhi: His life and message for the world*. New York: Mentor.

Friedman, P. (1981) . *Jewish resistance to Nazism: Its various forms and aspects*. In *European resistance movements 1939-1945*. New York: Pergamon Press.

Gandhi, M. K. (1961) . *Non-violent resistance*. New York: Schocken Books.

Gandhi, M. K. (1968) . *Gandhi: an autobiography*. Boston: Beacon.

Gitlin, T. (1987) . *The sixties: Years of hope, days of rage*. New York: Bantam Books.

Goldenberg, B. (1965) . *The Cuban revolution and Latin America*. New York: Frederick A. Praeger.

Guevara, E. C. (1961) . *Guerrilla warfare*. New York: Monthly Review Press.

Gutman, Y. (1980) . *The Jews of Warsaw, 1939-1943*. Bloomington: Indiana University Press.

Gutman, Y. (1983) . *Rebellions in the camps: Three revolts in the face of death*. In A. Grobman & D. Landes (Ed.), *Critical issues of the holocaust*. Los Angeles: Simon Wi esen thal Center.

Gutman, Y. (1989) . *The genesis of the resistance in the Warsaw ghetto*. In M. Marrus (Ed.), *The Nazi holocaust: Jewish resistance to the holocaust*. Westport: Meckler Corpora tion.

Gutman, Y. (1990) . *Partisans*. In Y. Gutman (Ed.), *Encyclopedia of the holocaust*. New York: MacMillan.

Hilberg, R. (1961) . *The destruction of the European Jews*. Chicago: Holmes & Meier.

Hilberg, R. (1985) . *The destruction of the European Jews*. New York: Holmes & Meier.

Horne, A. (1977) . *A savage war of peace*. New York: The Viking Press.

Hutchinson, M. C. (1978) . *Revolutionary terrorism: The FLN in Algeria, 1954-1962*. Stanford: Hoover Institution Press.

IDOC [Ed.] . (1970) . *When all esle fails: Christian arguments on violent revolution*. Philadelphia: Pilgrim Press.

Institute for Global Communications (IGC) . (2001) . *National prisoner statistics*. [WWW document] . Retrieved: http://www.igc.org/deepdish/lockdown/features/stats.html.

Jacobs, R. (1997) . *The way the wind blew: A history of the Weather Underground*. New York: Verso.

Katope, C. & Zolbrod, P. [Ed.] . (1970) . *The rhetoric of revolution*. Toronto: MacMillan Company.

Kaunda, K. (1980) . *The riddle of violence*. San Francisco: Harper & Row.

King, M. L. (1967) . *Where do we go from here: chaos or community?*. Boston: Beacon.

Kraft, J. (1961) . *The struggle for Algeria*. New York: Doubleday & Company.

Krakowski, S. (1984) . *The war of the doomed*. New York: Homes and Meier.

Lanning, M. L. & Cragg, D. (1992) . *Inside the VC and the NVA: The real story of North Vietnam's armed forces*. New York: Fawcett Columbine.

Laqueur, W. (1987) . *The age of terrorism*. Boston: Little, Brown and Company.

Laska, V. (Ed.) . (1983) . *Women in the resistance and in the holocaust: The voices of eyewitnesses*. Westport: Greenwood Press.

Latour, A. (1981) . *The Jewish resistance in France (1940-1944)*. New York: Holocaust Library.

Leiden, C. & Schmitt, K.M. [Ed.] . (1968) . *The politics of violence: Revolution in the modern world*. Englewood Cliffs: Prentice-Hall, Inc.

Levin, D. (1990) . *Abba Kovner*. In Y. Gutman (Ed.), *Encyclopedia of the holocaust*. New York: MacMillan.

Luis, J. G. [Ed.] . (2001) . *Cuban revolutionary reader*. New York: Ocean Press.

Mandela, N. (1986) . *Nelson Mandela: The struggle is my life*. New York: Pathfinder Press.

Mangold, T. & Penycate, J. (1985) . *The tunnels of Cu Chi: The untold story of Vietnam*. New York: Random House.

Marrus, M. R. (Ed.) . (1989) . *The Nazi holocaust: Jewish resistance to the holocaust*.

# REFERENCES

Westport: Meckler Corporation.

Mathews, H. L. (1975) . *Revolution in Cuba*. New York: Charles Scribner's Sons.

Maximoff, G.P. [Ed.] . (1953) . *The political philosophy of Bakunin*. New York: The Free Press.

Melville, T.R. (1970) *The present state of the church in Latin America*. Printed in IDOC [Ed.] . *When all else fails: Christian arguments on violent revolution*. Philadelphia: Pil grim Press.

Michman (1990) . *Belgium*. In Y. Gutman (Ed.), *Encyclopedia of the holocaust*. New York: MacMillan.

Miklos & Nyiszli (1960) . *Auschwitz: A Doctor's Eyewitness Account*. New York: Fawcett Books.

Military History Institute of Vietnam (2002) . *Victory in Vietnam: The official history of the People's Army of Vietnam, 1954-1975*. Lawrence: University Press of Kansas.

Minh, H. C. (1973) . *Selected writings: 1920-1969*. Honolulu: University Press of the Pacific.

Morris, A. D. (1984) . *The origins of the civil rights movement: Black communities organizing for change*. New York: The Free Press.

Moses, G. (1997) . *Revolution of conscience: Martin Luther King, Jr., and the philosophy of nonviolence*. New York: The Guilford Press.

Pankewitz, T. (1987) . *The Cracow ghetto pharmacy*. New York: U.S. Holocaust Memorial Museum Shop Memorial Council.

Payne, C. M. (1995) . *I've got the light of freedom*. Berkeley: University of California Press.

Pike, D. (1966) . *Viet Cong: The organization and techniques of the National Liberation Front of South Vietnam*. Cambridge: The M.I.T. Press.

Pike, D. (1986) . *PAVN: People's Army of Vietnam*. New York: Da Capo Press.

Powers, R. S., & Vogele, W. B. (Ed.) . (1997) . *Protest, power, and change: An encyclopedia of nonviolent action from ACT-UP to womens suffrage*. New York: Garland Publishing.

Rashke, R. (1982) . *Escape from Sobibor*. Boston: Houghton Mifflin.

Ringelblum, E. (1958) . *Notes from the Warsaw ghetto: The journal of Emanuel Ringelblum*. New York: McGraw Hill Book Company.

Ruiz, R. E. (1968) . *Cuba: The making of a revolution*. New York: W.W. Norton & Company.

Sharp, G. (1970) . *Exploring nonviolent alternatives*. Boston: Porter Sargent.

Sharp, G. (1973) . *The politics of nonviolent action*. Boston: Porter Sargent.

Short, J.F. & Wolfgang, M.E. [Ed.] . (1972) . *Collective violence*. Chicago: Aldine-therton.

Sibley, M. Q. (Ed.) . (1963) . *The quiet battle: writings on the theory and practice of non-violent resistance*. New York: Anchor Books.

Sitkoff, H. (1981) . *The struggle for black equality 1954-1980*. New York: Hill and Wang.

Spector, S. (1990) . *Lutsk*. In Y. Gutman (Ed.), *Encyclopedia of the holocaust*. New York: MacMillan.

Steiner, F. (1967) . *Treblinka*. New York: Simon & Schuster.

Stephens, J. (1999) . *The insurrection in Dublin: An eyewitness account of the easter rising, 1916*. New York: Barnes & Noble Books.

Suhl, Y. (1989) . *Resistance movement in the ghetto of Minsk*. In M. Marrus (Ed.), *The Nazi holocaust: Jewish resistance to the holocaust*. Westport: Meckler Corporation.

Tang, T. N. (1985) . *A Viet Cong memoir: An inside account of the Vietnam War and its aftermath*. New York: Vintage Books.

Taylor, S. C. (1999) . *Vietnamese women at war: Fighting for Ho Chi Minh and the revolution*. Lawrence: University Press of Kansas.

Teodori, M. (Ed.) . (1969) . *The new left: A documentary history*. Indianapolis: The

# REFERENCES

Bobbs-Merrill Company.

Thomas, O. (Ed.) . (1966) . *Walden and civil disobedience*. New York: W. W. Norton & Company.

Tolstoy (1967) . *Tolstoy's writings on civil disobedience and non-violence*. New York: Bergman Publishers.

Trunk, I. (1972) . *Judenrat: The Jewish councils in eastern Europe under Nazi occupation*. New York: The Macmillan Company.

Tyson, T. (1999) . *Radio free dixie: Robert F. Williams and the roots of black power*. Chapel Hill: The University of North Carolina Press.

Vague, T. (1997) . *Anarchy in the U.K.: The Angry Brigade*. London: AK Press.

Verney, K. (2000) . *Black civil rights in America*. New York: Routledge.

Walker, D. (1968) . *Rights in conflict: Chicago's seven brutal days*. New York: Grosset & Dunlap.

Warbey, W. (1972) . *Ho Chi Minh and the struggle for an independent Vietnam*. London: Merlin Press.

Weather Underground (1974) . *Prairie fire: The politics of revolutionary anti-imperialism*. San Francisco: Communications Co.

Weiss, A. (1990) . *Janowska labor and death camp*. In Y. Gutman (Ed.), *Encyclopedia of the holocaust*. New York: MacMillan.

Wells, L. (1963) . *The Janowska road*. New York: MacMillan.

Williams, R. (1970) . *Negroes with guns*. Printed in Katope, C. & Zolbrod, P. [Ed.] . *The rhetoric of revolution*. Toronto: MacMillan Company.

X, M. (1966) . *Malcolm X talks to young people*. New York: Young Socialist.

Yahil, L. (1968) . *Jewish resistance: An examination of active and passive forms of Jewish survival in the holocaust period*. In Y. Vashem (Ed.), *Jewish resistance during the holocaust: Proceedings of the conference on manifestations of Jewish resistance, Jerusalem, April 7-11, 1968*. Jerusalem.

Zaroulis, N. & Sullivan, G. (1984) . *Who spoke up? American protest against the war in Vietnam 1963-1975*. New York: Holt, Rinehart and Winston.

Zinn, H. (1980) . *A people's history of the United States*. New York: Harper Perennial.

Zinn, H. (1994) . *You can't be neutral on a moving train*. Boston: Beacon Press.

Zinn, H. (1997) . *The Zinn reader: Writings on disobedience and democracy*. New York: Seven Stories Press.

Zinn, H. (1998) . *The twentieth century*. New York: Harper Perennial.

Zuckerman, I. (1976) . *The Jewish fighting organization, ZOB: Its establishment and activities*. In Y. Gutman and L. Rothkirchen (Ed.), *The catastrophe of European Jewry*. (pp. 518-548). Jerusalem: Yad Vashem.

# Index